THE GREAT
GODDESS

THE GREAT GODDESS

REVERENCE OF THE DIVINE FEMININE

FROM THE PALEOLITHIC TO THE PRESENT

JEAN MARKALE

Translated from the French by Jody Gladding

INNER TRADITIONS
Rochester, Vermont

Inner Traditions International
One Park Street
Rochester, Vermont 05767
www.InnerTraditions.com

First U.S. edition published by Inner Traditions International in 1999

Originally published in French under the title *La grande déesse: Mythes et sanctuarires* by Editions Albin Michel, S. A. in 1997

Library of Congress Cataloging-in-Publication Data

Markale, Jean.
[Grande déese. English]
The great goddess : reverence of the divine feminine from the paleolithic to the present / Jean Markale ; translated from the French by Jody Gladding. — 1st U.S. ed.
          p.   cm.
Includes index.
ISBN 0-89281-715-1 (alk. paper)
1. Mother goddesses.   I. Title.
BL325.M6
291.2'114—dc21   99-40763
                      CIP

Printed and bound in Canada

10 9 8 7 6 5 4 3 2 1

Text design and layout by Priscilla Baker
This book was typeset in Stone Serif with Middleton as a display face.

Inner Traditions wishes to express its appreciation for assistance given by the government of France through the ministère de la Culture in the preparation of this translation.

Nous tenons à exprimer nos plus vifs remerciements au government de la France et le ministère de la Culture pour leur aide dans le préparation de cette traduction.

CONTENTS

INTRODUCTION
The Vast Mother

In the religious systems that emerged from the biblical substratum—that is, Judaism, Christianity, and Islam—the concept of a male god undeniably dominates the complex structure of theological speculation. The contributions of Greek, and then Byzantine philosophy, and the not inconsiderable influence of Iranian spirituality with its Mazdean component, have only reinforced this tendency to represent the Supreme Being with concrete masculine characteristics. Nevertheless, by reading the Hebrew Bible, it becomes clear that this victory for the masculinity of God was not won in an instant. The first books of the Bible, in fact, bear witness to a struggle among the Hebrews themselves, which would be constantly reenacted over the centuries, between those adhering to orthodox Yahwehism and those zealots of the divinities of Canaan, also called the dark goddesses of the Near East. And not even the wise Solomon could be kept from being seduced by the vertigo of the feminine divinities. All the time he was building his famous Temple to the glory of Yahweh, he saw to it that the country was sprinkled with sanctuaries dedicated to Ishtar, Tanit, and other Artemises springing up from the most ancient memory of the peoples of Asia Minor and the islands of the eastern Mediterranean. All this more than explains the distrust displayed by Saint Paul, the true founding father of Christianity, toward women and why they are excluded from religious ceremonies.

We should acknowledge that this conflict between masculine and feminine conceptions of divinity is not new, and that it can be found to varying degrees in all civilizations. If some evidence allows us to think that the feminine conception predominated originally, we would be equally justified in affirming that, at a certain moment in history—undatable and probably varying according to region—the situation underwent a reversal and the change from a gynecocratic state to an androcratic (patriarchal) state led to a conceptual transformation of the mother goddess into the father god. The best testimony for this transition is the founding legend of the Delphic shrine, which admirably summarizes all aspects of the problem.

In a very succinct way, this legend recounts how a god who came from the north and to whom the Greeks gave the name Apollo, fought and killed a serpent named Python, who resided in the area of Delphi. After this victory, the inhabitants of the country abandoned the cult dedicated to Python and devoted themselves to the vanquishing god, Apollo. But it is a woman, a priestess, the Pythia, who, by hiding herself away in a deep pit under the site of the temple constructed in honor of Apollo, becomes the interpreter of the god and the essential figure of the oracle, celebrated throughout the Mediterranean world.

For all its simplicity, one could almost say its naiveté, this story is rich in teachings. Moreover, it must not be forgotten that, since time immemorial, an upright stone (a baetulus, cippus, or menhir) has existed in the area of Delphi, and has served as the marker for the world's center, a symbolic center, of course, but still sacred in character. The battle that takes place at this site is, therefore, a *sacred* battle, bringing the equilibrium of the world into play. And it is this cosmic level that is confirmed by the very name of the serpent itself. In fact, *python* comes from a

Greek root that means "deep cavity," and then, by extension, "origin," having given us the Latin word *puteus*, "pit," or "well." So it is not by chance that the Pythia of Delphi functions in a "pit," and thus, a relationship is established between, on the one hand, the practice of digging funerary pits, and on the other, the megalithic mounds comprised of a central chamber. It is a matter, pure and simple, of the *primal matrix*, and the serpent is linked, in one way or another, without needing to resort to a psychoanalytic explanation, to the idea of parturition or regeneration. That opens an utterly revolutionary interrogation into the presence of the serpent trampled underfoot by the Virgin Mary in Christian iconography. And this interrogation goes even further still, since it also concerns the mythic battle between Saint Michael and the dragon, as well as all the other battles of "civilizing" heroes, such as Tristan or Siegfried, or hypothetical saints such as Saint Efflam or Saint David in Celtic countries, fighting against monstrous serpents coming directly out of the collective unconscious.

As to Apollo, his name—which may be compared to the Indo-European word for "apple"—is incontestably Greek. It comes from the verb, *apello* "to repel," and thus he is "the one who chases, who repels," a name that perfectly suits the role attributed to him at Delphi of eliminating the Python. Originally, Apollo is not a sun god at all. He will only become one through the contamination of the Mithras myth in Hellenistic syncretism. This is a god with primary Indo-European functions, at once a priest, poet, musician, seer, and doctor. He is the perfect archetype of all those civilizing heroes we find in various guises in the great legends and popular stories of the oral tradition, and, in this sense, it is completely natural that his luminous, solar aspects should develop when confronted with the dark powers represented by the serpent or the dragon, necessarily, the telluric monsters from the depths.

The victory of Apollo over Python has thus been interpreted as the substitution of an ancient telluric cult with a heavenly one. This is certainly not false, but it is incomplete. It disregards the femininity of the serpent (in fact, the very "serpent" we find in the myth of Melusina and in traditions surrounding the *vouivre*) who is the emblematic animal of the goddess of the earth, the primitive mother of gods and men. The victory of Apollo over Python at Delphi is thus the perfectly transparent symbol of a radical change in consciousness: the transition from the concept of mother goddess to father god.

Without claiming to do a sociopsychological analysis of Paleo- and Mesolithic populations, the ages that precede organized agrarian culture, we can outline certain hypotheses regarding this reversal, thanks to archaeology and the study of primal myths. It is plausible, though not certain, that the first humans were unaware of the exact role of the male in procreation, not having established a causal relationship between coitus and parturition. Thus, their attitude toward the female, apparently weaker than the male, but *mysteriously* able to produce life, was ambiguous: a profound respect, if not veneration, and, at the same time, a kind of terror in the face of incomprehensible, even magic or divine, powers. The statuettes called "Venus callipyges," of the well-known Lespugue type, are a decisive argument in favor of this thesis, because, in these representations, a divine maternal power is undeniably acknowledged. To put this another way, it is extremely probable that primitive humanity regarded divinity, whatever that was, as feminine in nature.

Everything changed when the individual male understood that procreation necessarily depended upon his participation in the sexual act. That realization must have taken place during the times of settlement, the Neolithic period, that is, from the eighth to the fourth millennia B.C., depending on the region, when the rudimentary techniques of agriculture succeeded those of gathering, and raising herds replaced hunting wild animals. The observation of animal behavior and herd proliferation were certainly determining factors in this realization. The individual male, long considered sterile, indeed even useless except for hunting and war, was then freed of his ancient "frustrations" and took his revenge, solemnly claiming his power and his essential role. This is what the legend of Apollo at Delphi expresses, along with many other analogous myths found through-

4

out the world. What is more, since everything rests upon concrete symbols, the sun, formerly considered to be feminine, became a masculine figure, and femininity was forced back into the night, taking the form of the moon. Ancient Semitic and Indo-European languages give the masculine gender to the moon and the feminine gender to the sun, as is still the case in modern German and in three Celtic languages that continue to be spoken, Breton, Welsh, and Gaelic. There is something troubling here, made even more so by the well-known legend of Tristan and Isolde, which, archaic as it is, fully restores the earlier conditions animated by a feminine solar divinity.[1]

We should not believe, however, that the situation was reversed in a single stroke. Ancestral customs are tenacious and only modified slowly in the collective consciousness. It is very likely that, with the appearance of agriculture and the rearing of livestock, early societies still retained their gynecocratic structures for a long time, even up to the epoch of the biblical fathers. Thus, it was among the elite of these societies that the idea of patriarchy, and with it, the downplaying of the woman, took hold. Now, the elite of these societies could only be the sacerdotal class. Without too much risk of error, we can thus conclude that it was the priests who imposed the concept of a father god, creator of all things, in an effort to eliminate the ancient concept of the mother goddess, as the legend of Delphi clearly reveals.

And all this is confirmed by Genesis, as long as we consider the first eleven chapters, which were written late, according to the patriarchal tradition of Moses, as a mix of primal myth and historical reminiscence reduced to the state of symbolic images. The episode concerning original sin, which can be read many ways, nevertheless contains some elements that are neither mythological nor moral, despite the obvious feelings of guilt they have caused for thousands of years. It is, in fact, a woman who commits the "error," before corrupting the man. The Greek equivalent of this figure is Pandora, held responsible for all the troubles that she let escape from her famous "box," even though she is, as her name implies, the one who dispenses *all the gifts*, thus the mother goddess herself. But what is still more revealing is that Eve commits the "error" under the influence of the serpent.

Western religious thought has been almost unanimous in making the serpent of Genesis into a concrete representation of the tempter, that is to say, of Satan himself, relying for support upon the Apocalypse where this "great serpent," whom the archangel Michael and his legions oppose, is the image of absolute Evil. Nothing could be less certain, however, since this interpretation deliberately ignores the feminine aspect of the serpent. And the phallic interpretation, which the psychoanalysts expound from all sides, quite to the contrary settles nothing. Once more, we must return to Delphi and the serpent Python, who is the image of the telluric maternal divinity. And most importantly, we must look to the innumerable representations of this divine mother in the Near East and the Aegean Sea. Very often, she is represented amid serpents, or taking two serpents in her hands. Moreover, the word *serpent* (which comes from the present participle of a Latin verb meaning "to slither") was feminine in gender for most of the Middle Ages, a usage that persists in local dialects. The classical Latin word *anguis* was feminine, as still are today the German *Slancke,* the Breton *naer,* and the Welsh *neidr.* This is surely not mere chance, anymore than is the presence of the serpent under the Virgin Mary's feet in Christian iconography.

Taking the female nature of the serpent into account can completely change the meaning of the episode of so-called original sin. The prohibition against eating fruit from the Tree had been proclaimed by YHWH, that is, the Tetragrammaton, the mystical symbol of God the father. But Eve breaks the "patriarchal" ban and listens to the serpent, the symbolic figure of the mother goddess. This is a case, pure and simple, of a return to the ancient mother-goddess cult, a true "apostasy" as it were, and thus a very grave sin against the patriarchal type of religion that Yahweh represents. "Thus the original sin of the Bible could well be considered the first act in this long struggle of God the Father against the mother goddess. Moreover, this first Fall, which will be followed by countless others, will be, like the others, severely punished by God the father."[2] And outside of the expulsion of Adam and Eve from earthly Paradise, the curses pronounced by God are perfectly revealing of historical, sociological, and theological reality.

First of all, there is the curse against the serpent, that is, against the mother goddess herself. The serpent is cast out, condemned to crawl. (Are we to understand that before that time, it did *not* crawl? This detail seems very strange, when you think about it.) Furthermore, enmity is established between the serpent and the woman, or to put it another way, not only will the woman no longer have the right to honor the goddess—and to obey her— but she will even have to struggle against her. Then follows the famous, "You will give birth in pain," which has caused much misunderstanding, including the denial, among certain people, of childbirth without pain. "Women, dominant up until then because of their fertility, which put them in a natural, biological relationship with the divine, were to be punished precisely by that which was their glory: their pregnancy and maternity. Henceforth, these would be sources of suffering rather than of glory."[3] In short, the woman, formerly triumphant because she alone possessed the power of procreation, would become the slave to man and provide him with sons (because the biblical text does not speak of daughters). And instead of arousing men's desire (as symbol of a sexual cult rendered to the goddess), it would be the woman who desired the men, or, who would be at the disposal of men, who would accept her or refuse her, but only with procreation as a goal.

This was a significant turning point in the history of consciousness, and not merely some rivalry—if not war—between two divinities, one feminine and the other masculine. In fact, the divinity is the same, eternal, infinite, ineffable, unspeakable, incommunicable through purely rational means. It is only to make it comprehensible that anthropomorphic—and therefore, sexual—characteristics are attached to this divinity. Human beings can only truly perceive what is concrete, and it is natural for them to project the familiar contours of the universe in which they find themselves onto a divine and abstract entity. When humanity considered the woman the sole possessor of procreative—and thus, creative—powers, it could not imagine divinity in anything but a female form. But beginning from the moment when the male's role in the phenomenon of life transmission was realized, the woman's primacy could no longer be accepted. Having lost her mystery and her sacred nature, the woman saw herself reduced to the subordinate role of "surrogate mother" to a masculine line that, believing itself to be cuckolded since the beginning, thought only of revenge. Now, as consciousness is not transformed at will by a simple decision of the ruling authority, it is clear that humanity was, over the centuries, the victim of an ongoing struggle for influence between those who held a gynococratic view and those who held an androcratic one. Genesis serves as incontestable evidence if we consider what the serpent, called "tempter," actually represents.

This is even more true in the Mosaic account:

> Since feminine religions have it that men desire women, which gives the latter mastery over the former, in the masculine religion that is now established, it will be woman whose "desires will be directed toward your husband, and he will have mastery over you." The woman becomes the slave of the man. This is a radical change. Another civilization begins when man is given predominance, since up until then, it had been given to woman. As to woman's familiar element, Mother Earth, it is cursed. "Because you have listened to the voice of the woman [that is, because you have turned back to the cult of the goddess], you must henceforth command her [in order to avoid falling into gynecocratic *heresy*], and cursed will be the ground because of you" (Gen. 3:17–18). The ground, that is, the earth, nature, Mother Earth, is cursed, and the reign of agriculture begins. Certainly it is agriculture (and raising livestock) that marks the historical beginning of masculine society.[4]

But that does nothing to prevent the bloody struggle that follows within masculine society between the pastoral state, represented by Abel, and the agricultural state, represented by Cain, which we will find in the collective unconscious as expressed again in American Westerns, films in which ranchers and farmers battle against each other.

The curse against the serpent and, consequently, against the telluric mother goddess, extends to women, suspected—rightly—of being the partisans of this deity. This suspicion gives rise to the Church Fathers' constant warnings against women, as well as their banishment from the priesthood and active participation in the church, and, in a more aberrant, vicious, and tragic form, the "witch-hunts" that began in the thirteenth century and continued until the end of the seventeenth century, at least in western Europe.

It seems as though this episode from Genesis is an *a posteriori* justification for an irrefutable social condition resulting from speculations of a religious nature. Actually, such a ban must always be backed by some form of divine intervention. Presented as a divine warning, or just simply as sacred, an obligation can only acquire more power. And no one would dream, at least at first, of contesting what conforms to the cosmic or divine plan that controls the existence of beings and things. And that is of considerable help to the dominant class, in this case, the sacerdotal class, in assuring its absolute power over the sectors of society. The temporal can never be separated from the spiritual, especially in those periods of history when no one would dare to distinguish the profane from the sacred. But what remains revealing in the biblical account is Adam's reaction after Yahweh pronounces the curse against the serpent, the woman, and the earth: "The husband cried out the name of his wife, Eve-Living. Yes, she is the mother of all living" (Gen. 3:20, Chouraqui translation). In fact, in spite of everything that has just been said, there can be no better expression of the primacy of the woman. It is also, in a roundabout way, a kind of homage rendered, through Eve, whose name means exactly "living," or more, *natura naturans* (naturing nature), to the mother goddess of the past without whom nothing living would exist. It is true that Lilith, Adam's mother or first wife, was probably eliminated in the Mosaic period. We only know about that burdensome figure from a few consistently derogatory biblical allusions and

9

a rabbinical tradition as continuous as it is obscure.[5] Clearly, the text of Genesis is cut, and we will never know the exact role the woman played in it, and consequently, the corresponding role of the mother goddess, before so-called original sin so cleverly took over to better control people through their sense of guilt.

What we can affirm is the importance of the sexual component in the worship of this mother goddess. This importance is justified by the fact that the goddess was considered the source of all life, thus emphasizing her sexual activity. Thus, the organs of procreation must be sacred, as the most diverse prehistoric statuettes make clear. It was perfectly legitimate not only to represent them, but also to worship them. Beginning from when the individual male is established as indispensable procreator, revealing the existence of a paternal lineage, it became important to hide the feminine genitals, too closely linked to the liturgies in honor of the Great Goddess, the idealized image of all women. Under these conditions, it was natural that Mosaism—and other theologies of the ancient world as well—should oppose what they called idolatry, that is, all the earlier forms of worship, notably the sexual forms, almost exclusively the prerogative of women.

A term constantly repeated in the Bible is "prostitution." The Hebrews are said to sometimes prostitute themselves to idols, and Babylon will rapidly become the "Great Prostitute." Now, in the biblical text, "prostitution" comes to designate anything involving sexual activity not directed toward procreation within an exclusively conjugal context (or familial context when concubines are legal, as was the case in the time of Abraham, Isaac, and Jacob). Sexual activity is obligatory to ensure the continuity of the race, and it is good in the eyes of the Creator ("Be fruitful and multiply," says Yahweh to Adam and Eve), even if it is subject to certain very strict conditions and gives rise to a certain impurity. But all other forms of sexuality are forbidden, and not so much for moral reasons, or "propriety," but because they recall too vividly those earlier forms of worship, which are "prostitutions."

It is not by chance that Babylon is called the "Great Prosti tute." Still, we must inquire into the exact nature of the prostitution practiced there. Herodotus is perfectly clear on this point, even if the traditions he describes offend him, solid supporter of patriarchal society that he is. "The worst Babylonian custom is the one that requires all women to go to the temple once in their lifetimes to have sexual relations with an unknown man. . . . The men walk past them and make their choices. The amount of money they offer makes no difference, the women will never refuse it, because that would be a grave sin. The money is rendered sacred by the sexual act. After this act, the woman is sanctified in the eyes of the goddess." Clearly he is describing the temple of Ishtar (Astarte), the Great Goddess of primitive Babylon, who, through the course of successive mutations, reappears in the character of Cybele, Demeter, Artemis-Diana, Aphrodite-Venus, and Dana-Anna in the Celtic world. But, the hierodules can also be found in the Babylonian temple, that is, the priestesses attached to the cult of Ishtar who had a very peculiar function. Organized into groups and presided over by a great priestess, they performed ritual prostitution in the temple or in the surrounding temple buildings, as if they were incarnations of the goddess. This prostitution was thus a liturgical act. Such intimate contact was considered a true initiation, and thus, men could be united to the divinity, could somehow participate in the divine. This idea is magnificently illustrated by the baroque poets of the sixteenth century, notably by Agrippa of Aubigné:

> Being only a mortal man, your celestial beauty,
> The violent lightning of your divine face
> Made me taste death, death and ruin,
> In order to come to immortality anew.
>
> Your divine fire burned my mortal essence,
> Your celestial being fell in love with me and ravished me
>   to the skies;
> Your soul was divine, and mine was also:
> Goddess, you raised me to the ranks of the other gods.

My mouth dared to touch the crimson mouth
To gather in, without dying, its immortal beauty;
I have lived on nectar, I have sucked ambrosia,
Savoring what is most sweet of the divine.

(Stanzas, 12)

This profession of lyrical—and passionate—faith is clearly the unconscious resurgence of Great Goddess worship such as it was practiced in ancient times. And we should note that this Christian (even, in this case, Calvinist) poet's reverie is far removed from the attitude ascribed to the Greek hero Odysseus when he is wary of the physical contact Calypso and Circe propose to him, or when he binds himself to the mast of his boat to avoid succumbing to the sirens' songs. It is true that Odysseus is the ideal model in an androcratic society that is trying, through every possible means, to eliminate the memory of the ancient mother goddess. The latter, still recognizable in the features of Penelope, is reduced to the role of passive and faithful spouse, forever taking up her work again and waiting patiently for the male's return, that is, if he so desires. In these times when the Greeks were entertaining themselves with recitations from the *Odyssey,* however, the famous sacred prostitutes of the temples of Artemis at Ephesus and Aphrodite at Corinth had not completely died out. They still officiated, though they had been reduced to the conditions of slaves. But that hardly altered popular opinion, which considered them sacred, as saints. Often, they were even referred to as *virgin saints*, which somewhat undermines the narrow idea of "virginity" as purely physical.

It was the same in India, where, during nocturnal ceremonies, the goddess Shakti, the feminine emanation of the divine, was supposed to inhabit the naked body of a young virgin shamelessly exposed and with whom one could have *sacred* sex. It was the same in Persia, before the Zoroastrian reform, in the cult of Anaitis, one of the names given to the Great Goddess:

A consecrated courtesan took the role of the goddess. She sat on a luxurious throne. Everyone could see her on the sanctuary's raised mound. With all the pomp and ceremony of the orient, her divine partner was brought to her, chosen from among the slaves. . . . The official union between the sacred courtesan and her lover, taking place in the presence of all the faithful, who joined in with elated cries, represented the high point of the religious festivities, and the invitation to a general orgy. For five days, all ties of marriage and relationships are suspended. Any woman can have sex with any man she desires and any man with any woman. In the ecstasy of the nocturnal celebration, each woman is the image of the divine Anaitis. At the end of the holiday, the lover is burned, a cruel illustration of the man's subservience to the woman.[6]

And these are only a few examples of the rituals practiced throughout the world to honor the feminine divinity of the beginnings, and to repeat through sacred gesture the primal act of creating life.

The relationship between the sacred and the sexual has always been ambiguous. The boundary between sacred orgy and depravity cannot easily be drawn, and the first can often serve as justification for the second. This debate shows no signs of being resolved soon, and we can understand why Greek and Roman censors were sometimes so severe in their opposition to what were labeled "Dionysian" cults. Not only did they call masculine society into question, but they really did disturb the public order. And when we consider how, during the first centuries of Christianity, many followers participated in the Liturgy and Mass before going off to attend ceremonies of various pagan cults, especially those of Cybele, Diana, and Isis, we cannot be the least bit surprised by the Church Fathers' constant and thundering condemnations of sexuality, nor by their repudiation of the woman, considered not only an object of temptation, but also the image incarnate of this great temptress, the Great Goddess, forever present in the memory of the people. The Church Fathers have often been called sexual obsessives. It is no doubt true to the degree that this struggle against femininity turned into a fixation and made the sexual act the great sin, but this attitude was fully justified within the context of their epoch. This was the price Christian religion had to pay to survive, faced with the neopaganism of the late Empire and the various Gnostic sects that flourished here and there, deviations of the evangelistic message that returned the woman to her primary role.

Such matters are complex, and Christianity did not impose itself on the remains of the Roman Empire without incident or vicissitudes. And this is not to cast value judgment on the content of the evangelistic message. It is simple historical observation that obliges us to note this fact: the greater the struggle, in the name of God the Father, against the very idea of the mother goddess, the more this idea took hold, and the more deeply it burrowed into the humblest layers of the social structure. What could be done to contain this invasion from within, since condemnations and curses did not suffice to purge the human unconscious? The response to this question was the same one all religions give for dealing with the fallout of an earlier order and gaining dominance. When a belief cannot be definitively expunged, it is rehabilitated by modifying it in some way so that it conforms to the new ideology. That is exactly what happened in the fifth century A.D. when the Virgin Mary finally supplanted, at least officially, the ancient mother goddess as Theotokos, that is, Mother of God. A page was turned, and it looked very different from the page before it, but the same story was continuing.

There is nothing astonishing about this continuity if we consider the history of consciousness alone, but it is a completely different matter from the theological point of view, because the concept known by the name of the "Virgin Mary" hardly asserts itself all at once. About twenty centuries had to pass to make the mysterious Mary of the Gospel of Luke into an entirely exceptional being, not divine, but somehow *deified*. This last term may seem shocking. Nevertheless, it is not an exaggeration to the extent that it corresponds to the slow development of an interpretive image revolving around an individual considered to be perfectly real, Mary, the mother of Jesus. Three dates mark this development. In 431, the Council of Ephesus (the location was

14

not chosen by chance) proclaims that Mary is the Theotokos, the Mother of God. In 1854, the pope proclaims the dogma of the Immaculate Conception, that is, birth without original sin by the one who would become the Mother of God. And finally, in 1854, Pius XII proclaims the dogma of the Assumption, that is, the sublimation, or it could even be called the apotheosis, of the woman Mary, after her physical death. But it should be pointed out that, in each case, popular religion—and thus, the deep belief of the faithful—preceded these official decisions by the Roman Church. It was as if Christian populations had imposed upon their elite the image of this universal Mother whose children we all vaguely feel ourselves to be. Twenty centuries of debate and more or less muddled delays to make one small Galilean who lived at the beginning of the first century A.D. into the "vast Mother," not a mother goddess, but the Mother of God, which, on the level of the unconscious, returns her to exactly the same place.

For, beneath it all, there actually is an individual considered to be historical—and there is no objective reason to deny that fact, even if there is absolutely no actual historical documentation: a Galilean, affianced to a certain Joseph, who bore the name of Mary, transcribed through the Latin, Maria, from the Hebrew name, Myriam. And this historical existence of Myriam presents many more problems than it resolves. Most of the so-called Church Fathers were perfectly aware of this, and often displayed their confusion, even their disapproval, regarding the religious *idolatry* (in the strict sense, and not the Catholic sense, of the term) that the faithful rendered to this Myriam-Mary, certainly mysterious, but not unlike the *Magna Mater* honored at Ephesus since time immemorial. And Ephesus was where, with an aptness loaded with innuendo, the house in which Mary supposedly lived—in the company of the apostle John—had been discovered. "The body of Mary is holy," wrote Saint Epiphanius (315–403), "but Mary is not divine." That great rationalist Saint Ambrose (340–397), maintained that "Mary was the temple of God and not the God of the temple," no doubt to emphasize that while she might be the absolute mother of God, she was no less the "Lord's servant" and not his "master," and that, in any case, she was, in the words of Saint John Chrysostom (340–407), "vain as all women are." There could be no better way to debase the woman, even if she was Theotokos.

We do not wish to ridicule or call into doubt the secular faith in that figure who would soon very rightly be called "Notre Dame." We only want to show how, through flagrant inconsistencies in canonical texts and commentaries—all differing—by the Church Fathers, the concept of mother goddess, as well as virgin mother and vast Mother, was sustained, and acquired, through the course of the centuries, a concrete form accessible to human comprehension. Because, without concrete representation, definite and perceptible, not only will a concept fail to evoke anything, it will also fail to be transmitted. Whereas this concept is transmitted and it does evoke something, even now at the end of this twentieth century when it encounters so many scoffers ready to regard "the eternally virgin Mary" ironically, without stopping to consider the significance of these terms or the place this concept occupies in the spiritual evolution of humanity.

Thus, it is necessary to begin from the historical figure of Myriam-Mary. Who was she? No one knows. The only person who could have told us anything much about her, the apostle John, who, the Christian tradition maintains, lived with the mother of Jesus, says nothing. John is absolutely silent on the conception and birth of Jesus, silent on Myriam-Mary's role in Jesus' life, except for a few details that, for that matter, reveal how little consideration Jesus had for his mother, a woman, and thus an inferior being, who had only to occupy herself with her own affairs and not those of her son. One expects more from a disciple "whom Jesus loved," and to whom he entrusted his mother when he was on the Cross. This is one of the Gospels' greatest absurdities. The principal witness of Myriam-Mary's life says nothing about her, and it falls to Luke (or those who wrote in his place: we must never forget the prudent *secundum Lucam* that the Church places at the beginning of this Gospel), who never knew either Jesus or Mary, to be the primary source of information. Certainly Matthew speaks of her as well, but in a more succinct way, and it is impossible to know which Gospel predates the other. In any case, two of the canonical Gospels out of four are silent on the circumstances of Jesus' birth, and not one of these Gospels mentions a single meeting between Jesus and his mother after his Resurrection. Only the Acts of the Apostles, which the tradition attributes to Luke, reports meetings between Mary and the disciples of Jesus.

And who was this Luke who provides so much information on Mary and the first years of Jesus' life? The Christian tradition answers unanimously: a disciple of Saint Paul. Now, as Paul never had actual physical contact with Jesus, which did not prevent him from being the true founder of the Christian Church, the testimony contained in the writings attributed to Luke cannot be considered firsthand. But, from all evidence, Luke was well read. It is reported that he was a doctor, but we do not know this for certain. All that can be confirmed is that he was Hellenized, probably Greek, and that he was a pagan converted through contact with Paul, who himself was indisputably Hellenized, despite his Jewish origins.

We know that the oldest of the Gospels is the Gospel according to Matthew, one of the Twelve Apostles. Matthew was Jewish, and wrote in Aramaic, which was a language of the people, the most widespread in all of Palestine and the surrounding regions, while the Hebraic language was reserved for priests and the intellectual elite. But the Aramaic original of Matthew's text has been lost, and only a much later Greek translation of it survives. Now, according to the opinion of all the exegetes, Matthew's translator knew Mark's account, which served as inspiration to him in many places, which makes the Greek text of Matthew unreliable. Interpolations are common in it, and, no matter what the text is, translating from a Semitic language—in which the vowels are not written—to an Indo-European language, in this case, Greek, is not easy. Interpretative errors could well have been made in all good faith. Thus, according to the documents available to us, the Gospel of Mark would seem to be the oldest, and that of John the most accurate with regard to Jesus, because of the privileged place John occupied as the "disciple whom Jesus loved." But, neither Mark nor John say anything at all on the subjects of the virginal conception, birth, infancy, or adolescence of Jesus. This is not a hypothesis; it is a fact. The two Gospels that give some information—however fragmentary—on the subject are the two accounts most influenced by Hellenism, that of Matthew, which is a translation, and that of Luke, which was certainly originally written in Greek. We can thus venture a hypothesis based on Luke's supposed personality. "As an ancient pagan, his concern was 'even to exceed, in terms of wonders, the religious stories that had lulled him to sleep as a child.'"[7] Thus, in some way, he would have wished to find in Myriam-Mary, mother of Jesus, the dominant traits of the pagan virgin mother of Ephesus, but free of all sexual components. And out of this desire comes the theme of the Annunciation by Gabriel and the idyllic description of a Holy Family that never existed except in Luke's imagination, Myriam-Mary having never married Joseph. In no canonical text is there any mention of such a marriage, to the great displeasure of certain translators, with regard to Sunday—and family—mass.

In fact, the figure of Joseph appears perfectly useless in the original schema. The principal role belongs to Myriam-Mary, whose maternity is an authentic parthenogenesis, even if it is explained by the intervention of the Holy Spirit, who "covers her with his shadow," as the Gospel's text so poetically puts it. But this parthenogenesis and the essential relationship between Jesus and his mother ran the risk of being misunderstood by new converts, too familiar with mythological accounts of ambiguous relationships between the mother goddess and her son. Thus, Luke intervened, making the schema more reasonable and, above all, supplying a historical context to make it understandable, memorable, and consistent with the new dogma that was taking shape among the heirs of the first apostles.

It is evident, nevertheless, that Luke did not adapt the stories of Christ's infancy to the myths of the mother goddesses. Rather, he wanted to show that some of these myths, which were only idealizations of deep human tendencies, had been realized, actually and historically, in the story of Jesus, and that the latter is, thus, the synthesis of the two religions: masculine (God is the father of the history of men) and feminine (the Goddess is the mother of nature). Therefore, Jesus must be regarded as the center and axis of all human history, as well as the creative principle in its entirety.[8]

And Myriam-Mary, then, is the incarnation, of *nature in the process of naturing*, in a state of permanent parturition. She is truly the vast Mother. And that is why, on Golgotha, Jesus entrusts her to John: "Woman, here is your son!" (John 19:26), signifying that he is giving her to all of humanity through the symbolic intermediary of the beloved disciple. This is a cardinal moment for the evangelistic message, and also an acknowledgment of the idea of universal mother, incarnated in the individual, Myriam-Mary.

This Myriam-Mary grows increasingly enigmatic. It is difficult to regard her as just a simple young woman of the common people, as the tendency has been, no doubt due to excessive populism. If we take Jesus' Davidic filiation seriously—and why shouldn't we?—we must conclude that Myriam-Mary belonged to a family of high nobility, a royal lineage.[9] She must have enjoyed undeniable privileges as compared to other women, social privileges that bent the customary rules by which women were entirely subservient to their fathers, and then to their husbands. Now, Myriam lives with Joseph even though she was not married to him, which is, in principle, unthinkable. Now she goes to spend several months with her cousin Elizabeth, which shows her complete freedom, something completely astonishing. All in all, she gives the impression of being a free , available, and completely self-aware woman. And these characteristics are exactly the ones that all ancient traditions attribute to the notion of virginity. The virgin is, in effect, a woman who does not depend upon a man. It is not a question of physical virginity, but of a state of consciousness. Moreover, the French word *vierge* [virgin] comes from the Latin *virgo*, for which the Indo-European root *werg* (from which come the Latin *vir*, "male," the Latin *virtus*, "courage," the Gaelic *fer*, "male," and many other terms as well) neatly expresses an idea of strength and power recognizable in the Greek *ergon*, "strength," and even in the word *orgy*, in the sense of a ritual religious ceremony permeated with divine power. The virgin is necessarily *strong*, and, since she is *free*, she is *available* to all: this is the vast Mother. Even if the Gospels provide scant—and probably deliberately abbreviated—detail on this subject, we must acknowledge that Myriam-Mary possesses all the characteristics of the traditional virgin.

As to Jesus' mother's name, it is obviously symbolic. Perhaps it was given to her later by the Evangelists, or chosen deliberately by the—unknown—parents of the Virgin. Moreover, in Latin and the Romance languages, this name acquires additional symbolic value lacking in Hebrew, as well as in Greek or the other Indo-European languages. *Maria* is, in fact, the neuter plural of *mare*, and means, first and foremost, "the seas," which immediately recalls Genesis (1:2), where it is said, "the breath of Elohim hovered over the surface of the waters." The allusion to the mother-waters, thus to a universal Mother, is perfectly clear, at least in the minds of Latin translators of the Gospels. In this connection, we should not forget that, from a scientific point of view, the origin of all terrestrial life lies in primordial waters. Latin translators were clearly aware of its ideological implications when they translated the Hebraic name of Jesus' mother as Maria.

But the French-English spelling of the name that is currently used, *Myriam*, is incorrect. It ought to be changed to *Miriam*, with two *i*'s, vowels, (not written in Hebrew), but also with a consonant *a (aleph)*. Thus, the Hebrew name is *mem-rech-aleph-mem*, which can be transcribed as MRAM, in other words, as a sacred tetragram, a counterpart to the divine Tetragrammaton YHWH. This observation is not without interest, especially when we consider the importance given to the vibratory power of letters in the Jewish tradition. Furthermore, without resorting to the subtle methods of the Kabbalah, we must observe that this feminine tetragram MRAM is composed of the key letters used in languages throughout the world to express *maternity*. Thus, it is not pure chance that the one who became the mother of Jesus, and of all humanity, was named Miriam-Mary.

Moreover, we can discover other women in the Bible who bear this name. First of all, in the Old Testament, there is Miriam, older sister of Moses and Aaron, truly a strong woman, and without whose influence, the two brothers would have sometimes fallen prey to despair and inertia. But this Miriam plays a curious role in an earlier story that is not at all clear, at least in the account given in Exodus. It seems as if Miriam had incited some kind of revolt to take control over the Hebrews. Punished by Yahweh, she was stricken with leprosy, then pardoned and healed. But could this not be, rather, a case of some kind of apostasy, a return to the worship of the mother goddess, to whom Moses, fierce partisan of the concept of the father god, proved to be the most virulent of enemies? The hypothesis is not at all improbable.

There are also some Miriams in the New Testament, in particular at the foot of the Cross, where, according to John (19.25), they numbered three: "Near to the cross of Jesus stood his mother, the sister of his mother, Miriam of Clopas, and Miriam of Magdala." John is the only Evangelist to note the presence of the mother of Jesus. The synoptic Gospels mention only Miriam of Magdala and the women who had followed Jesus since Galilee. Because John is the only Evangelist to witness the crucifixion, *a priori* the temptation is to prefer his version over the others. But there is much symbolism in John that is clearly Gnostic in flavor, and it is difficult not to wonder if this "triad" of Marys conceals meaning of a more subtle kind. In classical antiquity, but especially among the Celts, divine female figures usually appear in threes, constituting true "trinities." This is the case in all the Irish myths, especially with regard to the "triple Brigit," or "Brigit of the three faces" (Brigit, Badb, Morrigan), but it is much the same in Gallo-Roman statuary, which abounds in three-headed representations or groups of three *matrones*, that is, three mother goddesses. These three Marys under the Cross of

Jesus, couldn't they be an expression of this trinitarian concept, namely, the concept of the universal Great Mother represented in her three aspects? This is only a question, but it is an important one, especially given the presence—sometimes awkward for the commentators—of Mary Magdalene, the "Madeleine" so celebrated in popular Christian tradition.

It must be said that this Madeleine remains very mysterious. Is she a single individual or does she appear under three different aspects and three different names? The attentive reader of canonical texts cannot give a categorical response to this question because, in addition to the mother of Jesus, three Marys are named as the "holy women" coming from Galilee who, in fact, could very well be one and the same person. First of all, there is the sinner pardoned by Jesus at the house of Simon the Pharisee (Luke 7); then there is Mary of Bethany, sister of Martha and Lazarus, who rubs scented ointment on Jesus' feet (John 11 and 12); and finally, at Golgotha and at the tomb, the so-called Mary of Magdala (John 19 and 20). And nothing in the context disallows the identification of these three women as one and the same.

Whatever the case, these women are wealthy and of high social rank, including the "sinner"—that is, a prostitute—found in the house of Simon. We too often forget that, during his wandering public life in the company of his disciples, Jesus never had material difficulties. Now, he and his companions did not live on nothing, and Judas was even the treasurer of the group, proving that there was no lack of money. Was this a personal fortune, or the accumulation of "subsidies" granted by rich families? In this case, we would have to think that Mary Magdalene, no doubt one of the most important disciples of Jesus, could support his activities financially. Magdala was, at the time, a city whose prosperity seemed to rely on the presence of a certain type of establishment, and this Madeleine would have been a very wealthy proprietor of one of these establishments. These establishments are difficult to define, even though the shadow of prostitution continues to cling to Miriam of Magdala. But what is prostitution? Here is where, quite reasonably, the worship of the divine mother, considered scandalous by some, could make its reappearance under some other name. Miriam of Magdala has too often been considered an aging proprietor of a brothel. Wasn't she, rather, a great priestess of the Great Goddess, mistress of a group of hierodules, otherwise known as sacred prostitutes? It is not a far-fetched hypothesis. When, in the house in Bethany, the sister of Lazarus (a very dear friend of Jesus'), oils Jesus' feet with perfume, she performs a veritable ritual—which Judas, very shocked, judges severely[10]— an authentic ritual of royal unction. Recorded in detail in the Gospel of John, this event is of utmost importance because it does not constitute a simple sign of deference toward Jesus. It goes much further than that, as becomes clear from Jesus' re- mark to Martha as reported by Luke (10:42): "Miriam has chosen the good share, which will not be taken away from her." To understand this, we must not be satisfied with the limited inter- pretation of Miriam's act as a gesture of humility or repentance. The episode parallels the baptism of Jesus by John the Baptist. This first unction affiliated Jesus with the religion of the father god; the second affiliates him with the religion of the mother goddess. And implementing this synthesis (this reconciliation?), Jesus presents himself as the unique pivot for the spiritual life to come.

Decidedly, this Madeleine is very much of a nuisance, no less troublesome than the mother of Jesus, at least in the view of those who have refit the Christian message to an androcratic society's specifications, a society managed by men, and tied to the notion of an exclusive father god who is the sole life-giver, who punishes and rewards according to his pleasure, and who behaves himself, overall, like any vulgar Eastern despot. There is nothing of this in the words attributed to Jesus, and his public life is strewn with women, who are, without a doubt, ambigu- ous. It is for this reason that, in the first centuries of Christianity, the masters of spiritual power were forced to "cleanse" the texts of all that was too "feminist," or reminiscent of the ancient goddess religion that still survived. Thus, the figure of Miriam, the mother of Jesus, was minimized, reduced to no more than "servant of the Lord." Likewise, the role of Miriam of Magdala was reduced to only a prostitute's. But nevertheless, wasn't she the Initiatress? It is to her, not to his mother, not to the apostles, that Jesus first appears after his Resurrection. This could not be by chance.

Through these bits of information, intentionally scattered so that the great majority of followers would miss their meaning and import, it is easy enough to reconstruct the framework of initiation. Using all available means, this outline has been made to coincide as much as possible with actual and unquestionably authentic events. Born of a virgin (a woman not dependent upon a man), herself an incarnation of the Great Goddess (out of which arises, perfectly logically, the concept of Immaculate Conception), and from the breath of the father god (Elohim), the all-powerful generating principle, Jesus lives out his destiny as Christ (Messiah) to redeem and guide the humanity that he incarnates in himself. Revealed as the Son of the Father by the baptismal unction of John the Baptist, a highly symbolic figure for the ancient father-god (Yahweh) religion, he is then revealed as the Son of the Mother by the unction of the Magdalene, herself an emblematic figure for the ancient mother religion. He can then carry out what must be accomplished, that is, to submit to the trial of death and triumph over it. And it is clearly a woman, the great priestess of the mother goddess, who presides at his rebirth. Henceforth, it will be the Christ in Majesty who adorns the western portal of certain Roman Catholic cathedrals.

Now, since the very beginning of the apostolic mission, everything has been done to pass silently over this double—spiritual—affiliation of Jesus, feminine and masculine. The result has been a definitive rupture between the mother-goddess religions and the competing Christian message. And this competition has often turned into violent and bloody conflict. In the Roman Empire, the adversary was essentially a syncretic religion fusing Mithras and Cybele, which the emperors would finally adopt for obviously political ends. Too often we ignore the fact that the "persecutions" suffered by the new-born Church were not the work of the zealots of Jupiter; people had not believed in traditional Greco-Roman gods for a long time. They were carried out by followers of Cybele and political men under their influence. This fight to the finish ends, we know, with the victory of Christianity. But at what a price! Not only were the divine feminine images annihilated, but because women were considered entirely human, they were deliberately excluded from the religion and especially from the priesthood, which became the exclusive domain of the father god's sons. This exclusion, begun by Saint Paul, was maintained and sometimes amplified over the course of the centuries, and is manifested with just as much virulence today. Witness the Church's reluctance to grant priesthood to women, even within the apparently more liberal Anglican Church, as well as the total and absolute refusal to accept such an aberration in the minds of most "good" Christians. Despite feminist-sounding discourses, despite important concessions made to the female apostolate, the ruling order is always masculine. Only a man can represent Jesus, and thus, the father god. Admitting women into the priesthood would be a return, pure and simple, to those scandalous cults predating Christianity.

But this mistrust, sometimes edged with hostility, toward women originates as a sociocultural phenomena. Just as it has not always existed, it may very possibly be dying out. In this way, it is entirely unlike the concept of the divine mother that belongs naturally to human thought, no doubt because it touches the very depths of being, that is, the emotional as well as biological ties between mother and child. Here is a basic principle that, even if it is resisted and suppressed, constitutes one of the components of being human. Some thought the comforting, provocative image of the primal mother goddess had been chased from the Temple for good. She has returned, and her prominence there is sometimes even greater than before. No, the Great Goddess is not dead, and now more than ever, the shadow of the Virgin of the Beginnings falls over a world full of questions about its future.

It is clear that in the early stages of Christianity, the figure of Miriam, the mother of Jesus, had only relative importance, as the small place allotted her by the Gospels, Luke aside, proves. In the Acts of the Apostles, she evokes more interest, but we can see the personal influence of Luke at work even there. Most likely an old zealot for the Goddess, he must have been very much aware of what he was reverting to and very eager to cover the nudity or immodesty of the ancient divinity in "appropriate" attire, a divinity to whom the Jews, like the pagans, too often "prostituted" themselves. What is more, questions of great theological importance began to trouble the first exegetes of the message: Was it conceivable that she who had carried in her womb Jesus, Son of God, a divine being, could have been an ordinary woman, with all the faults attributed to her sex? In short, could the container of perfect contents be imperfect? The answer was "no," even if this "no" was accompanied by contradictory speculations.

To tell the truth, it was in Gnostic circles that this question had its greatest repercussions. The problem concerning Miriam, the mother of Jesus, would inevitably encounter the concept of the universal virgin, sometimes called Pistis Sophia, the Wise Creator, who was basically just an intellectualized form of the ancient mother goddess. In certain Gnostic sects,[11] there was even a resurgence of sexual worship that the Church Fathers condemned as aberrant (they commented on it at length), and which did nothing, of course, but reinforce their intransigence toward women and the concept of the mother goddess.

We know that the Gnostic sects, which flourished throughout the eastern Mediterranean during the first centuries B.C., set out to establish a link between the most ancient mystico-philosophical traditions and the Christian message. This link sometimes takes a very incoherent syncretic form, but more often, it constitutes a very serious attempt at in-depth synthesis. In particular, it gave full justification to the concept of a primordial feminine divinity, which the entire East would have venerated under many different names, especially in the city of Ephesus, which served, since high antiquity, as the most important sanctuary for all mother-goddess worship. Now, according to the Christian tradition, Ephesus was where the apostle John took Jesus' mother to live with her there in a house that, several centuries later, we are obliged to recognize as authentic. And why not? But the coincidences are curious, especially if we consider that in 431, Ephesus is where the notion of *theotokos* was officially attributed to Miriam.

In any case, for many Gnostic theorists, this image of the universal mother goddess, by whatever name was used to invoke her, crystallized all human drive for supreme wisdom. Thus, the Holy Spirit was considered a symbol of the Mother, included within the Trinity itself. The word used to designate the Holy Spirit was neuter in Greek (the language used to express these speculations), but feminine in Hebrew and Aramaic. Gnostics soon replaced the neuter Greek *pneuma* (breath) with the feminine *sophia* (wisdom), a term ordinarily used as masculine and feminine alike. And the term *sophia*, in the Gnostic tradition, clearly designated the feminine component of the divine. It was the divine creative wisdom and the primordial matrix of all that exists, the essential breath through which all living matter must pass before it can acquire its form.

Originally, Gnosticism was essentially Greek, though the contributions to it from Iran and Egypt were not insignificant. At the beginning of the first century A.D., the Hellenistic city of Alexandria was the great center of Gnostic speculation. Now, Alexandria was soon to become the favorite place for meetings between intellectuals of different countries and the place of asylum for Jews during the diaspora, at the same time as it was a seat of the Christian movement. The Gnostics were looking to reconcile their own traditions with Judeo-Christian traditions, and it was within this framework that it became necessary to find a place for the doctrine of Mary. We must point out, however, that the Gnostics did not express themselves in theological terms, but more often in philosophical terms, compiling elements of mysticism, mythology, and cosmological speculations in order to do this. It is a case, then, of a remarkable attempt at synthesis, aspiring to knowledge (gnosis) of the universe and the creative divinity. But this connection between Greco-Iranian and Judeo-Christian thought will soon lead to unexpected speculations.

The Gnostics seized upon the notion of "heavenly Jerusalem," the image symbolizing the future of humanity completely redeemed. Then, by way of comparison, they began emphasizing the *assembly* itself, the participants in this heavenly Jerusalem, otherwise known as the *ecclesia*, the Church ("assembly" in its etymological sense). It is Jesus himself who alludes to this heavenly Jerusalem, and he always speaks of it in terms that stress the *femininity* of this assembly of the chosen. Paul takes up the image and the name again, and he defines it as "our mother," which explains and justifies the well-known and often used expression, "our holy mother the Church." This has nothing to do with the institutional Church and its hierarchies and rules, as well as its dubious aberrations. It is an assembly, a collectivity, the "communion of saints." And, in all the traditions, this community is represented by the image of a woman, simultaneously mother, wife or lover, sister or daughter. So it is with Isis, Cybele, and the figure romanticized into Queen Guinevere who, less a representation of her actual being, remains the eternal incarnation of the social and quasi-mystical group of which she is the absolute center.

We can understand, then, how this concept of the assembly of the chosen, Christ's wife and mother, as it were, and at the same time, his daughter, slowly comes to be identified with the real individual, Miriam, mother of Jesus, but mother of all men as well. And if Miriam is the mother of all men, a feminine being perfectly historical and perfectly historicized (which, if you will, amounts to the same thing), she can only be comprehended in any real way in a known and recognizable form. From this, it follows that early on, she should acquire the essential characteristics, allowing for clever censorship, formerly attributed to the universal Great Goddess, the mother of all gods and all men. That is to say, the complexity of the individual, Miriam, then becomes the "Blessed" of Blessed Virgin Mary. A text from the end of the twelfth century, the Arthurian legend of Perceval, of Clunisian inspiration, but bearing the marks of Celtic influences, provides clear evidence that the intellectual elite—that is, the clergy—of the Middle Ages were well aware of the extraordinary role the Virgin played. In an episode coming at the beginning of the account, King Arthur finds himself at the door of a mysterious chapel. It is impossible for him to enter, because of his impurity (actually, because he has never submitted to any spiritual initiation), but, through a partly opened door, he can see what goes on inside: "The hermit said the *confiteor,* and to his right, the king perceived a child of extraordinary beauty; he was dressed in vestments and wore a gold crown set with precious stones that gave off sparkling light. To his left was a woman so beautiful that no earthly beauty could be compared to hers. . . . She sat the child on her knees and embraced him with infinite tenderness. 'Lord,' said she, 'you are at once my father, my son, my spouse, my savior, and the Savior of the world.'"[12] The roles attributed to the Virgin Mary can be no better enumerated than this, and, if examined closely, also prove to be those once attributed to the Great Goddess of the Beginnings.

Indeed, it is necessary to use concrete words or images to express a concept that is, by nature, incommunicable, and it was impossible to translate the problem of how the world or living beings originated into terms other than maternal, and thus, feminine. Abstract ideas are transmitted through concrete objects, what could be called "objects of meditation." When images, urges, feelings, or even inner convictions are projected onto them, these objects allow for comprehension or understanding. Obviously of a higher, unsurpassed beauty, this woman admirably embodies the concept of the maternal principle that presides over the appearance, over the *existence,* of all beings and all things. Within the Christian context, these perceptions of the feminine then crystallize around the historical, or historicized, figure of Miriam, and it could not be otherwise. But it is clear that the concept itself of the virgin mother predates the actual birth of the Galilaen, Miriam, existing since time immemorial. Furthermore, it is expressed again in the idea of the Immaculate Conception, even if this idea is not always clearly understood either by Christians themselves, or by Christianity's detractors.

The Gospel of John, which, we must not forget, prompts quite a number of Gnostic speculations, begins like this: "In the Principle was the Word."[13] That means that the Word, the Greek *logos* that corresponds to the Hebrew *dabar,* "effective speech," is not God himself, but that which is found in God. It is a matter, then, of the functional activities attributed to God, the Principle being identifiable with God himself in his entirety, God being the alpha and omega, the beginning and the end, which is aptly translated by the Eastern *om* and the Christian *amen,* expressions weighted with consequence and not to be pronounced lightly. But there are, *in the Principle,* other fundamental principles. If God is a totality, an absolute (equivalent to nothingness if he does not give rise to the Other opposite him, according to Hegel's famous dialectic), he must extract from himself a feminine part to accomplish the creative act. And, parallel to the phrase, "In the Principle was the Word," one could just as well say, "In the Principle was the feminine." Thus emerges the idea of a feminine, *matrical* component, a primordial divinity absolute and undifferentiated.

It is not a question, however, of coming around to the assertion that God is a woman. God is no more female than male (despite the widespread puerile imagery of God the Father). God *is.* If God is the Whole, he cannot be divided, "cut," since that is the original meaning of the word *sexual.* This "cut" is a feature peculiar to creatures who come from God but are projected outside of him into an autonomous and necessarily imperfect existence, that is to say, in the strictly etymological sense, not yet perfected, not yet come to fullness. Thus, God is not a woman, since this statement would be restrictive. By contrast, the feminine is within God, which does not mean, within Christian thought at least, that one can suppose the existence of a goddess who is hierarchically inferior. Thus, the Virgin Mary is not the Great Goddess of the religions preceding Christianity, but in the collective unconscious, she is the successor, especially on the level of concrete representation.

These are subtle distinctions, but they shed valuable light on the idea, dating back to the beginning of time, of a feminine component of the divine, sometimes anthropomorphized into an individual, sometimes remaining a pure abstraction. "This existence of a great universal feminine Principle, virgin and fertile, original Womb of all things, will seem absolutely logical to those familiar with the laws of analogy that form the basis of eternal harmony."[14] In one sense, this great feminine Principle can be compared to the *hyla* of Greek philosophy, but with Neoplatonic overtones. "Thus, the alchemists were being infinitely reasonable when they taught that, to obtain the Philosophers' Stone, it was necessary to procure the earth's *hyla*, the primitive Latex of things that carried the Word in its womb."[15] The Latin word *materia*, which denotes what we call "matter," does it not come from the word *mater*, the "mother"? Given these circumstances, "being the firstborn of God's works, and formed before time, the Virgin's existence could not be restricted to the short evangelistic period. Thus, it is not extraordinary that she was known on earth from the beginning, and even well before her terrestrial manifestation."[16] The Galilean Miriam existed before the dawn of time in the mind of God, and it is not merely a matter of historical chance that the Virgin Mary is supposed to have lived in Ephesus, home of the principal shrine to the Goddess of the Beginnings.

We must not ignore the fact that the concept of divine mother is linked to *matter*, thus to the earth, and that, consequently, this telluric aspect necessarily leads to a search for special places supposedly favorable to a privileged relationship between mother and child, between the "creator" and the creature. At Delphi, the sanctuary of the Great Goddess, an underground *womblike* sanctuary, is marked by the *omphalos*, the world's navel. It could not be otherwise. All the shrines of the ancient Goddess, like those of the Christian Virgin Mary, are, in one way or another, directly related to places possessing certain feminine characteristics: a grotto or manmade chamber (uterus), a natural or manmade knoll (belly of a pregnant woman), a deep, flowing spring (maternal milk). Actually, even though the symbolic significance of these places is clear, it is not primarily a matter of cultural traditions. In most cases, it is the places themselves that prompt the establishment or construction of a sanctuary.

Prehistoric peoples, which we too often have tended to consider "primitive" in the pejorative sense, in fact possessed a kind of knowledge now lost or deliberately ignored that might be called "geobiology," that is, the study of energies (vibrations) peculiar to a place, and the influence of those energies not only on the physical behavior of living beings, but also on their psyches, if not their spirits. Of course, this type of knowledge cannot be in any way rational, given the lack of technology and probable absence of any stable system of measurement, but this scientific "weakness" was compensated for by a far greater intuitive awareness of the environment. Living in constant and intimate contact with nature, prehistoric populations *knew*, without being able to express it logically, that places existed where one sensed more vividly a certain transcendence, negative or positive. Thus was manifested the feeling of the "sacred," this subtle relationship between human beings and all that surpasses them.

If we read the most ancient human texts—which are essentially mythological or religious—with a certain kind of naiveté, we are always astonished at the great degree of familiarity between gods and humans. In the Hebrew Bible, Yahweh is constantly showing himself to the "glebous" (that is, Adam, according to the translation of André Chouraqui) and his descendants. And when it is not Yahweh, it is his messengers, his "angels," who provide for these transmissions between the visible and the invisible. In the *Iliad* and the *Odyssey*, the divinities frequently "materialize" and intervene in human destiny. In primitive Celtic traditions, as represented by Irish tales from the Middle Ages, these "gods" (which, in reality, are only functional aspects of a single, unique divinity) permeate everyday life, where, in any case, there is already interpenetration between the divine and the human world. All this is absolutely obvious within the archaic framework. Moreover, similar evidence is found in the Christian tradition, as the *Golden Legend* of Jacques de Voragine and the numerous hagiographic accounts from all epochs attest to, all of which comprise the more or less official accounts of "apparitions," those of the Virgin Mary in particular.

It would be foolish, however, to take all this literally. Narratives exploit symbols, and it is through such means that the message

32

can be transmitted. The "apparitions" of pre-Christian divinities or of the Virgin Mary, whatever be the extent of their actual reality, are proof of the existence of privileged moments, in places equally privileged, in which subtle and mysterious contact is established between the visible and the invisible, between the terrestrial world and what we call the otherworld. Now, an attentive study of all these texts leads to an extraordinary finding: each time there is an apparition—or materialization—of a divine or spiritual entity, it is always within, or very close to, a place traditionally held sacred according to the collective memory. It is in the holy place of Shechem, at the oak of Moreh, that Yahweh appears to Abraham. It is with his head leaning against a sacred rock (a "bethel") that Jacob has his famous dream of the ladder. It is on Mount Sinai, the summit consecrated to the ancient Semitic moon god, Sin, that Yahweh shows himself to Moses. These are only three examples; there are countless others in all religious and mythological traditions.

Which is to say that those manifestations called, for lack of a better term, "supernatural," do not take place just anywhere. In a wonderful scene in *The Infernal Machine*, Jean Cocteau makes the ghost of Laertes appear at the miry, marshy, and mephitic spot where the sewage of Thebes is discharged. The spirit of the old king, assassinated unknowingly by Oedipus, takes on a vague human form in the nauseating vapors that the cesspool puts off. Marshes are well known, moreover, to be favorable sites for "apparitions" of all sorts, which makes rationalists snicker, because the more hazy and indefinite the environment, the more light breaks through suspended water droplets, and the more numerous are optical illusions. That's easy to say. Marshes are strange places where life and death are continually mixing with each other and delicate exchanges between dissolution and regeneration take place. There is no a priori logical contradiction involved in spiritual entities—whether good or evil is not the question—taking advantage of this environment to make themselves perceptible. It is in caves near springs or rivers, where likewise the atmosphere is humid and full of water vapor, that the mysterious "white ladies" appear throughout the Pyrenees.

And what happened to Bernadette Soubirous at Lourdes is a phenomenon of the same sort, without denying in any way the actual presence of the Virgin Mary.

We now know that magnetic currents travel throughout the earth's surface, currents termed telluric, powerful lines whose exact nature is unknown. We also know that the underground is crisscrossed with water that sometimes flows and is sometimes still, and that this water emits waves that can disrupt the normal behavior of living beings, not to mention natural radioactivity, especially in crystalline rocks, or faults in the earth's crust, sensitive places par excellence, or again, volcanic masses. The whole of these phenomena constitute a veritable vibratory tissue that cannot be without influence on the biological and psychological lives of individuals.

Now, these lines, these currents, inevitably run into each other, interpenetrate, and form what are called nodes. And depending upon how complex they are, these nodes are the source of turbulence that can be very powerful, whatever its polarity, positive or negative. It has been proposed, in connection with this, that the monoliths, those rough stones erected by Neolithic peoples, could be "fixation points" for telluric energies, acupuncture points, as it were, on the earth's surface, either to neutralize negative forces or to stimulate positive ones, but always to create equilibrium within the vibratory tissue. And we must not forget those points of junction between earthly vibrations and influences coming from the cosmos, cosmic rays or currents that, likewise, undeniably affect beings and things. Nothing in the universe is isolated, but so-called civilized humans have lost something of the ancient cosmic consciousness that belonged to our distant ancestors.

It is this cosmic consciousness, felt much more than intellectualized, that is the source of sacred places. People knew, without being able to explain, or even express it, that such and such a place was favorable for a meeting of the visible and the invisible, the *here below* and the *up above*, a fusion often symbolized by a hill, a manmade mound, an island, a clearing, a tree, a vital and perfect communication point between heaven and earth. And when human beings lost this cosmic consciousness to analytic consciousness, it continued, despite everything, to be put to use in establishing sanctuaries in the same spots. How many Christian churches are found situated where Gallo-Roman temples stood, which themselves were built on Gallic *nemetons*, ancient megalithic sanctuaries!

Everything takes place as if, in the unconscious order of the world, successive generations attached themselves, without knowing why, to a primal revelation completely lost to us today. But this "revelation" it seems, is much more the consequence of *sympathy* between man and the universe than of brutal and sometimes untimely intervention by an individual who was the incarnation—or the appearance—of a divinity. We know, of course, the forms this divinity takes are always cultural. They result necessarily from the projection of the imagination onto an "entity," by definition indefinable and ethereal, whatever be its true essence and intrinsic reality. In one sense, placed within certain social and psychological conditions, isolated in a place that provokes a rupture between the material and the spiritual, the individuals can only opt out and do their best within a dimension of consciousness totally different from that in which they would have normally developed. And since it is a matter of individual experience, they can only account for what they see by clothing it in garments that will be perceptible and comprehensible to others.

It is not a matter here of doubting the reality of these "apparitions," but of showing the subtle mechanisms by which these "apparitions" take shape in the imagination, and, beyond that, in artistic representation. Thus we come to the problem of the representation of the gods in general, and the visualization of the universal Great Goddess in particular, through all her historical, sociological, cultural, and even theological metamorphoses. Because, from the Paleolithic "Venus" to the pale Sulpician "Holy Virgin," it is the same phenomenon we can observe through countless mutations that the human spirit has prompted.

But still, nothing is gratuitous in these representations. They obey a completely implacable, if very often unconscious, logic.

The original design always shows through the successive ideological veneers, and it is evidently an obligatory design in which we find concentrated the two essential notions of the Great Goddess, femininity and maternity (which do not inevitably coincide). And just as the sacred place was chosen as a function of various factors, so the representation was usually chosen as a function of the place, where it would be situated in such a way that there would be harmony between the image and its immediate surroundings. With regard to this subject, it is useful to recall a motif often encountered in legends concerning the lucky discovery of a statue buried in the earth or hidden in a bush. Generally, the discovery is made by a peasant who is working his field, or who is astonished to see his cattle always stopping in the same place. The statue is unearthed. She is often ill-formed or very altered, but no one doubts that this is a statue of the Virgin (or of Saint Anne, who, we shall see, comes to be the same thing). In order that this statue be protected, and of course, worshiped, it is taken to the parish church where it becomes an object of veneration. But, every night, it disappears from the church and is found again the next day at the place it was first discovered, clear proof that this is where it wants to be worshiped. An isolated chapel is then built, which will become a place of pilgrimage. This legendary theme is rich with meanings.

As preposterous as they can seem, fables always take into account intellectual as well as historical reality. In the light of these stories of statues returning again and again to the places they were discovered, almost certain conclusions must be drawn. Let us pass over the "supernatural" aspect of this; it is only the result of a kind of symbolism that must captivate the imagination. The first certain conclusion concerns the place. If, in very ancient times, a statue had been erected in a carefully determined place, then its presence asserted itself there as an element of concentration, of crystallization, of different magnetic currents, telluric and cosmic. In this sense, the statue was indispensable to this precise spot. Once moved, even for clear reasons of conservation, even for the honorable purpose of worshiping it, this statue lost all its power. And if we follow this line of reasoning through to the end, we are led to conclude that all statues, so-called pagan as well as Christian ones, that have been saved from destruction and sheltered in museums have lost all religious or spiritual value. Nothing more than their artistic aspect remains, incontestable, but of very much less importance than the original whole. Any statue exiled in a museum becomes a lifeless object.

A second certainty concerns what, borrowing a term from magic, we could call the *charge* of the statue itself. A statue is made for one set purpose and as a function of the place where it must be erected. Thus, it is *charged* with particular intentions. A representation called Our Lady of the Marshes can have neither the same function nor the same characteristics as a statue called Our Lady of the Snows. And these deep intentions necessarily mark the construction of the work, the latter inevitably acquiring a certain "shape wave" in relation to both the charge and the place it is to be erected. Moreover, that is why so many statues of the Virgin, the originals of which were destroyed during religious wars or the Revolution and which were later reconstructed (even with inlays of the primitive statue), have absolutely no power. They are only reminders of an earlier place in the collective memory. As to the countless plaster statues scattered throughout churches and chapels all over France, they have no more value than the copies of ancient works that abound in archaeological museums. They are only interesting as documentation. But it is true that now, at the end of the twentieth century, sanctuaries are tending to become museums. We content ourselves with conserving (as securely as possible) what is no longer alive. Thus our nostalgia for times forever gone finds expression. . . . If the famous Lascaux cave is closed to the public—and if it is reconstructed in duplicate, not far away—it is with excellent intentions: to save an incomparable cultural heritage. But then, where is the spiritual heritage in all of that?

A third conclusion asserts itself: a sanctuary, whether it be Christian or it predate Christianity, loses all or part of its power to be effectual when it is emptied of the elements that composed it. The admirable care taken to safeguard artistic masterpieces by securing them away from possible theft or vandalism inevitably weakens the spiritual significance of a sanctuary, even if a statue made to stand in one precise spot in the sanctuary is only locked in a sacristy. As to the modifications and other innovations that are supposed to aid the faithful in comprehending rituals, they translate into aberrations and misinterpretations that do not even seem to touch the spirit of a clergy entirely focused on communication, to the detriment of spirituality. Moving the main altar, formerly placed in the most *energetic* spot in the church, toward the crossing of the transept represents total ignorance about the subtleties of the sacred. As for the statues that obstruct visibility and are relegated to any spot whatever, one no longer counts them. Thus it is that the churches and cathedrals, what sanctuaries they were, are nothing more than museums, only assuming a certain sacred aura, despite everything, and often simply becoming theaters. A sign of the times, when the sacred disappears under the false colors of the profane.

Certainly, it is necessary to adapt, but it is regrettable that the honorable desire to grant maximum accessibility systematically reduces its objects to the lowest common denominator. The end of the nineteenth and the beginning of the twentieth century, with its dose of atheism and anticlericalism, and consequently, the resurgence of a religious fanaticism cut off from all its traditional roots, fell into the pitfalls of badly digested scientism. Churches were constructed without regard to where or how, without reference to any sort of sacred geography. Thanks to technical progress, so-called Sulpician plaster statues proliferated, which lack intrinsic value as they do artistic qualities. And, on the purely archaeological level, sacred sites were cleared of all that was vital that remained there, to the profit of those new secular temples, the museums. As to the secondhand-goods dealers and antiquarians on all sides, they made fortunes reselling sacred objects at very high prices to enlightened amateurs, objects wrested from certain naive or incompetent clergy for ridiculous sums. The rupture, then, from the spiritual source that surged when time began and continued to manifest itself so forcefully for countless centuries, seems complete.

And yet, never has the cult of the Virgin Mary been more intensely alive, as much among the general populous as the intellectual elite. This is certainly not the great period of the twelfth and thirteenth centuries that saw so many sanctuaries dedicated to Our Lady open their doors. Enthusiasm is no longer so spectacularly displayed, and takes refuge in the individual mystic, but the image of the Theotokos blazes with all its fire there in the shadows where industrial society's attempts at explaining the world rationally are rejected. The "apparitions" of the Virgin, however debatable they sometimes are, as in the case of the La Salette, follow one after another with an astonishing rhythm, even if the official Church is very careful to issue warnings about this or that manifestation that they consider suspect or overzealous. Certain sanctuaries that had fallen into disuse are being restored. Ostensibly for cultural reasons, more and more places are being protected that, a hundred years ago, would have been classified as monuments to the glory of human superstition. It must be acknowledged that the "history of religions" continues to expand, thanks to new linguistic and archaeological discoveries, and that, very often, the historians themselves note with amazement that the Great Goddess of ancient times has never stopped speaking to humans in the language of timeless femininity.

And this language is accessible to all. Its emotional content exempts it from all considerations of a logical nature. Infants have not the slightest need to decipher the complex relations they maintain with their mothers. They are content to live them, even if, according to temperament, they find themselves favoring this or that characteristic. By nature, the Virgin is, in effect, capable of assuming all the features that her devotees wish to attribute to her. She is the vast Mother, at once collective and individual, maternal and filial, exacting and indulgent, suffering and glorious, physical and spiritual, lady of all origins and servant of the Lord. This is the message that the well-known, and too often trite, litanies of the Virgin try to convey, admirable synopses of the virginal functions: "Mirror of Justice," "Seat of

Wisdom," "Spiritual Vessel," "Mystic Rose," "Ivory Tower," "Ark of the Covenant," "Heaven's Gate," "Star of Morning," "Queen of the Angels," but also, "Comforter of the Afflicted," "Refuge of Sinners," and "Queen of All the Saints," otherwise known as the great queen who predates time and whose face will still shine forth even after the centuries end.

These litanies reveal a specific conception of the Virgin, as well as a symbol of a community. While borrowing from formulaic prayers that were Greek in origin, we know that litanies are an archaic Celtic ritual that then passed into primitive Irish Christianity, and from there, they swept through the entire Christian world. It is a matter, pure and simple, of crossing through the many names to find the lost unity once again, to reconstitute the "communion of saints," all the saints being, of course, the children of this universal mother, of whom Jesus of Nazareth is one of the exemplary members, the guide along the path of this return to unity. And with her multiple aspects, who better than the woman could express the interdependence of being and things within a cosmos conceived and created by the primordial God?

Clearly, it is necessary to go beyond the stage of piety, including within its features the most puerile and the most reductive. "Piety" does not consist of blindly following a ritual. It is a state of mind, an openness toward the whole, which inherent human weakness has trouble even glimpsing. Only those mystics and artists whose work becomes a means of grasping universal consciousness can raise themselves above the mists that blur appearance and essence. "The first creature issued from the thought of God, it is through her [the Virgin] that all the others have come into existence" (Thomas Aquinas). And, in the tormented mind of Gérard de Nerval, of lightning streaking a stormy sky, "I reported my thought to the eternal Isis, the sacred mother and wife; all my hopes, all my prayers met in this magic name, I felt myself revived in her, and sometimes she appeared to me in the form of the ancient Venus, sometimes with the traits of the Virgin of the Christians" (Aurélia). Here, the accusation of syncretism does not hold. It is a matter of a reality much deeper and more inherent to human nature.

Indeed, this reality of the vast Mother escapes all classification and is not satisfied by any dogmatic formulation, whatever religious system we consider. Thus, one of the most vibrant, sincere, just, and probably most moving of homages to the universal Great Goddess can be found in the strange story, *The Golden Ass*, by the late Roman Empire Latin author, Apuleius, initiate into the mysteries of Isis and steeped in Hellenistic culture. This is what he has his hero, Lucius, who is also his double, say:

> Queen of Heaven, whether you are the nourishing Ceres, mother and creator of the harvest . . . who now haunts the fields of Eleusis; or whether you are celestial Venus, who, after having united the sexes in the first days of the world by giving birth to Love and perpetuating the human species through eternal renewal, now receives worship in the sanctuary of Paphos surrounded by waves; or whether you are the sister of Phoebus, who, by relieving the pain of women in labor with soothing care, has given rise to entire peoples, and who is now worshiped in the illustrious temple of Ephesus; or the whether you are terrible Persephone, howling at night, with three faces, who puts down the assaults of the worms and keeps the underground prisons closed, who wanders here and there in the sacred woods, and who is propitiated by various rites, you who shed your feminine light on all the ramparts, nourish with your moist rays the fertile seeds, and dispense in your solitary evolutions an uncertain light—under whatever name, by whatever ritual, under whatever aspect it is rightful to invoke you—assist me in my misfortune (*The Golden Ass*, 12.2).

Such is the prayer of the believer, and which religion he or she claims to belong to doesn't matter. And the invocation becomes an evocation. The goddess appears and speaks in her turn:

> I come to you, Lucius, moved by your prayers, me, the mother of all nature, mistress of all the elements, origin and

principle of the centuries, supreme divinity, queen of the shades, first among the inhabitants of the heavens, *unchanging example of the gods and goddesses*. The sky's lit summits, the sea's good winds, hell's desolate silences, it is I who govern them all according to my desire. A single power, the entire world worships me in numerous forms, by various rites, under multiple names. The Phrygians, first-born of men, call me mother of the gods, goddess of Pessinus; the native Athenians, Cecropian Minerva; the wave-washed Cypriots, Paphian Venus; the Cretan arrow-bearers, Diktynna Diana; the trilingual Sicilians, Stygian Persephone; the inhabitants of ancient Eleusis, Actaeon Ceres; some Juno, others, Bellona, here, Hecate, there, Rhamnusie. But those who the sun god lights with his first rays as he rises, his last rays as he leans toward the horizon, the people of the two Ethiopias and the Egyptians, empowered by their ancient knowledge, honor me with the kind of worship which is proper to me and call me by my true name, Queen Isis (*The Golden Ass*, 12.5).

And if Apulieus had had some knowledge of the far western Celtic traditions, he would not have failed to add the names of Dana or Anna, of Brigit, of Macha, of Morgan or Rhiannon, the "great queen," or of Arianrhod, the "silver wheel," and that is to cite only a few names among so many, all designating the same unique female divinity of the Beginnings.

But the goddess is not satisfied with just talking to Lucius. She appears to him, and the description that Apuleius gives evokes wonder:

Marvelous apparition, which I will do my best to put into words, if the poverty of human language allows me to . . . First, her long, rich hair, in loose curls, spreading over her divine nape, hung with such softness. A crown of various flowers, braided unevenly, encircled the top of her head. In the middle of it, above her forehead, a flat disc in the form of a mirror, or rather, imitating the moon, cast a white glow. To the right and left, it was flanked by two coiled vipers with their heads drawn up, and above it also rested Ceres' ears of corn. Her tunic, with its changing colors and material of the finest linen, was, by turn, white as the day, yellow as the crocus flower, glowing red as the flame. But what especially and above all dazzled my eyes was her mantle, intensely black and shining with a dark light. Wrapped all around her body, it passed under her right arm to come just up to her left shoulder, from where it fell again, forming a knot in front and then descending in pleated folds to the lower hem, which was lined with a graceful fringe. The embroidered border as well as the hem was dotted with shimmering stars, in the middle of which a full moon gave off its fire. And all along the curve that this magnificent mantle followed ran a garland composed entirely of fruits and flowers. As to the attributes of the goddess, they were very diverse. Her right hand held a bronze sistrum whose narrow band, bent in the form of a sling, was crossed with three shafts which, after three shakes of the arm, gave off a clear sound. From her left hand hung a gold situla and on its handle was mounted an asp with its head raised, its neck flaring. Her divine feet were covered in sandals of braided palm leaves, the tree of victory. It was in this imposing form that the goddess, exhaling the lovely perfumes of Arabia, deigned to address me. [17]

It is all there. Thus, over the centuries, the Belle Dame will present herself to countless Christian "visionaries" dressed in the "color of the time." Nothing is lacking, neither the mantle, nor the crown, nor even the serpent (the latter, in Christian iconography, being expelled to the feet of the Virgin, of course!). As to the beauty of the apparition, it is imposing, and it will assert itself with even greater force when the "visionaries" of the Virgin Mary are shepherds or poor and tattered shepherdesses who would never take an apparition seriously if it had the aspect of an ugly woman or someone dressed in rags. Once again, we are not debating the reality of such apparitions here, but observing that these "apparitions" bear all the idealized—and fantastical—cultural projections of those who are, or who claim to be, their witnesses. The mystery itself remains intact.

Because despite the diverse and even divergent sociocultural veneers, one constant in the representation of the virgin mother remains. Diana of Ephesus, as she is represented in a statue at the New Conservatory in Rome, wears a tower for a diadem, has countless breasts, and a stomach covered with equally countless creatures, but even so, she is Mary, mother of all men, the "tower of David" of the litanies. The symbolic meaning is identical. As for the ancient Cybele, who laments as she holds the dying body of her son-lover, Attis, in her lap, we cannot help but recognize in it the pietà, so familiar in the Christian world, this Mater Dolorosa in which the maternal impulses of all women can be crystallized.

The Church Fathers did not shy away from denouncing this identification. While the

Apocalypse denounced Attis as the *monster*, and Cybele as the *Great Mother of prostitutes and the scum of the earth*, Saint Augustine considered her the most scandalous of all the divinities: "The Great Mother prevails over all the gods, her children, not by her divine excellence, but by the enormity of her crime. It is a monstrosity that makes that of Janus pale in comparison. He is only hideous because of the deformity of his statues. She is hideous because of the cruelty of her mysteries. Only in effigy does he have extra limbs. She mutilates actual human limbs. Jupiter's incest and licentiousness is nothing compared to this infamy. Seducer of so many women, Jupiter only dishonors one Ganymede's heaven, but she, by her professional emasculating, she defiles the earth and outrages the heavens." Saint Augustine alludes here to the galli, those priests who dress up as women and even castrate themselves, as did their model, Attis. But, in doing this, the bishop of Hippo forgets that, within the official framework of Christianity, priests castrate themselves morally and symbolically by agreeing to renounce all sexual activity. There is no lack of shared features between the cult of Cybele and Christianity. The sacrifice of the son who dies and returns to life is not missing from the latter. The Great Mother is not missing either, but she is split up into the figure of the Virgin, the sorrowful mother, and the terrible God who condemns his son to death. But it is, no doubt, because of these analogies that the cult of Cybele and Attis was so violently attacked by the first Christians.[18]

Finally, the great truth in all of this is what Gérard de Nerval so magnificently expresses in *Les Chimères*, "The thirteenth returns, it is still the first . . ."

PART I

Images and Sanctuaries of the Goddess

I

OUR LADY OF THE BEGINNINGS
The Paleolithic Period

For nearly four thousand years we have been living, intellectually at least, under the burden of an incredible deception: the deception that makes the sun into the symbolic image of creative and omnipotent masculinity. Now, if we carefully examine the oldest archaeological data and compare it with mythological motifs derived from the collective memory, which forgets nothing, we see that this deception is the result of a sociocultural disruption, occurring at various times according to geographical area. In fact, it involved a polar reversal by which the individual male began to dominate the woman and to bury the image of her in the depths of his unconscious, with all the negative repercussions that could carry with it. In short, this deception, which is truly a case of fraud, is only patriarchal societies' attempt to justify, through groundless assertion, man's superiority over woman, a claim that cannot be proven, and that is contradicted by archaeological findings as well as by analysis of the most ancient human traditions.

There are countless examples. In Japan, it is a goddess who

presides over the sun's course and who eventually becomes identified with that star by the familiar process that substitutes concrete expression for abstraction. Among the Scythians, it is the formidable Artemis of Tauris, who so impressed the Greek dramatists, and who we find again in the legend of the Nartes, so wonderfully illuminated by Georges Dumézil, under the already more or less "demonized" name of Sathana. Among the Germanic Scandinavians, it is the Valkyrie Sigrdrifa, sometimes appearing in the form of a swan, and later becoming Brynhild, asleep in an ethereal castle surrounded by walls of flame. Among the Celts, it is a mysterious, radiant sun-woman whose characteristics we find again in the Irish heroine, Grainne, whose name comes from the Gaelic *grian*, "sun," and who is the prototype for Isolde the Blonde. Moreover, isn't it worth noting that, in modern Germanic and Celtic languages, the sun retains the feminine gender while the moon is masculine? It is even said that Tristan, the moon-man, cannot live for more than a month without having physical contact with Isolde, the sun-woman. Because of her menstrual cycle, the woman has naturally been linked to the lunar month. That is valid, but it is a mistake to then identify the woman with the moon, because a woman's menstrual cycle exists only during those years when she is most fully a woman, and therefore fertile, and capable of being impregnated by a man. Where is the link with the moon for the prepubescent girl or the woman past menopause? This view is terribly simplistic.

The Hebrew Bible, we have seen, testifies to incessant struggles between the concepts of father god and mother goddess. As soon as the cult of Yahweh triumphed, the Goddess of the Beginnings was reduced to her simplest form, and the Lilith of the rabbinical tradition, consigned to the darkness. Thus the most shameful human impulses found themselves crystallized into the troubling image of "Our Lady of the Night,"[1] later becoming "Our Lady of the Underground," this incomprehensible Black Virgin of well-known Christian sanctuaries. Under the pretext that such divine feminine representations had been found in caves or at the bottom of dark burial mounds, these undeniably maternal figures were immediately relegated to funerary functions. But isn't the Goddess of the Dead also the Goddess of the Living?

In his *Cinquième Livre* (chap. 45), Rabelais, the inheritor of a great and uninterrupted tradition, has these words spoken to Bacbuc, the high priestess (and not the high priest) of the underground temple of the Dive Bouteille, which reveal this solar tradition: "What has become of the art of evoking lightning and heavenly fire from the skies, invented long ago by the wise Prometheus? You have certainly lost it; it has departed from your hemisphere, and here under the earth it is put to use." And the myth of the Grail admirably brings together the various strands of the solar conception of the female divinity. When, for the first time, Perceval finds himself in the dark (and symbolically, underground—hidden, or inaccessible to the mortal community) castle of the Fisher King, he sees, in the midst of a strange procession, a young woman, the most beautiful in the world, holding in her hands a grail from which emanates a light that eclipses all others.[2] The myth is incontestably Celtic, but more importantly, evidence of Gnostic influence contributes to its medieval formulation. This grail (a common term that can simply mean "container") will be carved into the emerald carried by Lucifer, the "light-bearer," also called Venus, and also, the primordial Goddess, before her descent into the darkness (to be read: "before the eclipse of the Goddess"). And in the darkness, this brilliant grail can shine more dazzlingly in some ways than in the world of habitual light.

And, despite everything, this light, an analogue for "the light under the bushel," is not about to be extinguished. "Up until now, humanity has experienced two types of civilization, the civilization of the chalice and civilization of the sword. . . . The civilization of the chalice represents the some sixteen thousand years of prehistory when the idea of God was female. These times of the Great Goddess mother are still very poorly understood . . . nevertheless, archaeological evidence abounds."[3] And something does remain: first, the famous quest for the Grail, a desperate attempt to achieve synthesis between the chalice and the sword, a passionate search for the chalice by men of the sword, and then, the mysterious game of tarot, in which the two civilizations of the chalice and the sword are carried on by two future civilizations, and finally and most importantly, the evidence supplied by female representations from the Upper Paleolithic period, before the polar reversal that moves humanity from the Age of Gold into the Age of Iron.

It is, in fact, in the Gravettian epoch of the Upper Paleolithic age, from 25,000 B.C. to 20,000 B.C., that the first manifestations of anthropomorphic art appeared. Now, it was nearly exclusively women who were represented, and not men, both by statuettes and the wall engravings found in specific spots in certain caves that seem to have served as sanctuaries. This is the case with the famous Venus of Lespugue, discovered in the Pyrenees, and which is only one example among many others, in France and throughout Europe. Thus, we could cite the Venuses of Grimaldi, in Italy, the Venus of Willendorf, in Austria, and again, the Venus of Gagarino in central Russia. In France itself, we could compare her to the Venus of Monpazier (Dordogne), the one of Sireuil (Dordogne), the one of Tursac (Dordogne), as well as the engravings in the cave of Pech-Merle in Cabrerets (Lot), which perhaps date back to the preceding epoch, that is, the Aurignacian (from 30,000 B.C. to 25,000 B.C.).

The term "Venus" that is applied to these figures certainly seems a bit surprising, since what characterizes them is the monstrosity of their forms. The Venus of Lespugue is an ivory statuette, fifteen centimeters high. The face is oval, and without a single feature, as if the sculptor wanted to show that what is essential is not to be found there. The neck is very long, overhanging a flat thorax from which thin, parallel arms meet above the enormous mass of breasts, which droop very low over a rounded belly. Seen from the back, the statuette presents two enormous masses encompassing hips and buttocks, which flow down from either side of the body, dominating the thighs, very close together and thin in comparison to the rest, and ending in very fine legs without feet. The whole thing is absolutely fascinating, and that is probably what the sculptor was aiming for in this accumulation of exaggerations.

There is much commentary on these representations that

insists, perhaps too much, upon their fertility symbolism. The parts of the body linked to maternity—breasts, belly, and hips—are definitely emphasized, but so are the buttocks, and in certain statuettes, like the Monpazier one, the genitals are too, with all the connotations that conveys. The Venus of Monpazier certainly poses the most problems concerning the exact nature of these female representations, and it is good to repeat, after Leroi-Gourhan, what we have reduced to a few hypotheses on the "profound meaning Paleolithic people gave to their Venus who could just as well be Juno or Proserpine." Because if Juno-Hera indisputably represents the divine Mother, Proserpine-Persephone, often mixed up with Hecate, has the alternative aspect of a nocturnal goddess, sensual, voracious, and terrifying.

The Venus of Monpazier is, in fact, is a model of the Lespugue one. The face is similarly blank, the neck less long, the breasts less large, but when we examine it in profile, we are immediately struck by the enormity of the belly and the curve of the back, which emphasizes the buttocks, protruding but small in relation to the whole. Now, if we look at it from the front, we cannot help by notice the importance given to the opening of the vulva, which is inordinately enlarged. We can attempt an explanation only by making a comparison with those strange feminine figures of Ireland and Great Britain that are given the generic name (in Gaelic) of Sheela-na-gig. These are relatively recent representations discovered in the churches, on the capitals of Roman or pre-Roman columns, but they seem to be reproductions of a much more ancient model inherited from druidic antiquity, and so, seem to refer back to a more distant era. The standard model of these Sheela-na-gigs consists of a feminine form whose appearance is often terrifying and whose hands deliberately hold open her labia to display her gaping vagina. The most beautiful and characteristic example is certainly the one found in the Kilpeck church in the county of Hereford (Great Britain), but countless numbers of them exist throughout Ireland. And here, again, fertility is always proposed when the idea that they are allegories for the horrible sin of lust is abandoned. But "there is not a single tradition or legend associated with the Sheelas that supports this hypothesis. Moreover, it is possible that they had been forgotten over the course of the centuries. And since they were generally placed up high (in the churches or on the exterior walls of buildings . . . it is possible to propose an apotropaic function for them: protection against evil or an enemy attack."[4]

Nevertheless, it seems that the Sheela-na-gig is neither a "scarecrow" meant to frighten away all kinds of enemies, nor a frightening and symbolic image of guilt-ridden sexuality, nor a simplistic representation of fertility as a means of reproduction. If no tradition of its own exists for this Sheela, we can find her in Gaelic texts from the high Middle Ages, nevertheless, appearing as the great queen, Morrigan in particular, this goddess of love and war, prototype for the fairy Morgan of Arthurian tales, and especially as the queen, Medb (Maeve) who, we are assured, "lavished the friendship of her thighs on all the warriors she needed to insure the success of an expedition." This is a well-known theme regarding the virgin (in the sense of "available") to whom young men go to prostitute themselves in order to acquire knowledge and power. This is the sacred prostitution so often denounced in the Yahwistic Bible because it gives value to the worship of the female sun. The Sheela-na-gig is thus even more of an initiatress, the one who allows penetration, thanks to her wide-open genitals, into the cave of knowledge, and who presides at the second birth, at the rebirth, by absorbing the dead-and-gone into her divine womb in order to transmit to them heat and eternal life. This is what emerges again and again from every Celtic myth, and can be very useful in clearing up the mystery of the Sheela-na-gigs.

The Venus of Monpazier is certainly very similar in nature. "The monstrous Venus is a *religious* representation—the reification of the Life Genetrix. Those parts of the body that in our eyes, seem exaggerated or grotesque are those parts of her that are most significant, magical, and sacred, the visible, productive source of cyclic life continuance."[5] The Goddess gives life, and also death, as well as regeneration. We will find this again with the Christian pietà, if we go beyond the stage of lamentation and understand that the Virgin—as is the case in certain representations in Brittany—reintegrates into herself the body of her Son in order to give him a second birth. And, regardless of whether or not we are shocked by this claim, the open sex of the Paleolithic Venus, like that of the Sheela-na-gig, is a religious symbol proving a belief in the immortality of the soul and in rebirth, or resurrection, after death.

What is more, the motif of the vulva seems to have been common in prehistoric art. At Saint-Léon-sur-Vézère (Dordogne), in the Blanchard-des-Roches cave, a small stone plaque was discovered engraved with three simplified but very recognizable vulva. By virtue of the principle that the part represents the whole, there is no doubt that these three grooves at the base of three vaguely rounded forms represented of a group of three mother divinities, as will be the case among the Greeks with the three Fates or the three Moirai, among the Gallo-Romans with the three Matres, among the Irish with the "triple" Brigit, and even among Christians with the famous triad of Saintes-Maries-de-la-Mer (Bouches-du-Rhône). Here, at Saint-Léon-sur-Vézère, appeared the tendency toward abstraction that would predominate in the Neolithic age, the concrete allegory giving way, little by little, to geometric simplification. The hypothesis of André Leroi-Gourhan was "that the most abstract forms derive from figures of masculine and feminine genitals. Some, like elongated lines, dashes, lines of dots, and later, arrows, daggers and swords, are masculine signs. The others, circles or triangles with a vertical line through them, ovals, rectangles with or without lower folds, and then pointed or concentric circles are feminine." The multiplicity of these examples proves that the sculptors, engravers, and painters of Paleolithic caves followed all the strict rules of a veritable religious vocabulary, symbolic in nature. And even if we know nothing of the actual thinking of these distant ancestors, we can be sure that metaphysical and religious speculation was far from absent among them.

In fact, we find representations of this type throughout, wherever traces of Paleolithic occupation have been detected. Corsica is particularly rich in this respect, with its many small stones cut into the form of rudimentary statuettes, the great majority of them sharing female characteristics. "The collected images are of many different sizes, and even though the majority of them measure between five and thirty centimeters, some Venuses exist on the island that measure .40 to .60 meters—dimensions never matched in all of the discoveries made in Europe. . . . By the specificity of the form itself and by the importance of their number, they attest to the intensity of the sentiment in Corsica that gave birth to them."[6] In Asco (Upper Corsica) in particular, many vaguely triangular stones have been found bearing the famous sexual "wound" in their centers. The same is true for Niolo, also in Upper Corsica.

Some Venuses, analogous to those of Lespugue and Monpazier but more crude, are found there as well. With certain Asco statuettes, the generous forms of breasts, belly, and buttocks are clearly recognizable. Astonishingly, there is even one in which a woman nursing an infant or holding it against her in the manner of a Christian Madonna can be recognized. Furthermore, this example is not unique, since others like them are found at other sites, notably at Niolo and Rocca-Poletra. Without any doubt, the artists were inspired by a common model, which assumes, if not a properly established dogma, at least a solidly embedded tradition. And even if the authenticity of certain finds might be doubtful, this clear fact remains: working with rudimentary tools and natural stones that already suggested the desired form, and with no knowledge of the "ready-made" technique so dear to the surrealists, Paleolithic artists permanently impregnated matter with their religious ideas.

On the Continent there exists another representation capable of provoking much comment. This is the one generally called the Venus of Laussel, from the name of a shelter that dominates the Beune valley, not far from the Eyzies (Dordogne). It is now found at the Aquitaine museum of Bordeaux. The shelter of Laussel was excavated at the beginning of the century, and interesting relics have been uncovered there. The Venus forms part of a group of limestone blocks sculpted into human figures. Thus, it is not a matter of a statuette but of an intaglio engraving showing traces of ochre on a block forty centimeters high. The

Venus is represented full face, her left hand on her belly, the other holding at head's height a bison horn pointed upwards. What seems to be her hair falls over the left shoulder, but the face, visibly turned to the left, is not defined. The fat of her buttocks and hips, very distinct, and the heaviness of her breasts recall the statuettes of Lespugue and Monpazier, even if this engraving can be considered more Magdalenian than Gravettian, that is, more recent by some ten thousand years. In any case, it marks the continuity of an art that is not gratuitous, and that is charged with more and more symbolic elements.[7]

The bison horn, ostensibly held this way to draw attention, is clearly very important. But what is its significance and what does it add to the representation of this fleshy woman? The woman of Laussel, with her copious form, must no doubt be added to the number of mother goddesses for whom maternity is emphasized at the expense of sexuality. Here, sexuality is neither indicated nor evoked, in contrast to the "shameless Venus," a statuette eight centimeters in height, coming from the Laugerie-Basse cave in the same region (Dordogne). This "shameless Venus," which is much less "shameless" than the one of Monpazier, is distinguished by her thinness and her lack of breasts. Is she prepubescent, or did someone wish to emphasize her genitals? We will never know. But, while the other Venuses are nude and carry no emblems, the one of Laussel holds this horn in what seems, very clearly, a ritual gesture.

There is a great temptation to see her as a prefiguration of the classical Diana with the crescent moon in her hair. But who, after all, is this Diana, this nocturnal and "lunar" huntress? It is Artemis of Ephesus, otherwise known as the Great Goddess, at once sympathetic and formidable, the one who gives life and takes it away. In the decline of Greco-Roman mythology, she became the twin sister of Apollo, the absolute model of the male god who appropriates the sun as his emblem. But, originally, Apollo is not a solar god, and he is not Greek. He was artificially integrated into Hellenic mythology by a sort of sleight of hand. In fact, he was born of Zeus, the Indo-European Great God father, and of Latona-Leto, who is one of the images of the solar pre-Indo-European Great Goddess. And when Latona-Leto fell into oblivion (limited to her parental role), her solar component was inherited by her children. But, as the society became patriarchal, it was the son who took possession of it, relegating the daughter to a secondary role, nocturnal and lunar. If the society had been gynecocratic, Diana-Artemis would have been presented with a radiating, solar head, and Apollo with a crescent moon. The polar reversal having been fully played out, Diana, endowed with the *horns* of the moon, was no longer viewed as anything more than a secondary divinity, when, in fact, the horns of the moon, attributed to Diana-Artemis, may have had an entirely different meaning.

They are not an emblem of the Goddess, in fact, but the symbol of masculinity, whereby she restores the primitive dyad, all the while affirming her primacy. The bison horn that the Venus of Laussel raises with so much show—and triumph—is quite simply the moon-man, her son-lover. She herself is the sun-woman who gives life and spreads her generous—ample, we could say—heat at once over the privileged being who is the son-lover, and all living beings for which he is the absolute synthesis. It is the great myth of Cybele and Attis, or again, of Aphrodite and Adonis. The virgin mother gives life back to her son-lover and presents him triumphantly, thus signifying the victory over death. The Christian image of Mary, taking Jesus in her arms in blessing, derives from the same idea.

This interpretation does not in any way contradict the others. "The method of mythology is analogy, and that the artists of the Paleolithic age were competent in analogy is surely evident in the statement of the Woman with the Horn, where a triple analogy is rendered of (1) the growing horns of a bull, (2) waxing crescent of the moon, and (3) growing child, *en ventre sa mère*.[8] And all this very clearly refers back to the triple representations of the mother goddess: mistress of riches (dispenser of the herds symbolized by the horn), sexually united to the moon-man (the horn is a symbol of virility), and mother. This tripling, so often noted in mythological legends and in the iconography, is crystallized in a single image in the Venus of Laussel.

In the following period, falling between the Solutrean and Magdalenian, that is, about 15,000 B.C., rock engravings ensure the permanence of this idea. Thus, in the cave of Angles-sur-l'Anglin (Vienne), a frieze (of which a reproduction is now found in the Musée de l'Homme in Paris) features, among horses, ibex, and bison, a triad of female silhouettes. They are worked in bas-relief just under the cave vault, without head or bust, and represented only from the waist to the knees. The forms are no longer rounded as in the preceding period, but, to the contrary, very slender, and the belly, genitals, and thighs are designed with much precision. What visibly dominates is the female sexual role, to the exclusion of all maternal connotations. We might be tempted to speak here of the "metaphysics of sex," just as we might for the two silhouettes of women without feet or head, also surrounded by representations of animals, which are painted on the walls of the famous cave of the Madeleine (Dordogne), whose languid posture clearly contains nothing that could suggest fertility.

> Considering further the interesting triad at Angles-sur-Anglin, one cannot help but notice that the sexual triangles are, all three, very well defined and that the mesial grooves are conspicuous. The triangles, furthermore, are distinctly equilateral, like the Pythagorean *tetraktys*, with the grooves then suggesting the point at the tetraktian apex as connoting the invisible source from which the visible form has proceeded . . . the analogy is impossible to miss. The triangle, furthermore, is the same as that which in Indian Tantric iconography is taken to connote the energy of the womb as identical with that of *maya*.[9]

It could be said that these remarks attribute very elevated spiritual preoccupations to prehistoric man, which perhaps he never had at all. But the coincidences are too numerous and too well distributed over time and place to be simply the product of chance. We are clearly in the presence of an "ideology" here, because this vision of divine femininity is found throughout, again and again, and in all epochs.

It is true that Pythagoras, who is said to be the inventor of the tetraktys, perhaps never actually existed as a historical figure, but Pythagorean thought is an incontestable reality that goes back even further in time. It is just that, with the Greeks, a form is given to this tradition that was transmitted for generations and generations, and survives today, sometimes even in the identical guise. The woman is always an unfathomable mystery that simultaneously attracts and elicits fear, that gives life and that becomes the devouring mother, which the Christian moralists have, in their spare time, identified with the devil, or at least with their puerile idea of it. This mystery was felt by prehistoric man, since Paleolithic sculptors and engravers were very careful not to design the woman's face. Who is the Goddess of the Beginnings, then, who has genitals but no face? Is it the eternal feminine, so dear to poets? Isn't it rather the result of an absolute determination to locate no reference point upon the mystery of sexuality and procreation?

Of course, we could claim that the head has broken off, but how does it happen, then, that no fragments have ever been found? Alternatively, the so-called Lespugue type includes the very clear form of head, but no face, which corresponds to a conscious desire not to represent precise individuality. Given these conditions, the best hypothesis would be to see in these statuettes and engravings a representation of femininity as such, anonymous and universal, a symbolic form of the ineffable divine. What is more, we know that the motif of the "woman without a head" is used to designate the prostitute. Wouldn't this be an allusion to sacred prostitution, the ritual by which the individual male attains a level of divinity and is impregnated with the supernatural powers that the Goddess, or the priestess who is her incarnation, possesses?

There is an exception, however, to the absence of heads among Paleolithic feminine representations. It is the famous "Lady of Brassempouy," discovered in the Landes region, at the back of the Cave of the Pope. It is now found in the Saint-Germain-en-Laye Musée des Antiquités Nationales. The body has disappeared. It is thought to have been the same type as the Venus of Lespugue.

Thus, there is simply a head that measures scarcely four centimeters, sculpted from ivory, whose face, though a bit pointed, is extremely fine, even though the eyes are just barely visible and there is no mouth. Most remarkable is the relief of a crisscross pattern that could represent the hair, or possibly a headdress falling over her shoulders, from which her nickname, "Lady of the Hood," derives. In any case, it is certain that someone wanted to represent feminine beauty here. It is the first link in the chain that emerges with the beginning of time and that, passing through the impassive faces of Greek goddesses and the ambiguous smiles of Gothic Virgins, will lead to the contemporary representations of the Mother of God. Henceforth, the Goddess of the Beginnings leaves the mists of origins and becomes individualized, as societies grow more and more sensitive to the look of the other.

2

OUR LADY UNDER GROUND

The Megalithic Epoch

From the end of the Paleolithic, that is, about 10,000 B.C., to the western European Neolithic age, that is, about 5,000 B.C., evidence of anthropomorphic art is almost completely lacking. It is only over the course of the fourth millennium that it reappears among societies undergoing massive transition, changing from nomadic to sedentary ways, from hunting and gathering to animal breeding and agriculture. This change entails, in fact, profound transformations in lifestyle, due in large part to the evolving climate and the possibility of living and surviving in comfortable conditions, especially in the regions of the Atlantic. But curiously enough, for all the transformations in lifestyle, the guiding ideas remained fundamentally unchanged. And the image of the Goddess of the Beginnings will reemerge, reinterpreted, of course, according to the new norms, but absolutely identical to her primitive—perhaps we might even want to call it her "initiatory"—outline.

Given the lack of pertinent information, it is difficult to imagine the mind-set of Neolithic populations, even if, thanks to the advanced techniques now used for archaeological excavations, we are able to reconstruct their everyday lives more or less faithfully. But the study of megalithic monuments found along the edge of the Atlantic (and a small part of the Mediterranean shore) from this same period allows us to venture serious hypotheses as to a very evolved spiritual religion: for these monuments are irrefutable testimony not only to funerary rituals, but to metaphysical ideas of a very high level. The architecture, the geographic distribution, and the ornamental graphics of these monuments reveal a perfectly coherent system of thought and a remarkably enduring notion of a mother goddess protecting the living and the dead. This ancient divinity in one way or another permeates what have sometimes been called dolmens and what would better be called cairns or megalithic mounds.

For a long time, it was believed that these dolmens, which are often seen standing in desolate moors, were erected solely as tombs. There is no doubt that they were burial places, either individual or collective according to their shape and dimension, but too often, their other function, that of sanctuary, has been forgotten. Moreover, it is consistently the case, especially in the Middle Ages, that temples were at once places of burial and places of worship. The great Christian churches have often been built over the tombs of saints and martyrs to benefit from the mystical *aura* that surrounded these holy figures, and, in any case, illustrious—and privileged—individuals were buried there because the prevailing opinion was, and still is today, that eternity is guaranteed when the corpse rests in a sacred place. Thus, it is not at all surprising to encounter representations of the Great Goddess of the Beginnings, called, in the language of archaeology, the Neolithic funerary goddess, in these tomb-sanctuaries, these dolmens and other megalithic mounds. But she is not only funerary, she is just as much the "source of life," as the various nuances given to her representation indicate.

What characterizes dolmenic art is the tendency toward abstraction and schematization, as if the builders of the megaliths had arrived at a point where they no longer wanted to express anything but the quintessence of beings and things. Most of the

NORTH SEA

ENGLISH CHANNEL

BELGIUM

PICARDY

Walcourt ■

Meuse

Beauraing ■

Rhine

Margut ■

LORRAINE

Moselle

ALSACE

Strasbourg ■
(Museum)

Ménez-Hom
(Brigit, Minerva)   Guernsey

Plouézoch ■

Dampmesnil ■
(Neolithic goddess)

Guiry-en-Vexin ■

Somme

Seine

Oise

Coizard ■
(Neolithic goddess)

Paris ■

BRITTANY

St-Germain-en-L. ■(Museum)

Brocéliande
(Morgane, Viviana) ■Tressé

Le Trevoux ┐
          ┤
Baud ■ ┘
(Venus of Quinipily)

Langon ┐
(Venus)

Rennes ■
(Museum)

PERCHE

Bellême
(Belisama)

Changé-
St-Piat

ILE-DE-FRANCE

Marne

Mont Donon

Rhine

Blavet

Orléans ■

Yonne

CHAMPAGNE

Châtillon-
sur-Seine ■
(Museum)

Sources ■
de la Seine

Vilaine

Sarthe

Loire

Cher

BURGUNDY

Dijon ■
(Museum)

Saône

FRANCHE-
COMTÉ

Berne ■

SWITZERLAND

Carnac■(Museum)

Gavrinis ┐
(Neolithic goddess)

Locmariaquer ■

POITOU

BERRY

Poitiers ■

Bourges ■
(Museum)

Autun ■
(Museum)

Lyon ■
(Museum)

Rhône

SAVOIE

■Aix-les-Bains

ATLANTIC

OCEAN

Lusignan ■
(Mélusine)

■Saintes
(Museum)

LIMOUSIN

AUVERGNE

Vienne ■
(Cybèle)

DAUPHINÉ

Bordeaux ■
(Museum)

Dordogne

Périgueux ■

Le Puy ■
(Annis)

Brassempouy ■
(Venus)

Garonne

Laussel ■ (Venus)
Laugerie ■ (lewd Venus)
■ Monpazier (Venus)

AQUITANE

Lespugue ■
(Venus)

Toulouse ■
(Museum)

Saint-Lizier ■

Saint-Sernin

Rodez ■
(Statues-menhirs)

Collorgues ■

LANGUEDOC

Nîmes ■
(Museum)

Rhône

Avignon ■
(Museum)

PROVENCE

Aix-en-
Provence ■
(Museum)

Marseille ■
(Museum)

100 km

SPAIN

Port-Vendres ■
(Venus)

■
Montserrat

MEDITERRANEAN SEA

GODDESS SITES IN FRANCE AND THE IMMEDIATE AREA
(Locations of Discoveries, Monuments, and Museums)

time it is a matter of intaglio engravings, which, certainly, lend themselves to simplification and two-dimensional display, mass being rendered by emphasizing certain fundamental particulars. That is how it is in the caves of the Petit-Morin valley, notably at Coizard (Marne). Actually, these caves are not megalithic monuments. They are cavities hollowed into a chalky ground. Thus, we find in the Joches area of Coizard a vast necropolis uniting thirty-seven hypogea. These are quadrangular burial chambers of about two square meters, connected by a narrow opening to an "ante-grotto," itself linked to the outside by an access trench exactly analogous to the entry passages of the covered walkways built under the surface of the earth. One of these grottoes contains the famous image of the "Neolithic idol," carved on the wall of the chamber. It is a feminine figure, consisting of a thick mass at the base, becoming thinner and rounder toward the top. The head is only suggested, following the Paleolithic method, but with a protuberance in relief that can only be the nose, a very simple necklace with an object that must be a pendant hanging from it, and a particularly visible pair of breasts. Since the genitals are totally absent from the representation, we can imagine that the essential role given to this divinity (because, given her location, this can only be a divinity) is that of wet nurse, the milk from her breasts clearly symbolizing an immortality potion meant to procure a new life for the dead buried in this chamber. At least, this is the hypothesis we can formulate without too much risk of error.

The hypogeum is itself an obvious symbol for the uterus. Thus, it is not surprising to find the universal Mother represented there. But it would be a mistake to consider her as simply Mother Earth, because the care Neolithic peoples gave to their dead, the arrangement of the burial place, the presence of this figure within that whole, all of this far surpasses the simple act of placing the dead into the earth from which they came and to which they return. It is not into the earth that the dead are placed, but into the womb of the universal Mother, where they can mature, but especially, from which they can be expelled toward an "elsewhere," so that they can be reborn into another life.

The hypogea of Coizard are not unique. There are many others distributed throughout France, and not only at Mornouards, Mesnil-sur-Orge (Essonne), and Fontvieille (Bouches-du-Rhône), where four hypogea are located beside a dolmen, demonstrating their similarity in function. But the hypogeum is the direct and logical successor to the natural caves of the Paleolithic. And it is only made more sacred by being intentionally carved out, following certain precise rules. Now, the megalithic mound goes a step further still, because it is constructed above the surface of the earth and not underneath. In fact, it is necessary to understand that the dolmens and covered walkways we now see out in the open were once covered by ground (a tumulus) or by stones (a *galgal*), or, again, by earth and stones (the classic cairn) and it was either weather or human need for easily available materials that stripped them of their outer layers.[1] Far from being crude and roughly made as some have imagined, all these monuments were, in reality, very complex structures built according to certain architectural rules and very precise religious imperatives.[2]

The megalithic mound is, in fact, the symbolic projection of the maternal womb, and, just by itself, constitutes a representation of the Great Goddess, especially if there is a covered walkway or what the Anglo-Saxons call a "passage grave." The entrance is always low and narrow, corresponding to the vulvar opening, the corridor initially very low, becoming higher and higher and opening out into a central, sometimes "dolmenic" chamber, covered over by an immense slab of stone, sometimes surmounted by a complex corbelled construction. In this central chamber, the dead were laid out, sometimes right on the ground, sometimes in some sort of stone basin. And, in certain monuments, the orientation was such that it allowed the rays of the rising winter solstice sun to penetrate to the interior and actually illuminate the central funerary chamber. It goes without saying that this was not mere chance, but skillfully calculated to allow the solar light symbolically to regenerate the dead, and to project them into another life by means of an authentic *regressus ad uterum*, as reported in numerous legends and traditions, notably in Ireland, where this type of monument is very common.

That is the case with the famous cairn of Newgrange, Ireland, in the Boyne valley, which occupies a special place in ancient Celtic mythology. In fact, it is often a question of a "sun chamber," ruled over by the god Aengus, master of places, whose regenerative powers are given prominence. The same feature can be observed in France at the monument of Dissignac, in Saint-Nazaire (Loire-Atlantique), differing only in that the mound contains two passage graves, evidently representing two wombs. These dark dens, flooded with solar light at that moment when the sun's course reverses polarity, are incontestably sanctuaries of rebirth and immortality placed under the patronage, or, we should say, the "matronage" of the universal solar Great Goddess. The latter gives back life by the heat and light that emanates from her. Here, there is not a maternal telluric divinity and a blazing masculine star, but one and the same divine entity, black and white, dark and luminous, who both devours life and generates eternity.

But megalithic mounds are not all oriented toward the winter solstice sunrise, far from it, and there are no general rules, as was the case for Christian churches up until the sixteenth century (oriented not toward Jerusalem as was foolishly claimed, but in accordance with Indo-European solar customs). Essentially, the mounds were built in places deemed sacred, and if the sun makes no symbolic entry there at specified periods of the year, the solar goddess is nonetheless present, engraved in the rock, generally at the entrance of the access corridor or in the central funerary chamber. That is how it is at Mané-er-Hroëg in Locmariaquer (Morbihan), which is not a dolmen, but a late Neolithic (ca. 2000 B.C.) funerary mound. At the chamber entrance, the builders deliberately placed an ancient pillar, from at least a thousand years earlier, the visible side of which includes a schematic representation of the Great Goddess.

This pillar constitutes one of the most mysterious, but also one of the most beautiful examples of megalithic wall art. On it, the goddess is represented in the form of a shield, with a bulge at the top to represent the head. In the interior of this "body" are some barely decipherable signs. We can recognize, however, two serpents, an ax, two crooks, and a design that could fall under the general classification of "ram's horns." Above and below this "idol," axes of different shapes are perfectly visible. The whole of the stela seems to emphasize the protective power of the divinity, represented by symbolic elements that probably refer to common objects of that period. But we know that animal horns and ritual axes are not rare among the objects uncovered in megalithic excavations. Must we consider them emblems of the divinity? This hypothesis certainly cannot be ruled out, especially if we take into account the lifestyle of the populations that, for lack of a better term, are called "megalithic."

The objection can be raised, however, that this representation does not contain a single truly female element. But the model of the idol in the form of a shield is found in many other monuments, with very carefully detailed female parts. Also, the serpent—which, remember, takes the feminine gender in many languages—is a representation of the ancient Goddess, as a careful study of Genesis, especially the temptation of Adam and Eve,[3] demonstrates, as does the legend of Melusina, the fairy with a serpent's tail (and not the tail of a fish), that is, the *vouivre* (from the Latin, *vipera*) so well known from popular traditions.[4] Finally, the local name of the monument is significant because Mané-er-Hroëg means "mound of the sorceress," and the legend claims that this mound was constructed by the fairies to allow a woman to watch for the return of her son gone to sail the seas. The idea of maternal protection is undeniably linked to this funerary monument, which could be a place of worship, a sanctuary for the Goddess of the Beginnings, as well.

The representation of this goddess can be simplified to the extreme. In the Barnenez cairn in Plouézoc'h (Finestère), one of the most ancient known monuments of its kind, it appears in the form of a triangle. But the triangle is found in a schematized boat, probably signifying the nocturnal navigation of the sun in the other world. This motif of the goddess in a boat reappears at Locmariaquer (Morbihan) in the Keverès cairn and also in the one at Mané-Lud. But, even more characteristically, at the Petit-Mont in Arzon (Morbihan), the goddess again appears as an idol in the form of a shield. As for the Ile-Longue cairn, in the Gulf of Morbihan, it contains many cone-shaped representations surrounded by hair, which can be identified as rays of the sun. This representation has sometimes been considered a "shamanic trance," which does not seem to correspond to the context at all. The solar character of this divinity is incontestable, and moreover, at Petit-Mont, beside a strange and complex representation of the idol, recognizable by her three necklaces, a perfectly clear solar wheel can be seen. This "fragmented" representation can be compared to the great stone slab in the form of a shield found in the chamber of the famous Table des Marchands, at Locmariaquer, at the center of which, among the crooks (which are perhaps stylized ears of corn), appears a very recognizable sun.

The engraved supports of the Mané-Lud cairn offer a great variety of images in which the goddess seems somehow "reduced" to certain characteristics that wanted emphasis. Besides the idol in the form of a shield, there is the U sign, treated in various ways, which could represent a stylized body, a necklace, horned headgear, or perhaps the line of the breast, or the maternal belly, this cup that contains the "mother waters," and into which all creatures must dive again before being reborn into another life. At first glance, these petroglyphs seem chaotic, disorganized, and crude, but, upon examination, we perceive that the smallest sign has its importance, and fits into a much larger framework. It is indisputably a matter of an artistic language meant to convey a religious message that, unfortunately, we do not know how to decipher.

Still at Locmariaquer, there is the cairn of the Pierres-Plates, which appears to be the great sanctuary dedicated to the Neolithic goddess. It has an angled, covered walkway, the mound that covered it having disappeared over the course of the centuries, and its many supports bear interesting engravings. On one of these supports, in fact, the classic shield-form of the idol can be distinguished, very square, with the bulge that indicates the head. In the body's interior, a sinuous curve surmounts two breasts, evoking the serpent theme. At the bottom, toward the left, a circle, smaller than the breasts, perhaps represents the navel, while at the right, a vertically elongated rectangle contains a double concentric circle. It clearly represents the uterus. Outside the body, below it and to the right, another vertical rectangle encloses a stylized ax, a symbol of power. The rest of the support is covered with four variations of the idol. On top, a simple U sign, which must be a cup; below that, a shield-form in which the head is no longer represented by a bulge, but by a neckline; lower still, the neckline is further emphasized; and at the bottom, finally, the idol belonging to the neckline head is doubled inwardly, inevitably evoking the theme of parturition.

But the other stone slabs of these same Pierres-Plates present us with the Neolithic goddess in all her splendor. We might be tempted to see in her a prefiguration of those astonishing Virgins in Majesty of the Middle Ages. The Goddess is, in fact, triumphant here, because she ensures the triumph over death. She is presented in ceremonial dress, which is why she is sometimes called "the chasuble idol." The body (the head of which is marked by a neckline) does, in fact, seem to be dressed in a sort of ceremonial "mantle," a little like the Virgins of Christian churches. Since everything is analogy, however, the circles that are drawn on this mantle (the source of that inelegant nickname, "the idol of buttons"!) are also breasts, indicating very clearly the "vast Mother" aspect of this divinity of burial mounds, whose name and cult we obviously know nothing about. One other representation is particularly noteworthy. The goddess is no longer dressed, but opened in some way, viewed from within, thanks to the treelike branchings that could as easily be a plant motif as a schematization of the lungs, a symbol of the vital breath by which the delicate alchemical metamorphoses of rebirth take place. More than ever, the Goddess of the Beginnings is present, watching over the fate of each of her innumerable children.

These representations, which tend toward pure geometrical design, seem charged with a message both magical and metaphysical. This is even more apparent in the magnificent cairn of Gavrinis, in Larmor-Baden, on an island in the Gulf of Morbihan, probably the most beautiful monument of this type in France, and even in the entire world, so very remarkable is the richness and the abundance of motifs.

Metaphysically speaking, it is a matter of expressing a perpetual process of metamorphosis that the Goddess personifies. She is not static, since she is endlessly creating new forms, undulations, vibrations, that emanate from a central point in a limitless universe. In Gavrinis, we recognize the famous shield idols, but doubled, tripled, multiplied. The waves of the sea, spirals, and, once again, treelike branchings have been seen in these, not at all contradictory, since the Goddess can only be perceived as manifested. She is thus, in herself, the divine or cosmic power, the first and absolute cause of all existence. All the supports at Gavrinis are engraved, and they all express this "ontological" presence of the Goddess. They explain creation.

But it is unthinkable that such metaphysical reflection was not accompanied by a form of ritual magic. Even though we can only make conjectures in this regard, we are free to imagine initiatory sojourns to the interior of this type of monument, if only to immerse oneself in the energy that permeates the space, in order to activate a kind of "uncoupling" from consciousness to achieve superior states, a true tuning into another world. Here, the double function of the megalithic mound, long considered a simple funerary monument, becomes evident. Obviously, it is a funerary monument, but it is also a sanctuary. And comparison with other cairns in different European countries, especially Ireland, can only attest to this other function as sanctuary, irrefutable prototype of the countless churches placed under the patronage of Notre Dame.

On one of the supports at Gavrinis, the divine representation is reduced to her most simple expression. There is nothing more than a female belly, with a vulvar opening. But surrounding it are representations of eleven axes without handles, which are phallic symbols, and V-shaped lines that evoke ears of corn or at least spelt. Is this the goddess's fertility for her many lovers? Without a doubt. The three higher levels of another support present the labyrinthine goddess (again a uterus symbol), while the lower level, very clearly set apart, presents semiconcentric circles, two axes and several serpents. We can easily recognize the ancient goddess of the serpents here, who has haunted humanity since the beginning of time. And on the wall at the back of the so-called funerary chamber (but which is a sort of holy of holies), the Neolithic goddess appears in all her splendor and multiple, labyrinthine complexity, hidden away, but inevitably linked to the serpentine designs and the ax. Simultaneously the axis of the world, protector and destroyer (the ax), she is also that which insinuates itself throughout (the serpent, or more, a *serpente*, a *"vouivre"* of infinite metamorphoses).

Thus, we can better understand what contours megalithic peoples gave to their principal (and perhaps only) divinity, despite our total lack of historical or philosophical documentation. These contours express all the multiplicity within the unity. Good evidence appears within one of the monuments, the cairn of Ile-Longue, in the Gulf of Morbihan, now nearly entirely in ruins. Beside a triangular idol with lines radiating outward (hair, or rays of the sun?), appears a second, much more rounded idol, with more radiating lines, then a third entirely in the shape of a shield, with two handles (arms or ears?) and topped with a small pointed addition (head or "third eye"?), and a fourth, very simplified, in the form of a square shield with a small point on top.

Again, a similar representation is found on the ceiling of one of the dolmens at the Barnenez cairn in Plouézoc'h (Finistère). But here, there is nothing more than a shield, this time rectangular, with two inner incisions and divergent outgrowths at the top. This vision of the goddess is not peculiar to the Armorican peninsula. In fact, similar motifs can be found on the strange monument at Changé-Saint-Piat, on the banks of the Eure, near Maintenon (Eure-et-Loir).

There are regional variations, however. In this regard, the monuments of the Parisian basin offer astonishing simplification of the forms. In the dolmen of Bellée (whose name evokes the Gallic solar divinity), at Boury (Oise), the shield idol disappears completely. Nothing remains but the representation of a necklace, very labyrinthine, surmounting some breasts in relief. It is the same on one of the supports of the famous Pierre-Turquaise, at

Saint-Martin-du-Tertre, in the Carnelle forest (Val-d'Oise), and also on the entrance to the cairn at Aveny, in Dampsmesnil (Eure), on the hillsides dominating the valley of Epte. The necklace, which has always been a sign of power and distinction, then becomes the emblem of a goddess with absolute mastery over the universe and the beings inhabiting it.

In fact, the combination of necklace and breasts is not new. It was already observed in the Coizard cave (Marne) on the chalk walls of this authentic hypogeum. But at Coizard, as at the dolmen of Collorgues (Gard), the face is not absent. In these two monuments, moreover, the face takes on curious significance. It suggests, purely and simply, an owl's head. This representation is not unrelated to images from the Aegean Sea area (found especially on the chalk cylinders), and we cannot help but thinking of the goddess Athena's emblematic animal. We can only conclude that this divinity, who protects the dead, is a birdgoddess who *sees* in the darkness of the tombs and guides the souls "toward the spaces of another life," as Chateaubriand says in a beautiful flight of lyricism. Thus, it is a matter of a double vision, of another world invisible to the mortal community. The great Celtic legends regarding fairy palaces and a parallel universe in the megalithic cairns can only confirm this.

But one of the peculiarities specific to Armorican dolmenic art lies in the treatment of the face, which is sometimes only suggested, sometimes clearly blind, as was the case for the Paleolithic Venuses. At the end of the Neolithic period, around 2000 B.C., engraving on stone slabs is gradually replaced by stela sculptures. One very curious example is a stela found in the cemetery of Catel in Guernsey, known as the "Grand-Mère du Chimequière." It was recut in a later period, proving that the functions of a female divinity who protects the dead continued to be assigned to her.

In structure, this Catel stela is like those that can be seen at Crec'h Quillé in Saint-Quay-Perros (Côtes-d'Armor), at Trévoux (Finistère) and at Kermené in Guidel (Morbihan). On all these stelae, a pair of breasts in relief leaves no doubt about the idol's gender. At Catel and Kermené, a necklace appears above the breasts, rising toward the neck, but not encircling it. At Trévoux, this necklace is no more than a simple crescent under the pair of breasts. But the stela at Kermené is the most impressive. Although it is no longer in one piece, we can easily reconstruct the head. It seems very stylized, cylindrical, as if the sculptor had wished to let the face remain mysterious. This is not a case of clumsiness or inability to represent reality, but of a conscious desire to blank out the face of an infinite divine being that cannot be conceived of in finite forms.

In the same period, representations of the same type also appear not on stelae, but on simple stone slabs. This is indicative of a tendency that will soon become dominant toward what are called "menhir-statues," or standing-stone statues. This is the case in numerous cairns, such as the Mougau-Bihan in Commana (Finistère), at the Prajou-Menhir in Trébeurden (Côtes-d'Armor), at the Mein-Goarec in Plaudren (Morbihan), at Kerallant in Saint-Jean-Brévelay (Morbihan) and at Tressé (Ille-et-Vilaine).

> At Tressé, on two stone slabs of the annex cell, two groups of two pairs of breasts appear in relief in a hollow. In each group, a necklace is represented under the pair of breasts on the right. This representation of a double idol constitutes another characteristic of megalithic art of this period at the end of the Neolithic. . . . The small annex cell of Prajou-Menhir is a true sanctuary. On the right is found one group of two pairs of breasts, as at Tressé. On the left, there is a square idol, marked off by an incised double line of cuplike forms. The shoulders are well defined. A curious square surmounts the top. At the center of this idol, two cuplike forms clearly mark the breasts. On the next stone slab, two complementary motifs can be found, one, an idol in the form of a pair of breasts with her necklace of pearls, and just underneath to the right, a sort of elongated pallet with a narrow handle. Mystery surrounds this last object. Long considered a representation of a spear head, an interpretation since disputed from all sides, it is in search of another explanation.[5]

All evidence suggests that it is a religious object related to the functions attributed to the Goddess, but what?

One fact remains certain: the permanence, throughout the millennia, of a mysterious goddess, whose concrete representations vary according to the period, but who is always ambivalent, generator of life and death, and also a transforming power, since she presides over the "passage" from the visible to the invisible world. This explains her presence, asserted more and more forcefully in the late Neolithic period, in the megalithic mounds, which are, it seems in the last analysis, as much sanctuaries as tombs. The two functions merge, just as they will later on when Christian churches are constructed over the tombs of saints and martyrs. But soon, this Goddess of the Beginnings will emerge from the darkness where she has been confined, from the caves and the cairns, to appear in the full light of the sun, which she alone invests with her creative and destructive forces.

Which means that these representations—even though some of them have been discovered in natural caves (like at Saint-Martin-d'Ardèche) or in the mine shafts (as at Collorgues, Gard)—are not necessarily linked to funerary monuments. These menhir-statues, as they are generally called, appear in abundance throughout the south of France, notably in the Gard and Aveyron regions. The masculine ones can be dated to the end of the Neolithic age, but those that are clearly feminine are more recent, from 2300 B.C. to 1850 B.C., that is, from the transition period between the end of the Neolithic and the early Bronze Age. Actually, these are more stelae than statues properly so called, because they are not cut in the form of human silhouettes, but assume a generally ovoid form that seems to be evolving from the primitive menhir toward a certain geometrization. Only the eyes and the nose render the face, while the trunk features arms done in sketchy relief, and the breasts are always very distinct. But, most of the time, only the front of the stela is carved. The back remains rough or very crudely adorned with hair. As to their height, they tend to be small, generally less than a meter tall, with a few rare exceptions. We cannot help but be reminded of those little statues of the Virgin Mary scattered throughout the countryside over the course of the Middle Ages, on small hillocks and even in hollow trees.

The most remarkable of these menhir-statues is, without a doubt, the one from Saint-Sernin (Aveyron), now kept in the Musée Fenaille of Rodez. It is a block of red sandstone 1.20 meters high, .70 meters wide, and .20 meters deep, which has the distinction of being carved on both sides. The head and the shoulders merge with the arch formed by the top. The eyes and nose are well defined, but the mouth is missing. Under the eyes can be seen horizontal lines that have been taken for a mustache, but which are actually tattoos, because the stela is female. Below the face, the megalithic necklace can again be found, and the breasts are indicated by small spheres done lightly in relief, between which a kind of fork takes form that descends to the very apparent waist, and continues around to the other side. The arms are displayed horizontally, with the fingers designated by five parallel lines of equal length. Finally, under the waist, the legs, drawn vertically, end in fingers similar to those of the hands. Thus the new vision of the Great Goddess of the Beginnings takes shape.

Following this model, there are many other menhir-statues. The one from Granisse in Lacaune (Tarn) bears a necklace with three strings, but not the mysterious motif in the form of a fork. The one from Mas-Capellier, in Calmel-et-le-Viala (Aveyron), now in the Musée des Antiquités Nationales in Saint-Germain-en-Laye, has no necklace, but the fork motif takes the form of a chalice this time, which cannot help but prompt certain associations.

From all evidence, the female represented here is sacerdotal in nature. On the back of the stela, the shoulder blades are clearly defined, and a sort of baldric joins the waistband to the neck. Is this a priestess? In that case, it is clear that the priestess must be identified with the divinity. Now, there is nothing to prevent us from comparing this representation with a much later one, the famous "Grail Virgin," so magnificently described by Chrétien de Troyes in his *Perceval*. This hypothesis may seem bold, perhaps, but it is not absurd. The Mas-Capellier stela is not an illustration of the Champagne storyteller's account, but a sculptural representation of the same theme: a young woman who bears a *grail* (the common noun means, etymologically, a "recipient") from which emanates a mysterious light. The theme of the Grail, integral to Authurian legend, we know, from the twelfth century on, goes back even further in time. We find it in various mythologies, Celtic, Germanic, Iranian, and Indian, and, by the first centuries of our epoch, Gnostic sects had already rediscovered it. Why not assume it existed during the transition period between the late Neolithic and the early Bronze Age?

This vision of the goddess-priestess as bearer of a vessel of light is not to be taken literally. Rather, it is a matter of interior light, and, consequently, the symbol's teaching involves penetration into another universe, which, for lack of a better term, we shall describe as "dark." Now, one of these menhir-statues, discovered in the Mas-de-l'Aveugle cairn at Collorgues (Gard), lets us propose an even bolder hypothesis. This stela is incontestably female, about 1.75 meters high, with only the top of it sculpted in an almost miniaturized way. We can discern what is perhaps a face in the shape of a rounded triangle, the upper arch representing either the eyebrows or a necklace, below which appear a nose and two eyes or two protruding breasts, and a mysterious object, replicating exactly the Saint-Sernin one, but reversed, presenting a double spiral too clear to be a matter of chance or of the artist's whim. Exterior to the face, there are two arms at right angles, and above, positioned horizontally, a sort of crook that could just as well be an ax, and thus, a symbol of power. "It would look more like the head of an owl than a human face and would readily produce a feeling of terror, no doubt the effect desired by the artists who will chisel these strange statues."[6]

This sense of fear is obviously linked to beliefs concerning owls and other night birds credited with the power to announce deaths or to bring bad luck. But the image of the owl also refers, once again, to the goddess Athena, as we can see in the Petit-Morin caves at Coizard (Marne). This is not the only example. The same motif appears on a vase discovered in the Los Millares necropolis in Spain, on numerous Hissarlik vases, on the Anatolian platter (Turkey), and especially on the famous Folkton chalk cylinder in Great Britain. Thus, the symbolic identification of the Goddess with the owl is not local, and it corresponds to metaphysical speculation concerning the "clairvoyance" of the divinity.

In France itself, the Bouisset stela in Ferrières-les-Verreries (Hérault) constitutes a perfect illustration of it. Here, the engraving is limited to a perfectly recognizable owl's head, very realistic, to say the least. Nevertheless, no one would claim to be in the presence of a "deification" of the animal known by the name of owl. It is the real powers of the owl, a bird capable of seeing in the dark, that are emphasized. The nocturnal world, invisible to noninitiates, is only accessible if some gaze pierces the darkness in order to reach light. Thus, the owl is the most appropriate animal to receive these messages coming from elsewhere, since it sees what others cannot see, and since it is capable of finding its way unerringly in a universe that completely eludes the rational categories of French Cartesianism.

In Greek mythology, the owl is the emblem of Athena, the Latin Minerva, goddess of the intellect and all the skills and methods deriving from it. She was born, it is said, fully armed, from the head of Zeus (logic: war is a method like any other!) who is the master of action in the world of relativities, but not the primordial god. Thus, Athena is the incarnation of the divine intelligence in the service of humans, and it is on these grounds that she protects the citizens (and not the other inhabitants) of Athens, a name that is plural in Greek, and whose etymology remains obscure. It is probable that sometime later, there was a desire to attach the name of the great Greek city to that of a more ancient divinity. So who is this primitive Athena?

She seems to have been identical to the archaic Artemis, who later became Diana of Ephesus, the place dedicated to the worship of the virgin mother since the beginning of time, and, not coincidentally, the site of the famous Christian council that affirmed the Theotokos dogma. No matter what name she goes by, Artemis is the original mother goddess whose solar character was later confiscated to benefit her twin brother, Apollo, and whose roots extend into the deepest levels of Indo-European mythology.

Now, in what remains for us of the mythology of the Scythians, an Indo-European people from the steppes of central Asia, namely, the traditional epics of the Ossets, with regard to the privileged Nartes tribe, there appears a completely extraordinary feminine figure bearing the name of Sathana, a sort of mother goddess, in so far as her magical powers and sexual transgressions place her outside the norm.[7] And, as is necessarily the case for all mythological entities beyond Christian redemption, her name, Sathana, probably very recent, results from a true "demonizing," made easier by a vague homophonic connection. This is not the only example of its kind. In the Hebraic tradition, the mysterious Lilith, probably originally the mother of Adam, and thus, the first human being, was also obscured and "demonized," likewise reduced to a night bird who comes to torment the living, to devour young children, and to mate with men in order to give birth to multitudes of demons. In one sense, the Hebraic Lilith, like Sathana of the Nartes, is a demoness, just as the "Scythian Diana" seems to have been, alluded to in the stories surrounding Orestes, Electra, and Iphigenia, and otherwise known as the solar Artemis, with mastery over wild animals and human destinies. The primitive Greek Athena, nocturnal and thus possessor of the secrets of the night (the inner intelligence), is a remodeled version of this universal solar divinity.

But in comparing all these menhir-statues, we cannot help but be troubled by a pervasive impression of ambivalence. Without a doubt, they represent the solar divinities, but nevertheless, these are Black Virgins. The Serre-Grand (Aveyron) one, in the Musée des Antiquités Nationales, has a face that merges with a sunbeam shooting from a mysterious forked object held in the divinity's hands. What kind of light is this? Light from another world or from this one? Probably both at once, because the goddess who gives life is also the one who gives death, and vice versa. Another stela, from La Verrière (Aveyron), and now in the Musée Fenaille in Rodez, presents a slightly different image. The object, more than ever analogous to the Grail, becomes a sort of hollowed-out rectangle at the base of the belly that calls up the primal womb where the subtle alchemical metamorphoses of birth and rebirth take place within the darkness. The posterity of this "Our Lady of the Night" will survive long into the Middle Ages.

This ambivalence of death/life, dark/light, depths/heights extends even into the sexual domain. One of the strangest menhir-statues we know of, the one from Trévoux in Laniscat (Côtes-d'Armor), is clearly female in appearance. The shoulders are well drawn, the arms clear, the breasts well defined, with a necklace below them. But the face is missing, lacking nose and eyes. On the other hand, at the back of the neck and the blind head, we can make out a sort of bulge that immediately suggests a phallus. Is this, then, a representation of the "phallic mother," so dear to psychoanalysts, always ready to reemerge from the unconscious, or even from the vestiges of the primitive state in which beings were necessarily androgynous?

A final ambiguity remains, that of joy and sadness. This divinity of the burial mound, is she "Our Lady of Joy" or "Our Lady of Sorrows"? We know that, in the Middle Ages, all representations of the Virgin Mary will retain this ambivalence, without which she would not be the universal Mother. No matter what the multiple circumstances in which she appeared,

> The Princess remains standing
> As a tree in which the sap rises,
> The Princess remains rigid
> And, passing over her cold brow,
> All the storms of terror
> Throw her straight hair to the sky. [8]

3

THE ECLIPSED VIRGIN

The Bronze Age, the Celts, and the Gallo-Romans

It is curious to note how, at the beginning of the Bronze Age in the third Celtic period called La Tène, that is, for sixteen or eighteen hundred years, realistic representation of the female divinity almost completely disappears, at least in western Europe. Yet, as we have seen, this female divinity seems to have been greatly honored since the beginning of *Homo sapien's* existence. How then, to explain this sudden absence in the archaeological remains that are, nevertheless, rich and numerous in this period of transition and profound change?

There is an immediate and obvious response. This disappearance of the female image must, theoretically, correspond to the time when masculine patriarchal society overpowered the ancient gynecocratic society, and whatever little remained of a matriarchal society within the Amazon tradition, if we can believe Herodotus.[1] There must have been an enormous reversal in tendencies at this time. The masculine cult of Apollo replaced the other, very feminine one, of the serpent Python and, in most languages, the word for sun, formerly feminine in gender, became masculine.[2] Once women had been lowered to an inferior social rank, they no longer held a place in the upper circles of divinity. This is a possible explanation for the virgin goddess's disappearance.

It is very likely that this response is accurate, but it fails to take into account the general phenomenon occurring in the Bronze Age, around 2000 or 1800 B.C., in artistic and religious expression (one is never far removed from the other), that is, the triumph of a kind of symbolization pushed to extremes, a geometrization that the Cubist painters at the beginning of this century and nonfigurative artists like Mondrian would reembrace; for in this period, we observe an almost total absence of anthropomorphic or even zoomorphic figures.

It is clear that this phenomenon is not the result of chance. Two complementary explanations assert themselves. One pertains to the intellectual evolution of humanity, the other to a broadening of its metaphysical or religious concepts. But "to pose the problem" as André Varagnac says so well,

> is to cast doubt upon all explanations of schematization as a "degeneration" of naturalistic representations. This last interpretation is truly peculiar to modern minds accustomed to asserting the superiority of the civilized over the savage. Because the slow psychological developments that separate us from populations called "primitive" have consisted in exactly this substituting of theoretical concepts for concrete visions full of detail, of naturalism. . . . Furthermore, it is in engraving or sculpting abstract signs that the Solutrean or Magdalenian hunter established himself as the distant but legitimate ancestor of our civilizations in which all power rests in our ability to conceptualize in abstract terms, to calculate, in order to anticipate and refine our actions. Let us stop talking, then, of a Paleolithic realism that would have "degenerated" into geometric designs. Not only are stylized realism and geometrism simultaneous, but there is no essential difference between geometrism and realism.[3]

It is all a matter of finding one's way, which is not easy when we know practically nothing about deciphering these symbol systems, these *analogies*, not only of form but of content. We will be able to understand, however, how the stylization of the galloping horse necessarily leads to the formation of an S sign, designating the sun in its course, the famous Sol Invictus that, in the period of neorealism at the end of the Celtic age, again takes the form of the mare-goddess Epona, in which it is not difficult to recognize the image of the primitive mother goddess.

The second explanation follows naturally from the first. The more the faculty of abstraction was developed within societies of the Bronze Age, and the Celtic period, the more the field of metaphysical exploration was enlarged and the more the thinkers of that time understood that it was difficult to express the absolute by means of the relative. We possess unimpeachable evidence on this point from the pen of the Greek Diodorus of Sicily (fragment 22), an author who took his information from a reliable source concerning the attitude of Brennus, the Gallic chief, in 279 B.C. Over the course of the Gallic expedition in Greece, "having once entered, Brennus did not even look at the offerings of gold and silver found there. He took only the images of stone and wood and began to laugh because they had attributed human forms to the gods and had made them out of wood and stone." This judgment says quite a bit about the mentality of the Celts, who, for a long time, would refuse to represent the infinite in any finite form. Their greatest challenge will come in the first century A.D., following their contact with the Greeks and Scythians of southern Russia, and then again, when subjected to the direct influence of their conquerors, the Romans, and the first Christian missionaries. But that does not prevent them, as Caesar and the Latin poet, Lucan, said, of representing their divinities by *simulacra* (and not by *signa* or *statuae*), shapeless sorts of pillars in stone or wood, and by simple or complex geometric motifs on their ornamental objects or even on their currency. And maybe we need to consider the possibility that simple natural rocks were the simulacra of gods and goddesses?

During the entire Bronze Age, there was intense solar worship in the Celtic world. Archaeological evidence, like the famous temple at Stonehenge in England, or the numerous solar ritual chariots (bronze or gold carts bearing the solar disc) and small solar watercraft (also bearing the disc, often in gold), are incontestable proof of this. But, considering the time period, this solar divinity could only have been female, as among the Scythians. And it must never be forgotten that the name of Allah conceals that of an ancient goddess of pre-Islamic Arabia, the solar goddess for whom the simulacrum was the famous Black Stone of the Kaaba, in Mecca, a meteorite, thus a gift from the sky fallen to earth, and which perfectly symbolized, in an entirely abstract way, the greatness and power of the divinity. Muslims have understood this so well that, with the exception of certain Iranians, they always refuse to represent the divinity in a "naturalistic" form, which is certainly not the case among Christians ever since the quarrels of the iconoclasts definitively ended.

Thus, it is impossible to find the least vestige of divine female representation throughout the whole of western Europe, unless we make an exception, of course, for the most recent menhir-statues, both from the Bronze Age and the beginning of the Iron Age. It is on certain Gallic coins, from the beginning of the first century A.D., that the figurative image of the Goddess of the Beginnings will slowly emerge from the darkness where she had been confined. Again, we must be very cautious with regard to any interpretations, even hypothetical ones, we might want to give to the women riders represented on the backs of gold or silver coins, which, among the Gauls, were not only objects of transaction, but veritable picture books, conveying ideas indisputably mythological or religious, though it is sometimes difficult to identify precisely what these are.[4]

It is in the Armorican[5] area of Gaul where we find the most examples of this sort. On one of the coins of the Cenomani (Maine), a nude woman, sword in hand and hair flowing, is running toward the right in an attitude we can only consider aggressive.[6] It is, in all likelihood, the virgin warrior, whom Caesar names Minerva, and the Irish will call either Morrigan (the "great queen") or Brigit (the "high" or the "powerful"), but who is a mother goddess, represented here in her warrior role of protecting the social group. Another coin of the people of Redones (Rennes) presents the same virgin warrior on horseback, nude as well, bearing a sword and shield.[7] A third, from the people of Unelli (Cotentin), represents her dressed and on her horse, with three horns on her head, brandishing a wheel with four rays (sun or shield?) in her left hand and an object (a sword?) from which light rays emanate.[8] It certainly seems as though the solar aspect of the female divinity is being stressed here, in connection with the horns, which are a symbol of power. Moreover, this solar character is apparent on another coin, this one not anthropomorphic, of the people of Ménapes (Flanders). Here we find a boat on which appears a figure perfectly reminiscent of the Neolithic idol represented in the cairns, hollowed and containing two small spheres, and from which solar rays indisputably emanate.[9] The ancient Goddess is ever present, even if her form evolves.

The Celts began to work figuratively in wood, stone, and metal when they came into contact with eastern peoples, first the Scythians and Greeks, later the Romans, and that was well before the Gallic conquest. Obviously, the wood images have almost completely disappeared, except when they are found buried in a marshy place, like at the source of the Seine or near Chamalière, in Auvergne. The ones in stone are mostly found together in the area of Marseille and the areas surrounding the Mediterranean. Those in bronze, much more numerous, are scattered throughout, but they are animal representations for the most part, not unrelated to the art of the steppes. As to various ceramics, it will not be until the conquest that they will appear in human forms, most often following Roman models, such as the countless statues of Venus buried in potters' workshops and in the ruins of Gallo-Roman villas. It is, however, difficult to date these objects with precision: everything depends on the place where they are found, at the beginning of the first century B.C. for the southern countries, toward the middle of the first century A.D. for the western and northern countries.

The most moving, and probably the most ancient of the stone

statues representing a feminine divinity is a nude woman, her genitals very apparent, her left arm squared, but half-covered by a long cloak. Her hair is very distinct and falls to her shoulders. Her eyes seem closed and her face expresses infinite sadness. One cannot help but thinking of a *Mater Dolorosa*. But we don't know what name, or more, what familiar name she was known by among the Bituriges (Berry), where she was discovered.[10] The bronze statuette of Neuvy-en-Sullias (Loiret) is totally different, discovered with many other ritual objects in a druidic sanctuary in the very middle of that Carnutes forest that Caesar took for the religious center of all of Gaul.[11] It is a woman whose body is very fine, slender and supple, with very distinct breasts and genitals, abundant hair. She is clearly adopting the stance of a dancer, and she necessarily evokes *la joie de vivre*. Isn't this the prefiguration of the triumphant Virgin of the Middle Ages, making the necessary allowances, just as the Bourges statue prefigures the grieving mother at the foot of the Cross?

For the maternal function is never truly absent, even when the representation seems entirely devoted to femininity. Moreover, it seems that before the event of realistic anthropomorphic representation, old allegorical images from the most ancient times were employed. That is the case with a very small sculpted stela, found at Chorey-Haut (Côte-d'Or) and now at the museum in Beaune. Here, we see a young foal nursing from a mare, and on first glance, this stela could be cited as an example of animal art. It is nothing of the kind, however, and, as Henri Hubert had already noted quite a long time ago, it serves as invaluable testimony to the Gallic worship of the goddess Epona in her most archaic form. This Epona, who, after the Roman conquest, became known throughout the Empire as the protectress of horses—and of riders—, is a purely Celtic divinity. Her name proves this, since it contains the term *epo*, which is the Brythonic equivalent of the Latin *equus*,[12] and her entire mythological history can be found in the first part of the Welsh *Mabinogi*, a very ancient account in which the goddess Rhiannon (the "great queen"), who is reproached for the disappearance of her son Pryderi, mysteriously hidden, and in fact, exchanged for a foal, is obliged to carry on her back the travelers who go to the fortress of her husband, the king Pwyll.[13] In Ireland, this same divinity appears in the character of the fairy, Macha, legendary founder of Emain Macha (Navan), capital and sacred site of the ancient Ulates.[14]

There are countless representations of Epona, especially in the Gallo-Roman period, in bronze, in ceramics, and in stone, the wood ones having largely disappeared. One of the most beautiful, and a fine example of distinctly Celtic technique, is a bronze, from Franche-Comté, and now at the Cabinet des Médailles of the Bibliothèque Nationale, Paris. The goddess, wearing a torque, a rigid, twisted, typically Celtic necklace, and draped in a great cloak, is seated on the back of a horse, not straddling it, but sidesaddle, toward the right, her two hands on her knees. It is a characteristic posture we will observe again and again for nearly all the representations of Epona, and much later, it will inspire the representations of the Virgin Mary's flight into Egypt. Another bronze, also at the Cabinet des Médailles, comes from Vienne. The workmanship is much more Roman, and the goddess carries fruit and flowers on her knees, while her mount resembles a ram. The presence of the flowers and fruit indicate that Epona is not just the goddess of riders (or the mare-goddess, as has been repeated entirely too often), but that she is, above all, the Provider, a sort of universal mother, with mastery over what the earth produces.

A stela discovered at Charrecey (Saône-et-Loire), and now at the Musée Lapidaire in Autun, presents a very rough Epona, in her classic posture, but with her feet resting on the back of a foal who is found under the belly of the mare. A bas-relief from Meursault (Côte-d'Or), now at the museum in Beaune, draws from the same inspirational source. A cloak floats around the goddess's head, but the foal is lying on the ground, between the mare's legs. The statuette from Loisia (Jura), now at the Cabinet des Médailles, presents an Epona naked to the waist, wearing a diadem, and the foal, carefully distinguished from the mare, faces in the same direction as the latter, that is, toward the right. It certainly seems that all these representations are illustrations of the myth of the mother goddess conducting souls in the otherworld, which is reinforced by the symbolic significance of the horse, considered to be a psychopomp. And that links back up to the funerary role attributed to the Neolithic goddess, who watches over the rebirth of the dead in the darkness of the mounds.

But Epona is only one of the names of the Goddess, one of her many metamorphoses. While Epona is associated with the horse, the goddess Artio is associated with the bear, as made evident by the Muri bronze (Switzerland), held at the Berne museum. The goddess is seated near a column that supports a vase full of fruit. The bear seems to be headed toward her, and, behind the bear, we can see a tree branching in all one direction, toward the left. Artio, whose name comes from one of the Celtic names for bear (like the name of the famous king Arthur), is a sort of mother of the wild animals, a "mother nature," not only protectress against the violence represented by the bear, but, according to the symbolic significance of this animal, the one who reawakens the beings deadened by their winter sleep. We could easily interpret this strange representation of Artio as a perfect illustration of the theme of King Arthur, mortally wounded at the battle of Camlan and taken away by his sister Morgan to the island of Avalon (where the fruit is ripe all year round), to be kept asleep until a future reappearance.

Another bronze statuette, now found in the Cabinet des Médailles, is just as revealing of the mythological themes underlying sculptural representation of the Goddess. This statuette, discovered at Margut (Ardennes), shows us a woman dressed in a short tunic, holding an arrow in her right hand, and seated on the back of a leaping wild boar. She can only be the goddess Arduinna, as indicated by several votive inscriptions, her name coming originally from the name Ardennes. If we are to believe the local legend of Wulfiliac, a Lombard converted to Christianity and now known as Saint Walfroy, a veritable sanctuary dedicated to this goddess existed at Margut. Unable to eradicate the pagan cult, Wulfiliac erected a pillar close to the sanctuary, on the top of which he installed himself, living on bread, water, and prayers, vowing that he would not descend so long as Arduinna remained preeminent. That shows the importance attributed to the Goddess in the eyes of the population of the Ardennes forest. It must be remembered, as well, that the wild boar, abundant throughout Gaul, constituted an almost inexhaustible food source, which fully justifies its becoming an emblem of the divine Mother, provider and nourisher. This cult looks back to very archaic traditions that are found again in the Welsh account of *Culhwch and Olwen*, the most ancient Arthurian "novel," in which the hero's mother is an image of the sow goddess, or the wild-sow goddess. The theme reappears again, in the same account, in the episode of the hunt of Twrch Trwyth, the monstrous wild sow, and in an Irish *Fianna* account, the story of the hero, Diarmaid, whose destiny is linked to that of a magical wild boar.[15] If the Gauls left no written texts, their traditions, along with those of other Celts, were maintained for a very long time and were available to the Christian monks of the Middle Ages who collected them, an enormous help to us in trying to understand how they honored this mysterious Goddess of the Beginnings, mistress of the wild animals.

There certainly seems to have been a strong desire to emphasize her omnipotence over nature. A strange stone statue at Courterel in Poulan-Pouzols (Tarn) shows this clearly. The statue's general form evokes the numerous menhir-statues of this region. It is undeniably female, and on the back are engravings of leaping animals, notably a stag and a wild boar. As for the bronze statuette of Kerguilly in Dinéault (Finistère), at the sacred site of the so-called Ménez-Hom mountain, it clearly resembles a Minerva, because of the helmet with its owl-like features, but the crest is in the form of a swan, which sends us back, not to Greco-Roman mythology, but to the more pure Celtic traditions of the "swan-women," magical or divine beings possessing a double nature, earthly and celestial.[16] Irish legends are teeming with anecdotes about these women of the *sidh*, the otherworld, who appear in the sky in the form of white swans and who, touching the earth, reveal themselves to be the most beautiful of all human creatures. The Gaelic tale of the birth of the hero

Cuchulainn reveals this theme. The mother of the hero, Dechtire, is, in fact, one of those ambiguous characters who wanders ceaselessly between the two worlds. And if the Ménez-Hom statuette, which is Gallo-Roman in technique, can be classified as a Minerva (the Gallic Minerva, of course, of whom Caesar speaks in his *Commentaries*), she evokes no less the Irish Brigit, daughter of the god Dagda, divinity of knowledge, arts and skills, mistress of the divine fire, and of whom the Christians took possession, making her into the famous "Saint" Brigit of Kildare. It must be known as well that Brigit, greatly honored in Armorican Brittany, bears a characteristic name that means "high" or "powerful," and that, moreover, she is often presented tripled, in the form of a triad, with three different names, and thus, three complementary aspects. She is in fact the same divine character as Morrigan (the "great queen"), Badb (the "crow"), Macha (the "rider," thus, the equivalent of Epona), Ethne (mother of the great multifaceted god, Lugh), Étaine (founder of a royal lineage), and finally, Boann or Boyne (literally, the "white cow"), the name of the deified Boyne River.

For if the Great Goddess has mastery over wild animals and thus reigns in the forests, she is also mistress of the sweet waters that give life, guardian of the sacred fountains, or resident of the lake bottom, living in a marvelous crystal palace. Here again we find the theme of Vivien, the Lady of the Lake of Arthurian legend, whose name derived gradually from Boann, or the ancient Celtic *bo-vinda*, the "white cow," who provides not only material food but also the divine milk of inspiration and knowledge. Thus, in Celtic, and then Roman, Gaul, we can speak of "pilgrimages to the sources," because, since earliest times, the fountains and the sources of rivers have served as heavily frequented sanctuaries where abundant archaeological traces remain, in particular, the ex-votos that attest to a fervent worship of this divine woman, provider, and healer; for the worship of mother-waters and so-called water cures are inseparable.

That is the case at the most famous of these sanctuaries, the Sources de la Seine, on the Langres plateau, near Saint-Seine-l'Abbaye (Côte-d'Or), the name itself providing sufficient proof that the worship of the goddess Sequana continued even through Christianization. At the site of these springs, an incredible number of ex-votos of all kinds have been discovered, which indicates that people came there from everywhere to ask the divinity to cure many different illnesses. But actual objects of worship have also been found there, in particular, a magnificent bronze piece representing a boat with the head of a duck for the prow, and with a crowned woman standing in front, dressed in an ample cloak, her hands open in a gesture that might be considered magical or propitiatory.[17] All evidence suggests that this a representation of the goddess Sequana, in other words, of the fertility function attributed to the universal Mother, symbolized here by the waters of the river. We must not forget that the name of the divinities is never anything but an epithet that reveals a function, and the same will be true in the Christian era for the many terms used to honor the Virgin Mary.

An essential comment: the sanctuaries dedicated to the Goddess are all more or less linked to a course of water or a spring. This is a tradition that continues to this day, since most churches and chapels dedicated to the Virgin Mary include a fountain or an inside well, as at Chartres, or a spring under the chevet, or a fountain or well in the immediate proximity. It is enough to travel the French countryside to be persuaded of this, but, in doing so, one would have to admit that it is very difficult to establish a boundary between Christianity and the religions termed pagan that preceded it. The Lourdes cave is hardly more than the Christian manifestation of a tradition anchored in the most distant past, when "white ladies" appeared at the thresholds of the caves overhanging a mountain stream in the Pyrenees.

The name of the Boyne, the river that flows through the most famous sanctuaries of pre-Christian Ireland, has been retained in certain places in France, which is not surprising, since it comes from a shared ancient Celtic name. Thus, on the borders of Auvergne and Velay, in the community of Saint-Jean-d'Aubrigoux (Haute-Loire), is found a very little known site, the Fontboine. Situated close to an abundant spring, it is a druidic settlement that endured because of its isolation throughout the Roman period. Now, the name Fontboine can only be an alteration of *fontem bonam*. Where did the *i* come from? More than likely, this is the "fountain of Boanne," the "white cow" divinity who distributes life and fertility. And what about Divonne-les-Bains, the famous spa in Ain? Don't we again find the name of the "divine Boann" there? As to the Gallo-Roman temple of Sanxay (Vienne), in Poitou, a temple that clearly replaced an earlier Gallic settlement, it is situated on the banks of a river called the Vonne, which refers us back once more to that mysterious divine woman figure who dissolves herself in the river to retrieve her lost virginity, according to curious Irish poems difficult to understand because the language is so archaic.[10]

Among the Greeks, the healer god is the handsome and benevolent Apollo, whose solar character only appears much later. In Romanized Gaul, this ancient Apollo presided over numerous sanctuaries located close to springs, everywhere taking on a different epithet. Thus it is in Grand (Vosges), where his name, Granus, goes back to the Gaelic—and ancient Celtic—name for the sun, *grian*, or, again at Aix-la-Chapelle (Aachen), in Germany, which is an ancient *aquae grani*. But elsewhere, this Gallic Apollo more often bears the name of Belenos, "brilliant," as at Beaune (Côte-d'Or) or at Saint-Bonnet-près-Riom (Puy-de-Dôme) which are the ancient Belenate. And, in the strange forest of Brocéliande (Paimpont Forest), the famous fountain of Barenton, around which so many legends revolve, was formerly named Bélenton, that is, Bel-Nemeton, "sanctuary of Bel." But is this "Bel" an abbreviation for Belenos or for the latter's *parèdre*, or counterpart, the goddess Belisama, the "very brilliant"? It is difficult to say, because this figure of Apollo seems to have very often usurped the place of a female divinity. Moreover, in the Irish tradition, if the god Diancecht, generally considered Apollo's equivalent, established the famous "fountain of herbs," which heals wounds and brings the dead back to life, it is his daughter, Airmed (which means "measure"), who insures its effectiveness by singing incantations. If we refer back to the Arthurian tradition, this fountain of Barenton—which has never been Christianized, but which is thought to cure madness—belonged to a

Lady of the Fountain who entrusted it to her husband. That is certainly significant. Barenton is, without a doubt, the *nemeton*, the "sacred glade" of the "very brilliant" Goddess.

What is more, the name Belisama appears widely throughout Gallic territory. At Saint-Lizier (Ariège), the ancient capital of Couserans, a votive inscription in Latin, now embedded in one of the pillars of the bridge, uses it as a name for Minerva. At Saint-Lizier, there is an interesting legend. During excavation at the Saint-Marsan chapel, located where there was once a temple dedicated to Mars, a statue of the Virgin was supposedly discovered, which, after being taken to the main church, returned to its original place each night. It is very likely that this so-called Virgin Mary was simply a "very brilliant" Belisama. At Vaison-la-Romaine (Vaucluse), another votive inscription is devoted to her, in Greek characters this time, which proves her antiquity, as do the many towns and villages bearing the name of this luminous divinity, beginning with Bellême (Orne). Now, in the forest of Bellême, near the pond of the Herse, is found a spring of ferruginous water with curative powers that has been used since antiquity, and which is dedicated to the "infernal gods, Mars, Mercury, and Venus."[19] Once again, the diversity of epithets covers a multitude of functions attributed to a single unique goddess. Thus, a strange bas-relief in the museum at Toulouse shows Epona on horseback, in her traditional posture, but galloping over stylized fish, and swimming among them is a bull with a fish's tail. The aquatic element is present, pure and simple, when it comes to representing the female divinity of the Beginnings. And that does not at all contradict the idea of light, and even of sun, since the sun, in Celtic and Germanic languages, is always feminine. At Bath, in England, the sanctuary of healing waters, the divinity honored there was a goddess, Sulis, whose name hardly needs to be translated.

Thus, the Goddess is Venus as well, that is, the beautiful one, the pale one, the one born from the sea foam (or from the sperm of Ouranos-Varuna, castrated by his son, Kronos). This is the goddess of the waves, the universal Mother, because she inspires the desire that leads to copulation, and thus, procreation. Her birth is supernatural, and constitutes a kind of *immaculate con-ception*. Perhaps this is Cesair, the primordial woman of the Celtic tradition whom we learn of in the Irish *Book of Conquests*, a compilation of Gaelic traditions thousands of years old. Now, an astonishing representation of this goddess exists—and oh, how pagan—in a Christian sanctuary, the chapel of Saint Agatha in Langon (Ille-et-Vilaine). Actually, it was in 1839, when the chapel was beginning to be rebuilt, that a fresco was discovered, very well preserved, on one of the walls, proof that this was a Gallo-Roman temple reused by the Christians. There we see Venus, nude, emerging from the waves, surrounded by fish, and Eros, astride a dolphin. The chapel was given its name in the seventeenth century, making it a place of pilgrimage for women nursing infants. Saint Agatha, the martyr with her breasts cut off, is actually the patroness of nursing. But formerly, the build-ing was dedicated to a mysterious "Saint" Vénier, or Vénérand, in which it is not difficult to recognize the name of Venus. It must be noted that the area of Langon contains important megalithic remains, in particular an alignment of monoliths known by the name of "Demoiselles de Langon." The local legend claims that these are young women who were turned into stone for preferring dancing to vespers, which reinforces the idea that Langon is located at the site of an ancient sanctuary devoted to the Goddess, served by many priestesses.

During the entire Gallo-Roman period, the worship of Venus was very important throughout Gaul, as is made evident by the multiple statues and countless statuettes of ceramic, mass-produced in the great pottery centers. On this subject, it is necessary to pose the problem of that strange statue known by the name of "Venus of Quinipily," which is now found in the open air, on a raised pedestal, above a stone basin in the gardens of the ancient Quinipily chateau, near Baud (Morbihan). This was not its original location. In the seventeenth century, it stood on the promontory of Castennec in Bieuzy-les-Eaux (Morbihan), above the Blavet, and it was the object of worship for a cult that was erotic, to say the least. Many couples went there to perform such acts under its shadow as Christian morality would find highly reproachful. This was the period of the Counterreformation in Brittany, when passionate missionaries raged against the obvious resurgence of paganism. Upon orders from the bishop of Vannes, the statue was thrown into the Blavet. But the inhabitants restored it to its place. It was thrown into the river again, wasted effort, because each time volunteers would remount it. Finally, the count of Lannion, an aristocratic libertine, took possession of the statue and had it installed in his chateau at Quinipily, after having it recut, it seems, to eliminate certain characteristics that were too shocking. But the "cult" devoted to this Venus did not die out for all that, and still exists even up until the present day.

The piece in question is a great granite statue, 2.15 meters high, which does not resemble the classical Venus in the least. She is presented nude, with breasts that have been visibly planed down. Upon her head appears a strip of cloth with a mysterious inscription, the three uppercase letters, ITT, probably added at the time of her "arrangement." She wears a kind of stole, as well, that goes around her neck, the two ends meeting at her belly. There has been much discussion over the origin of this statue. It is certainly not of Gallo-Roman design. Perhaps it comes from the Orient.[20] Whatever the case, it must have been the essential object of the sanctuary devoted to a feminine divinity. When it was found in Castennec, it was named the "couarde," an awkward Frenchification of the Breton *gwrac'h houarn*, literally, "virgin of iron," and we might well wonder why. But *gwrac'h* also means "sorceress," which implies a more heretical interpretation. This same place, Castennec, is the site of an ancient Gallic, then Gallo-Roman fortress, on the strategic spot in the Blavet valley at the intersection of Roman roads, the most important of which came from Lyon and Angers to head toward l'Aber-Wrac'h, passing by Rieux, on the Vilaine, and by Carhaix. Now, what is very revealing is the ancient name of Castennec, after the famous table of Peutinger: Sulim, from which it is not at all difficult to extract *Sulis*, one of the names of the solar goddess of the ancient Celts. In the end, this "Venus" is perhaps the realistic and erotic image of the Great Goddess in her solar aspect.

Sacred sites often take their name from the divinity that is honored there. We have seen this in the case of Bellême and Sulim, as we will see it subsequently with the many appellations given to "Our Lady," and to all the saints—sanctified or not—of Christianity. And even if all representations of the divinity disappear, the names maintain its memory. That is the case with the tower of Vésone, in Périgueux (Dordogne), a circular temple in ruins, at the site of a primitive city founded by the Gallic people of Pétrocores, and in which we find the memory of the Great Goddess, here known by the name of Vesuna. It is the same in Glanum, the ancient city (Gallic, Greek, and Roman) of Saint-Rémy-de-Provence (Bouches-du-Rhône). Here, the spring that feeds the area, and that is found in what is called the "local sanctuary," bears the name of Glanicae, a triad of protectress and fertility goddesses, such tripling being popular among the Celts.

In this regard, the strangest representation is, without a doubt, a block of stone found in Bourgogne and now at the Musée des Antiquités Nationales. Actually, this is not a sculpture, but an intaglio-engraved stela in which we can clearly discern three parallel female forms, not separated from each other, with torsos covered by a large X that clearly suggests crossed arms. The heads are well defined, with nose and mouth, but if two of them have two vertically hollowed eyes, the third, to the left, has only one eye. These figures are classified as the "three *matres*," but nothing in their attitude indicates a maternal function. They make us think again of those "triple goddesses" of the Gaelic tradition in Ireland, those famous triads sometimes called "triple Brigit" or "triple Macha." The mythological accounts attach great importance to these "triads," such as the Badb-Morrigan-Macha one, or the Boann-Ethne-Etaine one. This stone of "three *matres*" is incontestably the most perfect illustration of this theme of tripling. And, during just the Gallo-Roman period alone, the number of these mother goddesses grouped in threes will be considerable, which is solid proof that even under Roman domination, the ancient Celtic divinities were always present in the consciousness of the people.

This observation leads to another one: the absence of great

sanctuaries in honor of Venus during the Gallo-Roman period, however much celebrated she was among the Romans. "It has often been pointed out that, outside of certain southern ports like Marseille or Port-Vendres, Venus was hardly represented except by terra-cotta figurines, cheap pieces sold at fairs or markets; nothing the least bit honorific—putting aside the beautiful statues like the ones in Arles, Pourrières, and Vienne—attests to the presence of her cult."[21] The Gauls, no doubt, had a different vision of love than the Romans, who attached more importance to the physical beauty of the Goddess and neglected her metaphysical aspect. It will be the same, furthermore, for Juno, who protects mothers in all of Italy, but who will find great rivals in the famous *matres* so typical of Celtic worship.

Furthermore, the Celtic populations, even integrated as they were into the Roman system, seem to perpetuate a tendency observed in the Neolithic period: the skillfully proportioned excess of certain attributes or divine emblems, as a means to insist upon very precise functional aspects of the divinity. We have seen this with the goddess Artio, with the goddess Arduinna, both linked to the bear, with the swan goddess, with the goddess Epona, whether rider or mare. We find the same familiarity with animals in a statuette, very Roman in technique, discovered at Broye-lès-Pesmes (Haute-Saône), now at the British Museum in London. Here, a bronze represents a goddess bearing the antlers of a stag on her head and holding in her hands a horn of plenty and a peg. The deer is a symbol of abundance, as is the peg. The theme of the Grail is not far removed from this representation.

Thus, the Goddess is not only the mother of men (and of gods), but the universal Mother, the one who has carried in her womb the animals and even the plants. Certainly, the most beautiful example of this type of functional representation is one of the plaques of the famous Gundestrup Cauldron, the original now found at the Aarhus Museum (Denmark), and a perfect copy displayed at the Musée des Antiquités Nationales. It is a work done in silver, difficult to date (first or second century A.D.?), which seems influenced by the art of the steppes, illu-

ported by the Scythians, and that illustrates Celtic mythology in the most remarkable way possible.

The plaque's subject is the Goddess, and it presents a very well designed head of a woman, with long hair that seems to weave around a small female figure to the left. The torso is only sketched, but the breasts are clear. The left arm, very small, is folded against the bosom. The right arm is raised parallel to the head and a bird is perched on the fingers of the hand. This divinity wears a torque around her neck, and another small female figure is seated on her right shoulder, mounted on a four-legged animal. On her bosom, under her breasts, appears another four-legged animal and a human being, both of them probably dead. But on either side of the head of the divinity, there are two birds with spread wings, something like triumphant eagles, who give meaning to the scene. Indeed, it is the very figure described in Welsh mythology known by the name of Rhiannon, the equivalent of the Gaelic Macha and the Gallic Epona, who is not only the "rider," but also the mistress of strange birds that "waken the dead and put to sleep the living."[22] It is one of the fundamental aspects of the Goddess, mistress of wild animals and especially, possessor of the celestial power represented by the birds.

This vision can seem tormented. And it is so, to the extent that it conveys the creative or organizing energy that is the very justification for a divinity of origins. But as soon as "Roman Peace" is imposed in the Empire, this vision is going to become more reassuring, indicative of a certain political and economic stability that makes the metaphysical angst subside accordingly. Sequana of the sources of the Seine sails peacefully on the river, in the middle of a boat (which cannot help but evoke a certain megalithic representation), on the front of which appears the head of a duck, which reinforces the serenity and stability of this navigation on gentle water. And that goddess named Nantosuelta, on a votive stela from Sarrebourg (Moselle), seems to be a model and tranquil spouse at the side the god, Sucellos, the god of the hammer, the Gallic equivalent of the Irish Dagda with his ambiguous club. When the god strikes with one of its ends, he kills, but when he strikes with the other, he revives. Would Nantosuelta then be the mediator, the one who balances, who can stop—or put into motion—the formidable arm of her supposed spouse? The image of the Virgin Mary, mediator at the side of Jesus, is already prefigured here in a pre-Christian context heavy with mysticism. For the Goddess can also be the one who bears the grief of her children, as the Virgin of Compassion will be in the Middle Ages. The female statue at the Bourges museum (Cher) expresses this shared suffering and can be considered an Our Lady of Sorrows very much predating any speculations on the mother of Christ. Because if Jesus, on the Cross, made Mary the mother of all men, he is only following after the entire Middle East's belief in the universal mother goddess who takes the name of Cybele before coming to be installed in Rome and taking hold throughout the Empire. In Vienne, as in many other Gallo-Roman sanctuaries, the Metroac cult, resulting from a fusion between the religions of Mithras and Cybele, will leave many traces, particularly statues of the "mother of the gods." The stone statuette in the Borély Museum of Marseille, which represents Cybele seated, holding a lion cub on her knees, testifies to this attachment to a divinity whose function is maternal love and peace among living beings. As to the little votive stela in stone discovered at Grand (Vosges), and held in the museum of Epinal, even if it is anonymous, it very clearly conveys this desire for relieving suffering. Indeed, it presents a goddess seated in what seems to be a pharmaceutical dispensary or a laboratory, and we see, in a sort of tub, an instrument with a handle in the form of a caduceus. We must remember that Grand was an important Gallic sanctuary dedicated to the healing sun, and that the sun is feminine.

In the Gallic art of the Roman period, harmony, as much internal as apparent, was clearly an objective. At Neuvy-en-Sullias (Loiret), not far from the Gallic sanctuary of Fleury, magnificent bronze statuettes were found that are now in the Musée de l'Orléanais in Orléans. One of these is absolutely remarkable for its beauty, its fineness, and its technical elegance. It presents a nude woman, with long hair, dancing. The representation is not at all static, but there is nothing explosive about it, either. On the contrary, it is a matter of putting a world already created into harmony, as if the divinity were dancing through the stars to distribute to her countless children that vital light that renders the world "beautiful" in the etymological sense of the word. The fullness of the world is merged with the beauty of the divinity, since nothing would exist without her.

But this Roman period of Celtic art, in which, under the influence of lapidary techniques from the Mediterranean, abstraction and geometrization is going to give way to much greater concrete representation, is essential in the search for a nearly unique model of representation of the Goddess. The coexistence of different religious systems, with the multiplicity of interpretations that followed, is going to lead to a kind of synthesis, not only in the external forms, but also in the ideological content. The exact role attributed to the female divinity (no matter what the origin, Celtic, Latin, Greek, or Eastern) must then be redefined as a function of a new theological formulation, which nascent Christianity is going to reprocess to the extent that it can be made to conform to the decisions of the councils, especially those concerned with the concept of the Theotokos, by which the unforgettable image of the primitive mother goddess infiltrates the interior of an utterly masculine world.

For Christianity enters the Empire in force and changes considerably the exterior aspect of the divinity. Two diametrically opposed directions are now going to confront each other, in a quarrel constantly being updated with regard to images. Indeed, can anthropomorphic traits be given to a divinity that, by nature, even by its very essence, escapes any coarse realism? This problem had already presented itself at the time of the druids, who refused to define the infinite. But, the human mind needing concrete elements to make sense of the divine, divine forces began to be incarnated, given material aspects. The Evangelists themselves, by exalting the man-god Jesus Christ, went along with this realistic interpretation, perfectly conforming to the claims in Genesis with regard to man being created in the image of God. The great quarrel of the iconoclasts could only be settled with the victory of those partisans of the image; but what image, especially if it is to absorb the concept of the mother goddess, totally absent—as a result of internal censorship—from the first Christian texts? There lies the true problem.

All antiquity, be it Mediterranean or "barbarian," brought to light a divine figure, female in nature, under various names and with various characteristics. The Jewish people did not escape this intrusion by the Goddess, and the Hebrew Bible is full of conflicts opposing the partisans of the father god (Yahweh of Sinai, the ancient moon god of the Semites of the Middle East) to the partisans of the mother goddess, the Babylonian Ishtar who much later became Astarte and Aphrodite-Venus when she was not Diana-Artemis, a female divinity whose maternal function is necessarily paired with an erotic one. We are not wrong in thinking that this erotic function would be completely overshadowed from the beginning of Christianity, entirely centered as it was on a triumphant masculinity and an exemplary chastity, most of the time resulting in instinctive terror with regard to the mysteries of the woman.

Remaining completely objective, we can only note the nearly total elimination of the woman disciple of Jesus, the one it is customary to call, discreetly, the "Madeleine," and whose name and origin should be restored to her: Mary of Magdala. The commentators, cautious and distrustful, have made her into a repentant prostitute, seized by the love of Jesus and converted to his views. The reality must be completely otherwise. First, for the Hebrews, prostitution did not have the same meaning that is attributed to it now. To prostitute oneself is, in ancient biblical times, "to sacrifice to the Goddess," something unforgivable, since the Hebrews were entirely devoted to a unique male god, and since they struggled for centuries to establish his authority, despite all the deviances, made apparent in the Bible, in favor of the goddess of the Middle East, this Babylonian Ishtar for whom the temples were places of prostitution, otherwise called erotic worship, consisting of the union of a man with a priestess, the transitory incarnation of the Goddess. It is a matter of sacred, ritual, religious prostitution, and not of commerce. It is a matter of union with the divinity and not of simple carnal satisfaction.

Now, we know that Magdala was a place consecrated to the Great Goddess. It is probable that the enigmatic Mary of Magdala, so carefully kept in the background, was the great priestess of the temple of this goddess. From which comes the qualification of "prostitute" that she bears, even if, as first witness to the Resurrection of Christ, she is pardoned for her entire heretical past. Thus, the famous evangelistic episode at Bethany sheds particular light on the matter. Jesus was baptized in the Jordan by John the Baptist, in the name of the Father. At Bethany, at the home of Martha and Lazarus, who are the sister and brother of Mary (the latter, very wealthy, probably owned some property), Mary poured perfume on Jesus' feet, conferring on him an authentic sacerdotal unction, which was not to Judas's taste, relentless partisan of the religion of the father god that he was. Judas will then betray Jesus, under the pretext that Jesus betrayed the religion of the Father. If we understand this correctly, Jesus presents himself as the anointed one (that is the meaning of "Christ") of the father god (Yahweh) and the mother goddess (under whatever name she is invoked) at the same time, thus reuniting the two traditions that divide up the world. It is one of the manifest proofs of the universality of Jesus' teachings, and it is very surprising that Christian theologians never put it to good use. The shadow of the Goddess of the Beginnings, did she cause such fear for the hairsplitters?

That is why the time during which the Christian message gets introduced to the Gallo-Roman world is a transition period. From this duality—father god and mother goddess—a double vision of the Goddess of the Beginnings will be born: wise virgin or mad virgin? The question seems banal, but it will be asked in all the centuries that follow, not only on a purely aesthetic level, but also on the level of religious speculation, with much more serious consequences. In short, the primordial Goddess, is she a woman whose body has driven her mad, or a mother who doesn't know how she finds herself pregnant? To the sacred prostitute of the Babylonian temples and other sites in what is now French territory, henceforth is opposed the chaste virgin who no longer knows anything except her maternal function.

That denotes a considerable evolution in thinking. It all happens as if there was a desire, conscious or not, to eliminate the image of a strong divine woman to profit an all-powerful man whose relationship to the woman is restricted to one of son to mother. The ancient sacred prostitute, incarnation of the Goddess, is a virgin, in the strongest sense of the term, that is, free of all subordinating ties to any spouse, but she is no less continually sexually active. In fact, it is the Esther of the Bible (and not Racine's watered-down heroine) who uses her sexuality to put the plans of the divinity into effect. She is, thus, *active*, and she serves as a constant reminder that the role of the woman is necessarily carnal. One of the better examples of this type that endured throughout the Christian Middle Ages is, again, the famous Sheela-na-gig, found in the churches of Great Britain and Ireland, this nude woman displaying her genitals by holding her vulvar lips open outrageously wide as if to invite beings to reenter her womb to be reborn there. It is probable that representations of this type were made in France, too, but they must have been destroyed under the influence of the Roman Church. This image of the woman was then entirely "demonized" and became the medieval witch, suspected of all types of prostitution, including prostitution to the devil.

Under the Roman Empire, the counterpart of this "feminist" tendency was the exaltation of the god Priapus, in perfect accord with the androcratic character of the society. But, even if phallic worship survived in the strange devotion to the "Saints" Foutin or Phallus, its excesses provoked a puritan reaction and an eclipsing of sexuality within a young Christianity still looking for its doctrine. It was useless to pose questions on the subject of the sex of God, since he was all-powerful and since the phenomenon of creation did not need to be explained beyond being the result of divine will. Thus, a place for the divine woman no longer remained: the Mother of the Beginnings passed under the shadow where she rejoined all the demons of various mythologies of antiquity.

It is difficult, however, if not impossible, to get rid of concepts existing since the beginning of time, and the image of the woman could only resurface by taking on aspects conforming to the new thinking; which explains the dazzling ascent of the Theotokos, the Mother of God, this Mary, always virgin and mother of Jesus. But, in remaining necessary, she lost all her sexuality to her one unique function, maternity. Moreover, this situation permitted her role to be reduced to a singularly passive one. "I am the servant of the Lord," Mary is made to respond to the angel of the Annunciation. The many child-bearing virgins, like the sorrowful pietàs of the Middle Ages, are already germinating in the still-pagan mother goddess of Prunay-le-Gillon (Eure-et-Loir), a cast of which is now at the Musée des Antiquités Nationales. This is a seated goddess, her hands on her open knees. Between her thighs, she is holding a young child, also seated, its hands on its own knees. "This little monument is among countless votive statuettes of mother goddesses. While most of them only present her with the child at her breast, this one places her . . . in the posture that will be, a thousand years later, that of the Virgins in Majesty holding the seated infant Jesus and also viewed face on. The severe attitude and the heaviness of the robes also distance this object from the classical Gallo-Roman productions."[23] It is very evident that this representation conforms completely to the polychromatic wooden statue of Saint-Nectaire, the famous statue of the Virgin and child that dates from the twelfth century. Henceforth, the mad virgin will give way to the wise virgin before taking refuge in the dark forests to wait for the great witches' sabbaths that will not escape the wrath of God-fearing right thinkers.

Now, the reign of the Mother Goddess of the Beginnings seems to have come to an end, and the reign of the mother of all the gods, as well. Thus will begin the astonishingly prosperous reign of the Virgin Mother of the one, unique God, known by whatever names and dedications over the course of the centuries to follow. But appearances are sometimes deceiving.

4

THE TRIUMPH OF THE MOTHER

The Christian Middle Ages

Too often we forget that Christianity is essentially Jewish, especially since there is a sort of official anti-Semitism endemic throughout European civilizations. The Romans did not see it as anything other than a Jewish sect, this "abominable sect of Christians," in Pliny the Younger's own words, and the orthodox Jews of the first century A.D., considered it simply a deviance, a heresy, dangerous to both the doctrine and the public order. But we also forget that the ideology of this sect was transmitted to the West through Hellenism and that it had been cast in the mold created by ancient Greek philosophers. Saint Paul, the true founder of Christianity, was a Jew and a Roman citizen, but culturally, Greek, which is not without consequences for the events that followed, notably with regard to the internal contradictions within this new religion springing from a synthesis of such heterogeneous speculations.

Among these contradictions, two seem irreconcilable at first glance. The God of the Jews is "master of the armies," sole dispenser of justice, avenger, legislator without pity, jealous, sometimes racist, while the God of the Greeks is, first and foremost one of knowledge, of the dialectic and moderation, content with being many-sided, and submitting himself to a fate that is as much beyond his control as it is for all other living beings. Thus a paternal monotheism stands in opposition to a kind of polytheism, or at least to a multipurpose definition of divinity, this latter being much more abstract than it appears, clothed as it is in apparel meant to render it accessible to everyday mortals. Wedged between these two notions, Christianity makes its choices: God is love, it claims, because love is what unites the contradictions. And that is the deep meaning of the evangelistic message. That is the fundamental innovation Christianity brings to humanity.[1]

And, in the final analysis, that is what explains why the new religion spread among all the levels of the population. The language that will be used is no longer a legal language, as it was among the Romans and the Jews for whom relations between human and divine were governed by contract, and it is no longer an intellectual language relating to an invisible god as discussed by the Greek philosophers or even by the Celtic druids. Christianity is going to address itself to what is most deeply and commonly shared among human beings, the feelings. And if what Jean-Jacques Rousseau writes is true, that the origin of language is to be found in the expression of emotions and feelings, Christian discourse could only reawaken the impulses of love that centuries of intellectual speculation had a tendency to suffocate. Henceforth, the human being will no longer obtain salvation through meticulous observation of a contract with the divine, or through a comprehension of divinity, but through an act of love, even going so far as to sacrifice one's own life for the good of the other. And the ancient system of divine justice, marked by an eye for an eye, will give way to charity, the kind of voluntary act magnificently illustrated by the representation of the archangel Michael altering the weight of souls by leaning his shoulder on the lighter side of the scale.

But the Christian God is still the Hebraic Yahweh, revised and corrected by the images of Zeus or Jupiter. If not the father of the gods, he is at least the Father of All, and this absolute, total masculinity contradicts the notions of tolerance and pardon. Necessarily, the Father is the one who gives orders and chastises, and it is the Mother who intercedes, or who pardons. Now, the Mother was eliminated by the new religious language, because she evoked too many pagan rites. The disciples of Jesus are all men, even if that necessitated eliminating Mary Magdalene, and the Trinity is considered masculine. This could not last, and it is the very ground from which the ancient image of the divine woman is going to reemerge and take off with such force that the Church Fathers are going to have to channel the energy. Thus will be born the cult of the Theotokos, the Mother of God, which the Council of Ephesus will finally decide to make official in 431.

It is clearly not by chance that this doctrinal position was decided in Ephesus, since this city had been dedicated to the worship of the Great Goddess since early antiquity. She is called Diana of Ephesus in certain texts, and the name covers a multitude of feminine divinities coming out of innumerable traditions. By the same token, there have been serious attempts to find the house that the Virgin Mary supposedly inhabited—in the company of the apostle John—in that very same city. Where can the Mother of God be better honored than in the citadel of the ancient goddess of the Near East?

For the essential thing was to channel this outpouring of love that led the new Christians to implore the Mother to be their mediator, the one who could understand their weaknesses, their faults, the one who was the incarnation of a mother's love for her children, the one toward whom all eyes turned because she was the sun who gave warmth to beings wandering on the earth in search of light with her energy, her heat, and her love. The young child alone in the dark is afraid of ghosts who wander in the night, and he keeps calling for his mother, the one who reassures, the all-powerful. Thus, it was perfectly normal to present to the new Christians this serene and welcoming image of a mother who, not being in the least bit a goddess, was no less the Mother of God. Moreover, it was necessary, because the first Christian zealots, as much in Europe as on the coasts of Asia, felt no discomfort at all leaving a church where they had attended Mass to rush off to a temple dedicated to one goddess or another. That did not seem like a contradiction to them, and evidence abounds regarding this syncretism practiced over the course of the first centuries A.D.

It was very difficult indeed, if not impossible, whatever the usual hagiographies say, to obliterate the "false gods" without inheriting their legacy. As Corneille depicted him in his tragedy, Polyeucte—a model of the baroque bad taste of the classical period, besides—is the most perfect example of the intolerant, fanatical, and iconoclastic neophyte, conceited enough to bring down the ancient world with a single blow, possessed by a spirituality stripped of all attachment to the past. Real situations are never so black and white. The Church Fathers were not the imbeciles that Corneille makes the "Christian martyr," Polyeucte, out to be. To the contrary, they tried very hard to graft the new ideology contained in Paul's letters and the Gospels attributed to Jesus' disciples onto the ancient spirituality. We must at least admit that they did this with much ingenuity, taking the deep realities of the human spirit into account and providing what it had been wanting for so long. The human spirit awaited a new definition of the Goddess of the Beginnings. Whatever differences there were between them, however many details, the Church Fathers did respond, by and large, to this longing so deeply rooted at the very base of the soul.

In fact, it was impossible to erase the image of the Great Goddess of so many names, crystallized in this epoch under the two principle ones of Isis and Cybele. The latter was officially associated with the Iranian Mithras, within the framework of the so-called Metroaic religion, a religion adopted by the Roman emperors who were the first to benefit from their assimilation of the young god who kept dying and being reborn, the son of the Great Goddess, the mother of all the gods. The worship of Cybele was widespread throughout the empire, and in the first and second centuries A.D., it almost dethroned Christianity because of the enthusiasm it evoked. There was something entrancing about it, in that it plumbed the deepest spiritual depths throughout the Mediterranean, and unearthed the mysterious theology of those people considered "barbarians," who had always honored a female solar divinity as the giver of all life.

This divinity risked being a great nuisance within the Christian framework, all the more so because its image loomed so large in all the areas where the Gospels were preached. We know that the Jews, just as later, the Muslims, refused to represent God in a human form, aligning themselves in this way with the ancient Celts who did not understand how the perfect could be portrayed by an imperfect form, the infinite by the finite. In fact, in the earliest Christian times, the only image that was tolerated was that of a fish, a sign of recognition more than representation, and above all, a pure symbol, based upon the Greek name for fish, *ichthus*, in which appear the initials of *Iēsous CHristos THeou Hyios Sōtēr*, that is, "Jesus Christ, Son of God, Savior." And this interpretation did not contradict in the least the esoteric sense of the fish as the creature of earliest origin, thus capable of signifying "creator god." It is only in about the fourth century when, unable to eliminate the too-pervasive representational images around the first churches, there would be an attempt to recover certain ones and attribute entirely Christian overtones to them. This was the case with the Virgin Mary, and surely we must acknowledge that the image of the Mother of God owes much to Cybele, with equal regard to form as to context.

Actually, there are many analogies between the story of Cybele and the story of Mary. Cybele and her son, Attis, formed a perfect couple, but one never speaks of the father. Attis, of course, is a son-lover, conforming to the most ancient human myths, a concept absolutely rejected by Christianity, though it remains no less true that the relationship between Jesus and his mother retains great evocative power. But Attis dies, and Cybele is devastated, an image that cannot help but suggest the pietà, this Mater Dolorosa, so often represented through the ages. Now, the essential thing is that Attis is reborn, each year in fact, and his resurrection carries all his followers along with it. We can only be struck by this coincidence, which cannot, after all, possibly be a coincidence. And it becomes clear that the Metroaic cult must have been on the point of dethroning Christianity.[2] As to Cybele herself, the divine Mother, she could only prefigure the image of the Theotokos.

But the character of Cybele was blatantly sexual. Now, the notion of love expressed by the evangelistic message went far beyond sexual union and aimed at something universal and absolute. The problem that presented itself was how to adapt the model, how to purge it of all that called up, even faintly, the orgiastic celebrations and sacred prostitution ingrained in the memory of the Great Goddess with so many names. And strangely enough, the demands of Metroac worship would furnish the needed solution. We know, in fact, that during initiatory ceremonies, still largely a mystery to us, but no doubt orgiastic in nature, the priests of Cybele, the galli, voluntarily castrated themselves. They did so in order to better serve the Goddess, perhaps to better identify themselves with her by becoming female, perhaps to eradicate all other female temptation that could make them forget the one to whom they had consecrated themselves forever. This was an exemplary act, especially in a society that privileged virility. Moreover, by performing this sacrifice that cut them off from the warrior, and thus the active, working class, the priests of Cybele reenacted the myth of Attis, castrated by his own hand, dying symbolically at the end of the year, but being reborn immediately thereafter. Thus we can understand the whole significance of "voluntary castration," as it was expressed by Jesus in the Gospels, and as it has been practiced, at least in principle, by those who claim to be the disciples of Christ. We can also much better understand the hard-line policy of the Church Fathers in extolling the benefits of chastity and virginity, a tendency that will manifest itself later in the monastic vow of chastity and the priestly vow of celibacy. In eliminating those problems marked by their sexual nature, originating and emanating still from the temples of the Great Goddess, the organizers of the Roman Church emphasized the total commitment of all those who engaged themselves in the service of God, and on their voluntary renunciation of all sexual functions. This is the framework from which the Virgin Mary emerged, purified, renovated, modestly confined to her maternal role, but still endowed with all the components concealed within her image. If the primordial goddesses of ancient mythology were impregnated by the sky, the air, by fire, or even by a serpent, the Mother of Jesus was impregnated by the Holy Spirit, and this vague notion justified, without explaining, the strange birth of Jesus, God made man.

We should point out that the Annunciation, as it is reported in the Gospels, and especially by Saint Luke, is rich with symbolism. The angel is a *messenger*, but not an *agent*; Mary is a virgin and, even though she is engaged, she fully intends to remain one. And finally, Mary accepts her role as the Mother of God, the "bearer of infinity," which immediately elevates her to the rank of mother goddesses. As for Joseph, the "fiancé," who, if we are to believe the canonical texts, was never the husband, he embodies the chaste spouse, thus becoming the perfect model of the chaste man—or eunuch—who exclusively serves the divine. But that does not in any way prevent the commentators from continuing to speak of Jesus' *Davidic* filiation through Joseph, which constitutes, we must admit, a remarkable tour de force.

Whatever the case, the Virgin Mary took the place of Cybele—or of every other Goddess of the Beginnings. And just as her precursors were represented in human form, so she will be, since Western peoples need concrete images to reflect the ineffable. Thus, despite the various quarrels between orthodox and iconoclast, there will be representations of the mother of Jesus, who became, through the words spoken to the apostle John at the Crucifixion, the mother of all men, the one who loves the least of creatures equally and in whom all confidence can be placed, because she is essentially maternal.

According to a tradition solidly maintained throughout the centuries, it is Saint Luke the Evangelist who will paint the first portrait of the Virgin. Despite repeated claims by the Church Fathers, it is clearly impossible to consider the madonna of Santa Maria in Via Lata or the Madonna of Santa Maria Maggiore, in Rome, as authentic works of this Jewish doctor who was Saint Luke, disciple of Saint Paul, and who knew the Virgin Mary no better than his master. But the fact remains: according to tradition, all representations of Mary derive from an original portrait by Luke. Thus, homage is paid to the only evangelist who speaks at length about the Virgin and the circumstances surrounding Christ's birth. The evangelist John, who, according to the Acts of the Apostles, lived in the company of the mother of Jesus, is the only one who doesn't speak of her, which is rather strange, since it would seem as though he were in the best position to supply authentic testimony. In fact, the representations of the Virgin, paintings as well as statues, derive from a more ancient model, necessarily pre-Christian, and were embellished with details extracted by accounts considered apocryphal, such as the Protevangelium of James, dating from the end of the first century, or the Transitus Mariae, probably written in the fifth century. We are a long way from the details that some struggle hard to consider historically accurate.

But no matter, since the purpose here is to examine *how* the image of the Goddess of the Beginnings evolved under the name of Mary within the very heart of Christian society. There is no doubt that the origin of iconography relating to Mary goes back to the time of the catacombs, when Christianity was still only a Jewish sect lost in the decline of the Roman Empire. But in these crude, naive, but nevertheless moving representations, the Virgin plays only a very minor role. She appears as an insignificant figure in the midst of scenes illustrating the life of Jesus. We must wait for the fourth century to find the familiar features of the one who will later be called the Madonna. The first images in which Mary appears alone are found in the churches of Syria and the Near East. From there, they migrated to the West, following the trade routes and thus penetrating formerly Celtic territories where they would merge with images of mother goddesses to then give birth to an art completely original and containing much symbolic significance. Immediately following the Council of Ephesus, after Pope Sixtus III (432–440) had an ancient Roman structure made into an official sanctuary to Mary (the Santa Maria Maggiore basilica), most of the churches and cathedrals of France were also dedicated to the Virgin, just as certain abbeys were, like Autun, Tours, and Poitiers. Little by little, many sanctuaries took the name of the Virgin Mary, Mother of God, the Theotokos made official by the Council of Ephesus. This could only correspond to a conscious desire among the faithful to find, within the Christian message itself the image of the ancient Goddess of the Beginnings, momentarily brushed aside and obscured in favor of the Savior, who had to be masculine, since he had the capacity for virility and power.

Of course, it is the Byzantine Empire, that last reflection of the Roman claim to world dominance, but also a faithful mirror of the ancestral memory of the Near East, that will manifest the first representations of the Mother of God. Certainly, this representation was not accepted at once. It was a matter of knowing that it was acceptable to represent the divine Mother in a human form, because a simple uterine symbol, like those seen on the walls of Paleolithic grottoes would have been sufficient to perpetuate the concept of primitive maternal divinity. But, counter to the theological abstraction of the Jews, Greek philosophical realism and the historicizing methods of the Romans would prevail and put an end to all scruples. The most important thing was to render an abstraction concretely. What could be more natural than the image of a mother, underlying an infinite world of tenderness, resignation, hope, and love? The old mother goddess, who, even as primal parent was still a sexual woman, would find herself recast in the purified image of the Magna Casta, the chaste wife of the no less chaste Joseph, who played no other role than that of the castrated priests of the magnificent and triumphant Cybele, the eternal Rome from which Christianity would entirely recapture the will for power.

Whether or not they are attributed to Saint Luke, there is no doubt that we owe the first representations of the Virgin Mary to Byzantine artists, the last mystics of the mother goddess who knew so well how to secure the link between the Babylonian Prostitute and the Virgin free of all stain. It was enough to eliminate sexual instinct and, in its place, make *agape* the driving force. Thus, very soon, three basic types of representation became known, rising from the convergence between the mystical civilizations (Palestine, Mesopotamia, Phrygia, the so-called barbarian and the Hellenistic worlds) and the philosophical civilizations (Greece and Iran, indeed, even Brahmanic or Buddhist India). Thus dawned the day of paintings and sculptures representing the *hodgitria,* supposedly the bust of the Virgin, her right hand on her breast and holding the infant Jesus—the classical Madonna—then, the *nikopeia,* the "dispenser of victory," in a royal posture with her divine son sitting enthroned on her knees like a king, and finally, the so-called praying Virgin, the one who intercedes on the behalf of her many countless children who are all the human beings. These three types of representations are the most ancient and have given rise to an untold number of variations in the West, according to the motivations that inspire each individual painter or sculptor.

If it is impossible, however, to doubt the existence, beginning from the fifth century, of a multitude of representations of Mary, in the East as well as the West, it is rare to discover authentic ones among them. These gaps are not so much a product of time as the result of the systematic destruction that continued for more than a century, between 725 and 842, at the time of the famous quarrel of the iconoclasts. Moreover, from this apparently formalist quarrel emerged even more profound ideological theses concerning the antagonism between Monophysitism, which recognizes Jesus Christ has having only a single nature, and Nestorianism, which distinguished his human nature from his divine nature. Furthermore, we must note that in their destructive fanaticism, the iconoclasts aimed first at the countless vestiges of paganism apparent throughout the representations then known as the "false gods." We shall have to wait until 843 for the worship of images, paintings, statues, or sculptures, now officially admitted into the Christian religion, which took as its starting point the principle that anything that has been seen can be reproduced, the scriptural testimonies authenticating this visible reality. Henceforth, there would be no more opposition to representing the Virgin Mary, Mother of God, and the same would be true for Jesus himself, and all his apostles, as well as the saints and martyrs.

But the problem arises, and is still far from being resolved, of knowing if these representations are Christian creations or pre-Christian cult objects recovered. The period of the iconoclasts provoked countless anathemas against the worship of idols, stones, trees, or statues, but, despite various condemnations by the councils, especially under the reign of Charlemagne, the practice and the objects of idolatrous worship were maintained throughout the West, to such an extent that the clergy, unable to exterminate them, resigned themselves to "baptizing" them. Besides, the only thing to do was to apply the famous formula of Saint Augustine (*Letter to Publius*, 47): "When the temples, the idols, the sacred woods . . . are diverted from their first purposes and put into the service of the true God, theirs is like the case of men who are diverted from sacrilege and impiety, to be converted to the true religion." This is an admission. How many Virgin Marys, once miraculously discovered, and sometimes lightly retouched, always repainted and redressed, indeed, even crowned, are, in reality, pagan idols put into the service of Christian religion?

It is just as difficult, and nearly always impossible, to place the various representations in any chronological order. Some of them are only more or less faithful copies of earlier representations. Others were completely redone and corrected according to sociocultural demands. Some are even restorations based upon conjecture, as is the case for the statues burned at the time of the religious wars or the Revolution. But they all testify to the permanence of this worship of the mother goddess, whatever her denomination, as evidence bears out since the beginning of human history.

In this regard, one of the most fantastic realizations, and at the same time, one of the most beautiful, even if it is among the least well known, is the Virgin in Majesty found in the church of Saulzet-le-Froid (Puy-de-Dôme). Characteristic of medieval art from the Auvergne, this grouping of the Virgin holding her son on her knees in an attitude that suggests deep inner vision, is unforgettable. The way the Mother is dressed cannot help but recall dolmenic engravings like those of Gavrinis, in Brittany, thus testifying to the permanence of a symbolism issuing from the dawn of time. Featured on many Auvergne Virgins, these semiconcentric curves are, at the same time, hair, the waves of the sea, undulations in a ripe field of wheat when the wind blows, and the great power lines of the universe so often emphasized in megalithic engravings and in Celtic ornamentation. We might be tempted to say that the Virgin of Saulzet-le-Froid is a copy of the ancient goddess of the dolmens. Even the Mother's hands, which seem to protect the Son, indicate clearly that the center of the universe is located in the Son, pressed flat against the womb of the one who has given birth to God—and, consequently, to all living beings. Here, metaphysical speculation seems more intense than ever, and it goes beyond all strictly aesthetic interpretations that we might venture to make on the subject. This Virgin dates from the twelfth century, but nothing indicates that she is not a copy of an earlier representation. She plumbs the very depths of the mystical past of the West, to an even greater extent that the Virgin of Saint-Nectaire, who is so famous and whose beauty is indisputable.

The former statue of Notre-Dame-du-Puy-en-Velay (Haute-Loire) must have been an entirely different matter, if we believe a rustic replica made of it before its destruction during the Revolution.[3] This one belongs to that category of representations called the Black Virgins. The Mother is standing, Jesus as well, right against her, and both of them are wearing strange bonnets on their heads, as if recalling the tower above Cybele, the famous *turrigère* Cybele, so popular during the early Roman Empire, mother of all the gods and all men, heiress to the Goddess of the Beginnings of the Near East, to the Germanic Herda, and to the Celtic Dana-Don all at once, as well as, we too often forget, to the mysterious *turanna*, the "tyrant" of the Etruscans, the one who gives life and death, otherwise known as the mistress of fates.

This type of standing Virgin, with a standing child, is not very common, and we have to wonder if the rustic copy from Craponne really represents the ancient statue of Puy. Concerning the latter, doubt remains: was there only one of them or at least two? One tradition claims that it was given to the cathedral of Puy by Saint Louis himself and that he had brought it from the Orient. But then how did it happen that, before Saint Louis's return from Egypt in 1254, the Puy-en-Velay pilgrimage was already well known because of the presence of a miraculous statue of the Virgin? It is true that the Puy setting occupied the same site as the ancient Gallic sanctuary of Anicium, a name in which it is not difficult to recognize that of the mysterious Anna or Dana of the Celts, the primordial Goddess, mother of all the gods.

The so-called Auvergne style is, however, the one that comes closest to the earliest traditions of the West. The great lines that mark the folded robes of the figures cannot help but evoke those great megalithic undulations. This is clear in the statue of Notre-Dame-de-la-Bonne-Mort of Clermont-Ferrand (Puy-de-Dôme) and in the one of Notre-Dame-de-la-Rivière of Beaumont (Puy-de-Dôme), which dates from the twelfth century and was recently rediscovered,[4] and especially in the very beautiful Notre-Dame-la-Brume of Tournus (Saône-et-Loire), also from the twelfth century. This last statue represents the Virgin seated on a throne and holding on her knees a Jesus already grown, despite his small size, and seeming to teach more than to bless. It is impossible not to notice that the hands of the Virgin are immense, as if they indicated her protective powers and her power over her divine Son. But there, again, it is difficult not to admit how striking the parallels are between this Christian Virgin Mary and that mother goddess of the third century A.D., discovered in a funeral pit, near Bernard (Vendée), if only in their general attitudes and the folds of their robes.

These examples refer to the Virgin in Majesty, in which the attitude of Mary is that of a queen, or more, of an empress triumphantly holding the god-child. At Beaulieu-sur-Dordogne (Corrèze), the representation of Notre Dame that is found in the parish church superbly expresses this majesty through accentuation of clothing and the noble and serious face of the Mother. Even though it is from the twelfth century, this statue already predicts the exaggerations of the baroque period. Completely opposite, the Virgin in Majesty of the northern portal of the cathedral of Reims (Marne), which no doubt dates from 1175, retains a remarkable simplicity that emphasizes the mystical, regal quality that Mary possesses within herself. The humble expression, the half-closed eyes, the somberness of the decor, all point to this desire to make Mary the queen of the otherworld, a world invisible but nevertheless very near. This is very different from another Virgin in Majesty, dating from the thirteenth century, located on the portal of Saint Anne at Notre Dame in Paris. Here the Theotokos appears in all her glory, surrounded by angels and bishops. And abandoning all traces of humility, her attitude is truly one of a triumphant victor bearing the scepter of the world. It is true that the Gothic style marks a significant transformation in religious devotion, going from solitary meditation to communal ceremonies amid much pomp and circumstance. In fact, the Virgin in Majesty of Reims represents an eternal personal quest, the one of Paris, a triumphant success, a certainty. These allow us to appreciate the evolution of attitudes over the course of one century within the very bosom of the Catholic Church.

It is, however, the maternal aspect that dominates all the representations of the Middle Ages. At Rouen (Seine-Maritime), a statue now at the Musée des Beaux-Arts shows the Virgin nursing Jesus. The same will be true for a statue from Orléans (Loiret), also at the Musée des Beaux-Arts. Admittedly, it had almost been forgotten that the Virgin Mary was a woman, that she had a body, even genitals. Certainly, this nursing remains very discrete in the case of these statues, but it constitutes a kind of recognition of the only sexual function that was acceptable for the blessed "ever virgin" Mary. It will be an entirely different story with the paintings at the end of the Middle Ages, in particular in the picture by the Flemish master, *La Vierge et l'Enfant*, now at the Musée des Beaux-Arts of Dijon (Côte-d'Or). Here, the right breast of the Virgin is very full and round, very visible, even if the child, with a faraway look in his eyes, seems completely disinterested in it. A certain sensuality is apparent in this composition, and it is still further accentuated in the famous painting of Jean Fouquet, *La Vierge á l'Enfant*, now at the Musée Royal des Beaux-Arts of Anvers (Belgium), in which the Virgin's very low-cut dress can strike one as unseemly for a religious work. But was this painting by Fouquet really meant to be a religious work? We know that the model for Fouquet's Virgin was Agnès Sorel, the Dame of Beauty, the official mistress of King Charles VII. The time is not far off when the forms given to supernatural beings are going to be more and more deeply imbued with a passionate sensuality. But these works are the exceptions. One type dominates by and large, that of the classical Madonna of whom there are countless examples. Among the most remarkable, we can point to the Virgin of Trumeau, on the northern portal of the western facade of Notre Dame in Paris, or, again, the gilded Virgin, with the strikingly gentle face, of the cathedral at Amiens (Somme).

Because even if attitudes do not change very much and tend to produce stereotypes that are perpetuated through time, more and more we arrive at a sort of "transfiguration" of the Virgin's expression. What we see is no longer the passivity of primitive statues or the mystery attempted in certain representations that emphasize the hieratic character of the Mother of God, model of perfection and purity, but the passionate quest for that look of tenderness that is expected in a human mother, the mother shared by all men, if we are to believe the Gospel, since before his death on the Cross, Jesus made Mary the mother of the apostle John, and through him, all human beings. At the end of the Middle Ages, we find this tenderness continually. The Virgin Mary can be only good, wanting happiness for all her children. She can be only gentle, as we imagine she was with the child Jesus. And since the role of a human mother is to feed, to raise, to educate, to comfort, the role of Mary can be no different. From these ideas, which amount to widely held beliefs among Christians, will spring the essential concept of the mediator. If Jesus, and consequently, God, is distant, sometimes demanding, always just, it is better, when you are not so sure of yourself, when you believe yourself to be a sinner, to bring along an advocate to defend your case. And who could be a better or more effective advocate than the very mother of the Savior? That is the message we find in the tympanum of the royal portal of the Chartres cathedral (Eure-et-Loir). It is a depiction of the Last Judgment, and the supreme judge is Jesus. But to his right is

Mary, on her knees, her hands joined, imploring her Son to be generous, indulgent toward the humans who crowd in front of him. Thus, this type of praying Virgin will very often appear on the portals of churches, especially in representations of the Last Judgment. On the northern portal of Notre Dame in Paris, where we find the famous story of the cleric, Théophile, who sold his soul to the devil and was redeemed by the Virgin, the latter clearly appears as the one who intercedes, the one who, because of filial love, is devoted to saving the least of her children, no matter if he is a criminal, no matter if he himself has renounced eternal salvation. This theme will appear widely in all subsequent Christian iconography, even up to our own time.

The Mother of God is thus one more woman among women, with all the human feelings that entails. Whatever the symbolic significance of the supposed events in Mary's life, these events could affect the life of any woman in the world, no matter where or when. The theme is universal, and, even as we saw in antiquity the pagan Demeter mourning the loss of her daughter Kore, or Cybele lamenting over the body of Attis, we shall see Mary holding the body of Jesus on her knees after his descent from the Cross. Thus appear the numerous pietás scattered throughout the world, of which the one from Villeneuve-lès-Avignon, now at the Louvre, is the most famous example. And also the most moving one, with an intensely sad face, infinitely sorrowful, but also infinitely tender and resigned, as the Virgin, her hands joined, addresses her ultimate prayer to the heavens that the Son be admitted into his Father's house. What woman has not been, at least once in her life, and for any number of different reasons, a Mater Dolorosa?

But these popular representations, accessible to all the faithful, do not dispense with more intellectual, not to say esoteric, interpretations of the theme of the Virgin Theotokos. It is not only the sublime, but nonetheless human, Mother of Jesus who is honored in these statues, bas-reliefs, engravings, paintings, and illuminations, but also the ancient possessor of sovereignty over the universe, the first cause of all existence, coming well before the manifestation of the Word, which, according to the

Gnostic Gospel of John, was the *principle* (and not the *beginning*) of the world of concrete relativities. The art of the Middle Ages reflects a kind of thinking, and this thinking, despite the weight of Roman dogmatism, is far from being univocal. Even if she never ceases to be comforter, indeed even soother, the medieval Virgin transmits a message that goes back to the dawn of time and sometimes manifests itself through speculations deemed heretical, or even through fantastical aberrations such as the concept of eternal creation that can only be female in nature. If Mary was truly what, as "surrogate mother," generated the divine, she could only be the incarnation of a preexisting concept that had become incomprehensible, incommunicable, and inexpressible, which appeared throughout the various myths concerning the creation of the world.

This is what emerges from the Christian tradition itself, what it draws from the Old Testament. "I was created from the beginning and before the centuries," according to Ecclesiastes. A passage from Proverbs is even more specific: "Adonai possessed me at the beginning of his ways before he had done a single rudimentary act. I was rudimentary from before the centuries, at the beginning, before there was earth. The chasms did not yet exist and I was already conceived, and the springs of water did not yet surge, and before the hills, I was already brought forth" (8:22). The popular artists of the Middle Ages, possessors of a knowledge transmitted in a more or less secret manner since the beginning of time, knew how to express this idea of the anteriority of Mary-Miriam. The theologians did not say anything different. Thus, Anselm of Canterbury writes in his *De excellentia Virginis* (chap. 9): "Even as the Lord, in creating all things, is their sovereign, *Dominus omnium*, so the Virgin, in restoring all things according to their merits, is the Mother and the Mistress of all things, *Domina rerum*." And, based on these traditional ideas, Grillot de Givry can allow himself this commentary that is, in fact, an observation: "Thus, to incarnate his Word, God made use of this great universal female Principle that had already received the Spirit of God within her womb at the time of the creation of the world; he concentrated it and confined it within the form of a human creature who was Mary [because] only the wife of the Father before the beginning of time was worthy, indeed, of becoming the mother of the Word."[5]

Within this context, it is appropriate to examine the strange "Hunt of the Unicorn" a bas-relief from the thirteenth century found in the church of Saint John in Lyon. We do indeed see a hunter there pursuing a unicorn who comes to hide at the feet of the Virgin. But this representation has a double meaning: first, the Virgin welcomes the unicorn to protect it; but also, the supernatural and phallic aspects of the mythical animal's horn necessarily evokes a sexual union of a mystical nature. Here, we are in the presence of the perfect illustration of the Virgin who, at the dawn of time, received the divine Spirit, even before *materially* becoming the Mother of God. And that is the case, despite the disturbing presence of the hunter who can be considered the negative Spirit, the old Satan who struggles perpetually against the God of light. The theme is most certainly Gnostic, and throughout the Middle Ages, it will be developed in the iconography, often being charged with alchemical elements or influenced by the occult. The final outcome, somewhat secularized, will be the famous tapestry of the Lady and the Unicorn, one of the major works exhibited at the Musée de Cluny, in Paris.

If the Virgin was imbued, from the first, with the divine Spirit, she inevitably plays a sacerdotal role. Having received these powers, she can, to a certain extent, take the place of the priest at the altar and celebrate Mass herself. This is what is represented in a magnificent painting of the Amiens school, dating from 1437, *The Virgin's Priesthood,* now at the Louvre. But it is not the Host that she is consecrating, it is simply her Son, whom she takes by the left hand, while he, with his right hand, seizes the hem of the robe. This astonishing scene will be recaptured much later, in a more classical style, by Ingres in his *Virgin with Host,* at the Louvre as well. There, the divestment is complete, and the face of Mary, with her half-closed eyes fixed on the Host where all the lights of the world converge, indicates clearly the painter's desire to unite the worship of the Virgin Mary with pre-Christian traditions surrounding the mother goddess, primordial divinity from which emanates the energy that spreads throughout the universe. This same idea is found again in the famous *Burning Bush* in Saint-Sauveur Cathedral in Aix-en-Provence, attributed to Nicolas Froment. The Virgin, holding her Son on her knees, is, in fact, surrounded by branches, as if by a crown of flames. This is nothing more or less than the image of the solar divinity, such as she appears in the various Nordic mythologies, in particular, among the Scythians and the Germans. It is true that the Christian Middle Ages close in a state of great ambiguity, marked by a clear return to a sort of humanistic "paganism" that will triumph during what will be called the Renaissance and that will endure, sometimes very covertly, up until our own time.

5

THE ETERNAL RETURN
OF THE DIVINE WOMAN

The Sixteenth to the
Twentieth Centuries

From the beginning of the sixteenthth century, the rediscovery of Greco-Roman Antiquity in France greatly contributed to the further humanization of the Virgin's image by emphasizing exterior harmony and the perfection of forms. Memories of Athena, Hera, and even Aphrodite-Venus flow behind the somber robes adorning the Theotokos. But, this is only a matter of expression; it doesn't represent a change in attitude regarding the way the divine Mother is conceived. *The Nativity* by Jean Courmont, exhibited at the Louvre, is a characteristic example of this return to humanism, with all the exaggerations that entails. The architectural decor is baroque, tormented, tortuous, the sky literally encumbered with a throng of little angels, strongly resembling the cupids who surround Venus, and the Virgin no longer occupies the center of the canvas. The event depicted here is a human event, like so many others, the supernatural element inherent in this strange presence of angels, which also make it border on the ridiculous. This mix, resulting from the confrontation between pagan antiquity and Christian mysticism, is even more striking in a painting by Antoine Caron, *The Sibyl of Tibur*, also at the Louvre. The scene is completely earthly; everything there is arranged to represent a ceremony in honor of a goddess, who appears in the form of a statue of a naked woman at the center of a fountain. Water flows from the breasts of the woman and a kind of radiant sun is poised on her head. Obviously, this is a matter of a religion devoted to the solar goddess who dispenses water and fire. We don't know what goes on in the small temple situated in the far corner. But, in the foreground, in very modest robes, the sibyl prophesies and points to a part of the sky in which appears, in fantastic glory, the image of the Virgin with her child. Traditional ideas nurtured Antoine Caron's work, and he attempted a synthesis that would emphasize the continuity of religious beliefs, outside of all ideology. Nevertheless, this representation continues to be enigmatic, the symbols employed being so numerous and heterogeneous.

But no matter how it is expressed, the idea that dominates is that of the mother of all men. The theme of the cloaked Virgin certainly reveals this vision the most clearly. The painting of Enguerrand Quarton, which comes from the transition period between the Middle Ages and the Renaissance and which is found in the Villeneuve-lès-Avignon museum, is one of the most remarkable on this subject. The Virgin, immense and in the very center of the work, opens her mantle in a gesture that seems not protective but more an offer to let us see her children. Under the cloak, they are numerous, including many popes and bishops, as if Mary opened her maternal womb to give birth to humanity. On either side of the Virgin stand Saint John the Baptist and Saint John the Evangelist. When we consider that the Christian calendar divides the year into two sequences centered around Saint John of summer (the Baptist) and Saint John of winter (the Evangelist), two symbolic festivals that mark the position of the earth at the highest and lowest solstice points, we cannot avoid interpreting this extraordinary and ecstatic vision as the expression of the totality of the universe within the very bosom of the Theotokos. The Virgin is not only the Mother of God. She is the universal Mother, and on these grounds, we are all Christ. This is the message delivered by the Gospel. Here is the deep meaning of the Christian quest, a message often lost in the twists and turns of a religion blighted by a primary and dualistic morality, but the sense of which reemerges from the human subconscious through the work of artists, clearly inspired by the Spirit.

Nevertheless, in the centuries following the Renaissance, those works that do not obey the rules of a rigid formalism are rare. Henceforth, the models are established by the tradition, and all those who depart from this tradition, if they no longer risk finding themselves on the stake, are condemned to a certain imposed obscurity. This is the Age of Reason, and, as a result, nothing can escape the rationalization of the image that comprises the divine Mother. The Madonna, the praying Virgin, the pietà, the Mater Dolorosa, all these merge into a conventional imagery from which all sexuality is excluded, the Virgin becoming a sort of disembodied entity, totally abstract, and which can only be represented by a neuter woman, ascetic, thinned out, watered down, nonexistent. It is a long way from the ample Virgins of the Renaissance to the Sulpician stereotypes that became fashionable with the Lourdes apparitions, but this way reveals an incredible censorship reinforced by what was called the Victorian period in Great Britain, and marked by nothing other than excessive prudishness and emasculation. Forgotten were the mystical and sensual nuns of early times who claimed to *enjoy* Christ. Forgotten were the mother goddesses with so many breasts, because they were the "vast mothers." The image of the Notre-Dame of Lourdes, revised and corrected by the Roman Catholic clergy to justify and spread the ideology of the Immaculate Conception, was finally imposed as a required model that was not allowed to be modified. Having become the official art, often encouraged and authorized by the thinkers of the secular—and finally agnostic—French Republic, religious art was going to become an ornamental motif much like Irish interlacings or the decorations on Corinthian columns. By the same token, the concept of the Virgin Mary, universal Mother, would become completely blurred, giving way to a nonexistent individual whose femininity could be reduced to an absolute passivity in the face of the too-obvious androcratic power within the Roman Church. The vile statue of Notre-Dame de France that dominates the sacred site of Puy-en-Velay, isn't this the best example of this secular and so-called patriotic rehabilitation of the concept of divine maternity, bad taste aside?

During this entire period that will extend from the end of the Middle Ages to the beginning of the twenty-first century, it is not the official art, secular or religious, that best testifies to a Mary cult, but the popular art, such as it appears throughout the rural areas, in the smallest, isolated chapel or in the middle of the fields or woods, in the humblest, forgotten parish church. Most Christian sanctuaries were built on sacred sites known as such since prehistoric times. That is what insured the permanence of a spirituality, and, most of the time, it is in the collective unconscious of rural populations that the beautiful figure of the divine Mother is maintained, taking on various tones and complexions according to the area or the period. And these are all the more significant as they were not imposed by a dominant ideology but emerged naturally from a tradition that has never been lost.

Even as it is impossible to give a complete list of these Virgins born of popular fervor, it would be fruitless to draw up an organized catalogue. All models and styles have their place in this wave of tributes to the Mother of God, where, in each case, the motivation is linked to local history, or more exactly, local legend. What is more, among the various statues of the country churches, it is difficult to say which were created especially for that site, and which were brought in from elsewhere. Still others have been discovered in the hollows of trees or in the ground, these last probably being pre-Christian idols bearing some resemblance to the Madonna model, but most of the time recut, retouched, Christianized, and very often readorned in such a way as to camouflage pagan characteristics.

A statue like the one of Notre-Dame-des-Avents, however, in

the parish church of Chissey (Saône et Loire) indisputably bears the mark of the sixteenth century. Here, a woman with an expression of great serenity is presented standing, her hands joined in an attitude of meditation and prayer. There is something very sober about the folds of her robe, but on her belly appears the engraved image of the child Jesus, in an embryonic state, surrounded by solar flames. Clearly, the emphasis here is on the eternal parturition attributed to the Virgin Mary. The not-yet-born one is, however, fully alive, and moreover, he is himself the sun that gives his energy to the world. We can consider this Virgin of Avents as a kind of "repository," a "Holy Grail," that contains the ineffable, the God who gives life to the entire world and who only appears outside the womb as the sculptural transcription of the concept of the eternal mother. Despite its apparent orthodoxy, the image takes us back way beyond the evangelistic message.

All these wooden or stone statues that derive from a popular art tradition more closely conform to the deep beliefs buried in the collective unconscious than to modes imposed by an intransigent clergy. In fact, beneath orthodox exteriors, there are always heretical or archaistic tendencies manifesting themselves, because appearances, accommodating as they are, can be very deceiving and always allow for an interpretation that goes without saying. That is how it is with the many representations of the Virgin and the serpent. The proper response is to claim that Mary crushes the serpent, who is responsible for the misfortunes weighing on humanity. Functioning as the Mother of God, the Virgin was allowed to neutralize the effects of the Temptation and the Fall, since Christ, by his sacrifice, does away with the works of the devil. But it is necessary to examine this image of the woman and the serpent more closely, because originally, let us repeat, the serpent is female. It is a feminine serpent, *une vouivre*, with the bust and head of a woman, that is represented, for instance, on one of the ancient doors of the parish church of Mauron (Morbihan). In this case, another equally orthodox interpretation presents itself: the Virgin Mary triumphs over Satanic femininity. It is the celestial virgin who asserts herself to the detriment of the telluric virgin, otherwise called Eve, responsible for the first sin and forever entrapped in the material world, thus trampled underfoot. Looking below the surface, however, and taking into account images like the mysterious stone of Oo, now at the Toulouse museum, a kind of hermaphrodite whose sex is extended in the form of a serpent up to the left breast, don't we have to consider the Virgin with the serpent as an expression of divine femininity completely restored? Simply because it has been repeated so often that God is the Father of all, he has arbitrarily been made masculine. And as for the question that is continually posed these days, "Is God a woman?" another can be substituted, "Is God androgynous?" Logic would have the response be affirmative.

But, it happens that the serpent is replaced by a siren, as in the statue of Notre-Dame-de-Bréac-Ilis in the parish church of Brennilis (Finistère). This is a Notre-Dame-des-Marais (Our Lady of the Swamps), the name being justified by the presence of the Yeun-Ellez marsh, below the village of Brennilis. According to popular belief, this marsh is supposed to be one of the doors of Hell. We cannot help thinking of a poem by François Villon dedicated to the Virgin, "imperial over infernal marshes." And as is the case with the representation of Saint Michael struggling against the dragon (but not killing it), isn't this image an expression of the equilibrium that must be constantly maintained between celestial and telluric forces? In this sense, the Virgin Mary, eternal mediator, guardian of the gate of Hell, only restrains the power of the siren (with the tail of a fish, or of a serpent, that is, Melusina), thus allowing for the equilibrium of the Creation. More than ever, she is the "mother goddess." What is more, not far from this statue, there is a stained-glass window representing Saint Anne carrying Mary within her. Now, in all Celtic countries, Saint Anne is the Christian transposition of Dana-Anna of ancient mythology, the mother of the gods and of men.

The Virgin is really and truly the eternal Mother. In the territory of Edern (Finistère), at the Koat-Kaer ("Pretty Woods") site, on the slopes of a wooded hill, stands a remarkable cross

4.80 meters high. It is very simple and, on one side, presents Christ with an angular face and seemingly drowsy expression, and on the other, a very unusual pietà. Indeed, what we see here is the body of Jesus folded in upon itself, in fetal position, in such a way that it doesn't extend beyond the spread knees of the Virgin. It seems that this eighteenth-century sculptor who signed his work, "G. Le Foll, 1756," wanted to show that the dead Jesus was, in some way, reintegrated into the maternal womb in order to be reborn. This idea is reinforced by the strange labyrinthine figure placed between the legs of the Virgin, a figure indisputably evoking a womb. This image recalls the dolmenic engravings, in particular, those in the Gavrinis cairn, and, although we are dealing with a relatively recent work, it cannot be denied that the sculptor has recaptured a thousand-year-old tradition here. Moreover, this type of labyrinthine representation is found on the capitals of the porch columns of the Yvignac (Côtes-d'Armor) church. It is possible that this is a case of the stones belonging to the ancient Roman building, but we can never know for sure that these are not copies or variations on an earlier theme. That recalls the motif, not appearing on the Continent but found throughout the British Isles, of the Sheela-na-gig, this female representation with her genitals wide open as if to invite the deceased to reenter the maternal womb in order to be able to be reborn. The so-called pagan elements are indisputable. The Virgin Mary is no longer simply the "servant of the Lord" here, a woman who passively accepts being the medium for a single instance of divine incarnation in the course of history. She is the eternal Virgin, absolute, the one who, as *natura naturans*, plays the active role in uninterrupted creation.

This idea of uninterrupted creation can be interpreted in a more orthodox fashion. There is the famous example of it in the parish church of Yaudet in Ploulec'h, near Lannion (Côtes-d'Armor). Yaudet, or rather, Koz Yaudet ("Old Yaudet") as it is called in the country, is a place charged with history and legend. The name is an awkward transcription in Breton and French of the Latin *vetus civitatem*, the "old city." The present-day village, at the mouth of the Léguer, is located on the site of a

Gallo-Roman city that must have been very important and, before the immigration of the Breton islanders, had been the seat of a Gallo-Roman bishopric, later moved to Carhaix, and then to Locmaria-Quimper. Historical documentation is lacking on this subject. But the Yaudet church, rebuilt in 1860 with some of the original elements from the ancient structure, houses an altogether astonishing sculptural grouping in an alcove above the main altar. There is a Virgin with child lying on a bed of lace, and above them soars a dove. We know of only a few examples of this genre, but in Brittany, we find the same theme in the church of La Martyre (Finistère), from which the child nursing from his mother has been removed, because of prudishness, it seems, as well as in the chapel of Notre-Dame-de-Guedoet in Lanrivain (Côtes-d'Armor). Now, the name Gueodet, like Yaudet, comes from the Latin *civitas*. To discover the same recumbent Virgin in two sanctuaries both bearing the name of a "city" cannot help but prompt certain reflections.

The grouping at the Yaudet church bears the markings of a touching naiveté. Now popular art, as we know, only reproduces—sometimes very awkwardly—traditions of which no one knows the exact origin and for which the meaning has been forgotten. We should note that at the summit of the promontory upon which the village of Yaudet was built, corresponding to the site of the ancient "city," can be seen a great flat rock, strangely engraved: a circle with rays. It seems that this petroglyph belongs to certain megalithic groups of engravings found in Morbihan and Ireland, which represent the ancient Goddess of the Beginnings, female solar divinity, possessor of heat, light, energy, and finally, life, which she dispenses to all creatures. The bridge is thrown across the gap between the megalithic and Christian eras, and the representation of this resting Virgin, like the petroglyph of the Yaudet promontory, suggests that in the past there existed in this area an important sanctuary devoted to the solar Goddess of the Beginnings. The mouth of the Léguer opens toward the west. Isn't this the ultimate point where human beings can gather to honor the sun goddess who lies down to sleep somewhere in this mysterious ocean where we are

hesitant to venture, but which delivers the hope of a resurrection, that of the son who will be born the next day, otherwise
known as the Young Sun? Isn't this the fundamental idea that is
represented by the recumbent Virgin with child, under the inspiration of the dove, that is, the divine Spirit that soars over the
primordial waters? As to the "city," derived etymologically from
civitas, which refers to the "community," it undeniably evokes
the emblematic image of the queen. This "great queen" that the
ancient Bretons called Rhiannon is the visible incarnation of
collective whole, what Christians would call the "communion of
saints," and which, in the Armorican tradition, manifests itself
in the belief in Anoans, those deceased peoples who haunt the
moors, forests, and shores. The Anoans are, literally, the "children of Anna," those famous Tuatha dé Danaan of Ireland, who
brought from the "islands of the north of the world" wisdom,
science, magic, and druidism, along with four symbolic objects,
the spear that never misses, the blazing sword, the inexhaustible
cauldron of food, and the stone of sovereignty. The peoples of
the goddess Dana, or Anna, always remembered the presence of
the Mother, and whatever the dominant ideology, whatever the
current dogmas, they have continued to honor her as the Mistress of Life.

But if this fidelity to an ideal is characteristic of popular art,
the same is not true for official art. The nineteenth century is
going to fix the image of the Virgin according to the imposed
norms. It could be claimed that this official representation,
catholic in the sense of universal, is the result of "visions," which
is not to call them "apparitions," arising from the period that, in
a kind of counterreformation destined to struggle against the
skepticism of the Enlightenment and the atheism of the Revolution, provoked, consciously or unconsciously, a codified resurgence of the concept of the divine Mother. Certainly, the descriptions we owe to the visionaries of the Rue du Bac, La Salette,
and Lourdes depended heavily on the elaboration of a new
image of the Virgin, but as these descriptions, no doubt sincere,
were revised and corrected by a clergy concerned with maintaining a prudent orthodoxy; the variants observed here or there fell

away before the necessity for a single model in keeping with the motivations of a Church on the defensive. And, with the help of the industrial phenomenon, it became possible to mass-produce a single model. In the same way, as required, that secular education dispensed *the* truth, singular and indivisible, religious education could only give rise to *the* truth of a Virgin completely purged and cleansed of any stench of an underlying paganism. That is the origin of what is called Sulpician art, which has inundated most of the sanctuaries. The image of Notre Dame of Lourdes obliterated local and particular Virgins so much more easily once it could be infinitely reproduced and distributed.

And even if certain artists have continued to dress the Virgin in clothes they believe suited to her, if they have lent to her attitudes they consider in keeping with the evangelistic message, the representation of the Mother of God has become such a pathetic banality that it is better not to speak of it.

6

THE SACRED PLACES
OF OUR LADY

It is probably true that human beings, when they became conscious of the existence of a world beyond the senses, considered the notion of sacred as inherent to everyday life. But, as metaphysical thought developed on the margins of material existence, it is also probably true that they finally admitted that the sacred could be separated from the profane and hide itself away in special places. How were these places determined? No one knows, but there is no disputing that they were recognized as sacred since the earliest prehistoric times. No doubt, a type of sensitivity came into play, a kind of sixth sense connected to cosmic or telluric currents, to the energy that emanated from certain places, to the landscape itself. This hypothesis cannot be rejected when we know that the sanctuaries, regardless of what religion is practiced, are always situated in the same places. And since the sacred seemed to be confined there, it was good to go there on certain occasions to be "recharged," to be regenerated by coming into contact with the invisible powers that pervaded these special domains. This must have been the origin of pilgrimages that began in the earliest periods of prehistory, as evidence shows.

As inheritor of so many earlier rituals, Christianity would not depart from this practice. "Visits" very soon developed to the very places of Christ's Passion, to the sites where martyrs and saints were buried, along the paths taken by the apostles, and, of course, by Mary, in particular to Ephesus where her house is supposedly found. These pilgrims all try to become permeated with the sacred aura left by divine or blessed individuals. It is a constant among all peoples of the world to seek out intimate contact with exceptional, if not divine, beings in order to benefit from their influence. That is what explains the worship of relics: an object that once belonged to a holy person is necessarily blessed and the mere act of touching it may be enough to insure direct communication, true communion, between the one who has achieved and the one who desires to achieve the highest level of holiness. For, although not everyone can be holy, everyone desires to become so. And then, whatever the ideology, there is the sense that a place is charged and that this charge can be distributed among all who come in contact with it. Far from being naive or ridiculous, this idea attests to a factor inherent to the human spirit; that the creature must, at one time or another, merge with its creator—or what comes closest to the creator—to obtain the power to pursue the work of creation.

That spiritual condition could only favor places consecrated to the Theotokos. But, as it wasn't possible to make claims for the actual presence of the Mother of Jesus in western Europe, it was through roundabout ways that a worship devoted to Mary was successfully established. That is where the legend of the Virgo Paritura came from, this Virgin on the point of giving birth, who had been worshiped by the druids, and who, as a clerical creation, only dates back to the ninth century in Chartres. However, the very fact that pre-Christian religions worshiped a mother goddess made the transition from one ideology to another easy: the ritual remained the same. It was enough to endorse the legend of the Virgo Paritura and to find manifest proof of it in the form of statues preserved from the beginning of time or miraculously rediscovered, if not brought back from the East by some pious pilgrim returning from his journey to the source.

NORTH SEA

ENGLISH CHANNEL

Boulogne

PICARDY

Meuse

Somme

Laon
Avioth
Moselle

LORRAINE

Le Folgoët
Brennilis
Le Yaudet

Oise
Reims

Seine
Miraculous medal
(Paris)

Sion

Douvres
NORMANDY
Pontmain

BRITTANY
Querrien
La Pesnière
Josselin
Gueodet
Sainte-Anne
d'Auray

Blavet

Vilaine

Sarthe

Loire

Montugeon

Chartres

ILE-DE-FRANCE

Yonne

Marne

Rhine

Vézelay

BURGUNDY

FRANCHE-
COMTE

Cher
Pellevoisin

Saône

POITOU
Poitiers

Tournus

Rhône

ATLANTIC

OCEAN

LIMOUSIN

Dordogne

Riom
Marsat
Clermont-
Ferrand
Orcival

Le Puy

Rocamadour

Notre-Dame d'Ay

DAUPHINE
La Salette

Garonne
Penne d'Agenais

AQUITANE

Rhône

100 km

Garaison
Lourdes
Bétharram

Rennes
le-Château

LANGUEDOC

Saintes-
Maries-
de-la-Mer

PROVENCE
Noves

La Sainte-Baume
Marseille

MEDITERRANEAN SEA

SANCTUARIES AND PILGRIMAGES DEDICATED TO THE VIRGIN
MARY, SAINT ANNE, AND MARY MAGDALENE IN FRANCE

Since antiquity, there have been countless statues of Gallic, or rather, Gallo-Roman, mother goddesses. During Christianization, some of them were destroyed as demonic idols. But others were hidden, buried in the ground by peasants who sincerely desired to adhere to the new religion without, for all that, renouncing their ancient customs. When the worship of Mary was officially established in the fifth century, we can easily imagine the excitement and emotion the faithful must have felt when they rediscovered a statue buried in the earth or hidden in some inaccessible place. The virgin mothers of antiquity so resembled the new images of the Virgin with the child that a miraculous manifestation of the Mother of God only had to be claimed for a certificate of authenticity to be issued for these finds. It has always been true that the discovery of a lost statue is surrounded by elements of the marvelous. And, in the case of the statues of the Virgin, these elements of the marvelous fall into two categories.

The first involves the discovery of a statue thanks to the intervention of an animal, a ruminant in most cases. The scenario is very specific: an ox insists on browsing at the same spot or even stops stubbornly on the path or in one part of a field it is plowing, or, again, kneels down instead of going forward. Sometimes it happens that an ox or a cow begins lowing at the foot of the same tree, which excites curiosity. Then, a statue is discovered in a bush or in the ground, generally ill-formed or damaged, in wood or stone, which is solemnly declared to be a Notre Dame hidden away in a safe place during the heroic age.

> Similar legends inevitably remind us that we have worshiped Isis of the cow horns, Cybele associated with the Mithraic bull, and the pre-Celtic horned god, Cernunnos. It is true that one myth can be spontaneously generated many times, but it is also true that the ruminant, in the mythologies in which it figures, is always associated with the worship of the earth. This was already true among Neolithic populations. Now, a tradition can be maintained even when it is no longer understood. The bullfights are proof of this, and also the procession of fattened cattle.[1]

The second category is that of the "return," and it is widespread throughout nearly all of Europe.

> The image having been discovered in some deserted, sometimes uninhabitable, indeed barely accessible, place, the finder, who is never a priest, carries it home. During the night, it returns to the place it was found. The peasant then speaks to the parish priest, who takes it to the parish, but the next day, it has returned to its original spot. The parish priest then comes back for it with the cross and the banner, but it escapes yet again. Thus, it becomes necessary to build a chapel exactly at the spot where it was found.[2]

Thus, there is a miracle, and the place of discovery becomes a sacred place of pilgrimage. That is also the explanation for the numerous names such as "Our Lady of the Nettles," "Our Lady of the Brambles," which testify to the place of origin.

But the supernatural has limits, and the Church is wary of it. Not only is it reluctant to recognize this or that marvel resurfacing from distant times and impossible to verify, but also it prefers to rationalize this type of discovery. That is why, very often, the miraculous statue is said to have been brought from the Orient by a devout individual or by a king. This is the case at Puy-en-Velay, and in many other famous Christian sanctuaries. Or again, as in the case of Sainte-Anne-d'Auray, the discovery of an ancient statue is explained by the presence of a forgotten, destroyed chapel that is declared to be Christian, but which, upon analysis, can only be a pagan sanctuary. The process of reclamation advanced by Saint Augustine serves as a basis, all the more so because there is something in it for everyone, clergy and lay populations, pilgrims and merchants. In the Middle Ages, the places of pilgrimage were important economic centers as were the centers of religious education, and we know this is still the case today.

The Puy-en-Velay is certainly one of the oldest sanctuaries we know of in France dedicated to the worship of Mary. Local tradition relates that, in some unspecified distant time, a woman suffering from fever was invited in a dream to go lie down on a dolmen located on the southern side of Mount Anis in order to be healed. Having accomplished the required rite, she then heard an angel declare to her, "Out of all the places in the world, the august Mother of the Savior has chosen this one especially in order to be honored and served here until the end of time." And the woman was healed of her fever. In memory of this miracle, a sanctuary was built on this spot, which, after many transformations and improvements, became the admirable Romanesque cathedral that we know today, as celebrated for its architecture as for the importance of the pilgrimage that takes place there on August 15 each year.

Any legend is significant, but it is necessary to read between the lines. The town of Puy-en-Velay is found on the slopes of Mount Anis, and, during the Gallic period, was called Anicium. Anis and Anicium, without a doubt, refer to the name of the great Celtic queen, Anna or Dana, which means that, since time immemorial, the Goddess of the Beginnings was honored at this site. Anicium was the religious center for the people of Vellaves, but when the Romans came to occupy this region, they established their capital a little farther away, at Ruessio, which today is Saint-Paulien. It was at the time of the Christianization that this center was moved back to Anicium, which then took the name of Podium, which became Le Puy. Here is a remarkable example of cults succeeding each other, a succession that takes place without a single problem, as if it were natural for the Celtic Anna to become the Virgin Mary, since she represented the same divine entity, especially within the context of popular devotion. And it is not for no reason that the statue that dominates Mount Anis today bears the name of Our Lady of France, because, beginning with Charlemagne, most of the French sovereigns came to this place to render homage to the Theotokos, including Saint Louis, who is said to have brought a Black Virgin given to him by an Egyptian emir. This statue was apparently burned in 1794 during the Revolution, and later replaced by a group that seems to bear hardly any relation to the original. Whatever the case, this new 1844 statue, which contains, it seems, a bit of the old one, perpetuates the ancient devotion to the divine

Mother that rises in a great, undeniable wave of fervor.

Another place of pilgrimage, probably as ancient as Puy-en-Velay, is Chartres, restored to its place of honor after the famous poem of Charles Péguy. It seems that the original Mary cult can be located in the crypt of the modern-day cathedral, where there was a well, called "the Well of the Holy Forts," and more importantly, a Black Virgin called Notre-Dame-de-Sous-Terre, (Our Lady of the Underground) burned in 1793, and since 1856, replaced by a work that remotely resembles what is known of the old one. At the end of the Middle Ages, in 1497 to be exact, to keep the crowds of the faithful from descending into the crypt, another statue was erected in the nave, a statue called Notre-Dame-du-Pilier (Our Lady of the Pillar). The cathedral, as it appears today, is one of the masterpieces of the Gothic period. Two earlier sanctuaries preceded it, a basilica from the fourth century, standing against a Roman wall of the oppidum, which was destroyed by fire in 743, and another, pre-Romanesque Carolingian in style, which was burned in 1020.

According to local tradition, the crypt is said to represent an ancient pre-Christian sanctuary where druids were already worshiping the Virgin even before her birth. She supposedly came from Palestine to bless them and ask them to build a temple where she would always be present. And the story goes that when the first evangelists of Chartres, Saint Savinien and Saint Potentien, or their disciples, Altin and Edoald, came from Sens to introduce the new religion, they discovered an edifice containing a statue that bore the inscription *Virgini pariturae*, a typically Roman dedication that means, "to the Virgin on the point of giving birth." This legend seems, *a priori*, to be logical and testifies to an incontestable reality. Chartres, then called Autricum, was a sort of sanctuary-fortress as existed throughout formerly Celtic territories, and in the country of the Carnutes (from which comes the name of Chartres itself). Now, thanks to Julius Caesar, we know that it is in the country of the Carnutes that we find the great forest where, once a year, the druids of all of Gaul assembled. It was, in short, the great central sanctuary of all Gallic peoples. Given these circumstances, why not suppose that the druids had established a special worship devoted to the mother goddess in this place?

In fact, things are not so simple, and a problem presents itself. According to a 1609 document, the statue that the druids supposedly worshiped depicted a Virgin with the child, which clearly contradicts the notion of Virgo Paritura, the second term being a future participle meaning "on the point of giving birth." Logically, this statue would have had to represent a pregnant woman. Moreover, we know very well that the druids never represented a divinity in a human form. The statue in question could only be Gallo-Roman. Thus, it must be acknowledged that the statue burned in 1793 was not a copy, but a forgery. Other documents from the seventeenth century, which mention the local legend, specify that the dedication was not found on the statue, but on the base.

It even seems that, over the course of the ninth century, the legend of the Gallic Virgin was spread by the Chartres chapter, who had little tolerance for the competing Puy-en-Velay pilgrimage and wanted to prove at any cost the preexistence of Mary worship in Chartrian country. This would not be the only example of this kind, the invented legend serving not only to ensure the clergy's prosperity, but also to confirm the popular fervor directed toward the divine Mother. Whatever the case, the sanctuary of Chartres was built on ground held sacred since earliest antiquity, being one of those *nemetons* that the Gallic territory is so rich with. It isn't a matter of a lie, or even fraud, but a simple rehabilitation of a recurring religious theme.

The Chartrian tradition, both in its popular and clerical version, indicates that the famous statue was found in a cave. That has prompted much speculation on subterranean Chartres. Secret temples have been imagined, the holy of holies reserved for initiates who alone knew the hidden entrances to it. Mystery always excites speculation. In fact, and without recourse to the wildest fantasies, it can easily be supposed that at the site of the Chartres cathedral there existed a megalithic monument of the dolmen type with passages. This would not be the first time that a Christian church would have been built over a Gallo-Roman sanctuary, which was itself erected on top of a megalith. We know that the well that is in the crypt had a square opening, which indicates that it was Gallo-Roman in origin. Now the well—or the spring—is inseparable from the cave where the mother goddess is worshiped (and, incidentally, where she appeared). The *fanum* only serves to replace an earlier dolmen, collapsed or destroyed. But if we accept this hypothesis, it carries with it another. Something of the ancient edifice always remains, either the materials may be reused, or a part considered sacred is kept intact, and it is very possible that the primitive image was only a simulacrum, that is, a megalithic engraving like the ones that exist in so many cairns, notably in those that survive, not far from Chartres, at Changé-Saint-Piat, in the Eure valley. For these megalithic engravings always present, in symbolic form, the protector goddess of the deceased, and thus, a female divinity who has power over life and death. Thus, female worship at Chartres would have originated with this ancient engraving, this petroglyph going back to the Neolithic, which would then have to be transposed into the form of the Virgin with the child. And, of course, this sacred place is healing. It was claimed that Fulbert, the builder of the cathedral, was healed of *le mal des ardents* by the water of the well. It was then that the sick began to flock to Chartres in hopes that the Virgin would relieve them of their pains. Everything contributed to this rush, since the presence of the "tunic of the Virgin," donated by Charles le Chauve in 861, added to the miraculous aura of the site. If the cathedral of Chartres harbors artistic treasures, it contains many mysteries as well, and it cannot be denied that this is one of the most powerful places where the devotion to Our Lady manifests itself.[3]

There was a third famous "Mary" pilgrimage in the Middle Ages, to Rocamadour (Lot), which is now a special tourist site. It is a matter of the ancient *vallis tenebrosa*, the "dark valley," a cliff, two hundred meters high, which rises abruptly in the Causse, with a great castle on the edge of the chasm, a cluster of churches and chapels on the rocky slope, and below, a medieval village. At the bottom of the valley, the Alzou, which is perhaps the "river of alders" winds through the site of an ancient forest. Not only did crowds throng to Rocamadour to honor the Virgin, but also men recognized as guilty by the ecclesiastical tribunals were sent there, in irons, to do penance. This was the very place that Henry II, on his knees before his army, had to perform the rites necessary to atone for the murder of Thomas à Becket.

There is a Black Virgin at Rocamadour. It is a statue of the Virgin in Majesty from the end of the twelfth century, blackened and very roughly cut, partially recovered in gold flake, hollowed out as a reliquary. Tradition claims that the publican, Zacchaeus, brought a statue sculpted by Saint Luke into the Causse from Quercy. In fact, the sanctuary does not seem to have originated with the presence of a statue. In 1166, a body perfectly preserved was found at the entrance of a chapel dedicated to the Virgin Mary. For very obscure reasons, people took it to be the mortal remains of a mysterious Saint Amadour, for whom the site was named. This "saint" was buried before the altar of the Virgin, and another legend spread according to which Amadour was said to be the spouse of Veronica, the one who mopped Christ's face with her veil. But in the sixteenth century, Amadour was simply merged with Zacchaeus, which allowed the two traditions to combine. There is no need to point out that Amadour does not figure into the Roman Catholic calendar any more than do Veronica or Zacchaeus.

We now know that the Rocamadour hermitage existed well before the discovery of the "saint." The primitive chapel was dedicated to the Virgin Mary alone, and a bell, said to be miraculous, has been preserved that was made before the thirteenth century. Furthermore, a popular local legend claims that in the past, human sacrifices were made in this place to a "Black Mother," named Sulevia or Soulivia. Her sanctuary was located in a cavern, and it is there that Zachée would have placed the statue sculpted by Saint Luke. Thus, we find ourselves right in the midst of Gallo-Roman religion. Indeed, the Sulèves were feminine divinities of the uncultivated earth and the name of Sulevia clearly indicates that, in this arid region, there was a cult dedicated to these savage gods. It is also said that the village of

Alysses, not too far away on the banks of the Alzou, was founded by a mysterious Lady who continued to wander about in the night, especially in the "Combe-de-la-Dame" area.

This mysterious Lady, probably a funerary goddess, a "black queen," is certainly linked in more than one way to the Black Virgin, whether it be Sulevia or any other Roman or Celtic divinity, protectress of the dead and guardian of sacred waters. In earlier times, during dry years, the peasants from the surrounding areas came to Rocamadour for water. They left in a procession from the source of the Ouysse, clergy at the head. After many prayers, one of the priests plunged the foot of the processional cross into the spring, and each started off with new hope that the rain would soon make its appearance. Numerous rituals of this kind exist almost throughout France, notably in Brittany, reminding us again that the worship of Mary can never be separated from the ancient water cults. Near the sanctuary or within it, there is always a well or a spring.

This is once more the case at Saintes-Maries-de-la-Mer (Bouches du Rhône), one of the strangest sites that exists as much for the traditions associated with it as for its clearly mythological origins. In principle, it is not the Virgin Mary who is honored here, but the three women saints, Marie-Salomé, Marie-Jacobé and Marie-Madeleine. Legend has it that, after the death of Christ, these three Marys, accompanied by Lazarus, arrived at this site and erected an altar to the mother of Jesus, near to which the first two Marys finished out their days with their servant, Sara the Black. This legend seems a replica of the one of Marie-Madeleine of Vézelay, which does not go back beyond the eleventh century, but it gives another location for the disembarkation, Marseille. Now this story, which was not known in the great Phocaean city and which ended at the mouth of the Rhone, was grafted onto local traditions and spread rapidly, to such an extent that in 1448, King René had excavations done under the altar of the church, which revealed a crypt, with a spring. As primitive as it was, the archaeology was found to be in agreement with the popular tradition.

In fact, the Saintes-Maries occupies the site of a part of an ancient fortified town, *priscum oppidum Ra,* according to the writings of the geographer, Avienus, Ratis, according to the ecclesiastical documents of Arles. We might be tempted to see in this name Ra the divine solar disk that the Egyptians worshiped, all the more so because Saintes-Maries became the special place for a strange pilgrimage of the Gypsies. But it would be wiser to refer back to the Latin word, *ratis,* which means "raft," an allusion to the disembarkation of the three Marys, or better still, to the old Celtic word, *rad,* "wooded island," which we find again in the name of the town of Ratisbonne, the "wooded fortress." Whatever the case, Ra was a great city with fortifications on its high ground to protect a port that offered, for the amber and pewter routes, the surest and fastest access to the center of Gaul. That there was a mix of Eastern and Celtic traditions here should astonish no one.

All that remains of this ancient city is the summit of the oppidum where the church stands. To the north of this rock, the alluvial deposits have built up the ground and diverted the water. To the south, the sea has eaten away or engulfed the shore. This is a historical and geological reality, but a certain sense of the lost city lingers in the air, as with the Breton town of Is. Until the thirteenth century, the church bore the name of Notre-Dame-de-Ratis; it became Notre-Dame-de-la-Mer. But the legend of the three Marys was so strongly anchored in the minds of the population that it never stopped invoking three Marys and not just one, to the point that the name Saintes-Maries-de-la-Mer was made official in 1838. Thus, here we have a dual origin: first, the worship of the Mother of God, as she was honored in the East, at Ephesus in particular; then, the worship of the three Gallic mothers so typical of Gallo-Roman religion and that we see so often in the statuary.

All that led to a composite worship at Saintes-Maries, with certain, seemingly aberrant, characteristics. On May 25 and October 22, two of the saints (Marie-Salomé and Marie-Jacobé) are carried in a small boat to the sea. The boat is launched and splashed by those present, while the priest performs a blessing with a silver reliquary arm. That obviously makes one think of certain Isis liturgies in which the statue of the goddess was carried in a boat, before which was waved an open left hand. We also know that the saints were invoked by neighboring towns in time of scarcity, but that it was especially to Sara the Black they prayed for intervention. Now Sara, according to all evidence, is the heir of the Great Goddess of the East. Where exactly is the place of the Virgin Mary in these liturgies, which are ambiguous, to say the least?

Very ill at ease with the slightly heretical presence of this mysterious Sara, the Roman Church has tried to make her Jewish, the wife repudiated by Pilate, arriving with the three Marys. But popular tradition, here in agreement with the Gypsies, claims that Sara inhabited the ancient city well before the boat reached it. It is easy to decipher this legend: Sara represents an ancient divinity that was honored in this place before the arrival of the three Marys.

> Although it is situated in the middle of an area that seems to be exclusively sandy, the present-day church is actually built on a rock that has always been able to support one establishment or another. At a few hundred meters from the sea, it contains a spring of fresh water that comes out of the rock, nearly at ground level. In the garden and in various outbuildings of the presbytery can still be seen the debris of columns and sculpted capitals, of very beautiful marble, that tradition says belonged to a temple of Venus. . . . We have observed a block of very white marble . . . that could well have played an important and characteristic role in the ancient worship of Astarte or some other ancient divinity. In earlier times it was simply deposited in the crypt, where the "Boumians" came to scrape it with a knife for a little of the dust which they absorbed to protect themselves from sterility. It is now embedded in a pillar.[4]

What is more, there is nothing very "Catholic" about the Gypsies' pilgrimage. It even seems as though the Marys hardly interest them at all. They don't pray to them.

During the cheering, when everyone cries, "Long live the Saint Marys," the "Boumians" remain quiet. It is even more striking to note that most of them insist on responding by the single cry of "Long live Saint Sara!" While in the middle of the silence . . . the preacher pursues the panegyric of the saints, the "Boumians" fill the crypt and occupy it very carefully, sitting on the steps, the stairway that leads into it. Not listening to a word said by the priest, to whom they turn their backs, it seems as though they perform a ritual of their own. The women, especially the young girls, it seems, hold in their hands large lit candles for a certain time that they then pass to their neighbors. At what seem to be regular intervals . . . they move forward . . . in groups of three or four toward the well that is in the middle of the church . . . and very reverently drink a few sips of water. From there, they descend into the crypt, in the company of as many young men whom they pick out as they go by. What ritual are they going to perform?[5]

Christians are not actually allowed into the crypt while the Gypsies perform this rite. We know, but only since 1912, that they cover the statue of Sara with scraps of fabric and that they leave before her rags hanging from strings. This closely resembles certain popular customs of rural France, where bits of clothing and even whole cloths are left at sacred places in order to obtain a cure or ensure the success of some project.[6] And we should point out that the statue of Sara always remains in the crypt. It was not until 1935 that the Gypsies were authorized by the Church to carry it in procession during the May festival. Still, they restricted themselves to dipping it into the sea and lowering it again into the crypt. We cannot help but be reminded of certain Indians of Cape Comorin who are certainly of the same origin as the Gypsies. They do the same thing with the statue of the goddess Durga, otherwise known as Kali the Black. The Saintes-Maries-de-la-Mer sanctuary truly retains all its mystery.

It is just as astonishing to note that if the Marys arrived as a threesome, only two of them are still honored, Sara not being a Mary. The third, Marie-Madeleine, followed her own itinerary and went away to finish out her days in meditation and contemplation in a cave in the mountain of Sainte-Baume, a site which, if it is not historic, has nevertheless become a sanctuary dedicated to this "penitent sinner" who is the mysterious Mary Magdalene. The official Roman doctrine has had a hard time admitting this figure and has, to a great extent, worked to camouflage her, if not obscure her completely. Who was she exactly? No one knows, but, in all probability, she was a former great priestess of the Goddess who became one of the first disciples of Jesus, who, because of her fortune, provided material support for his work. It is certainly not by chance that the Gospels make Mary Magdalene the first witness of Christ's Resurrection, and whatever the case, she remains one of the essential figures in Jesus' public life. It is for this reason that there have been various hypotheses concerning her, notably the one that makes her the concubine, if not the wife, of Jesus. However outrageous this hypothesis seems to orthodox Christians, it is not at all impossible or even unlikely. How else to explain the devoted following, throughout Christianity, of this Mary of Magdala? The fact that she is "repentant" is not sufficient cause and it certainly must be recognized that the figure all by herself reembodies one of the images of the Goddess of the Beginnings, otherwise called the Sacred Prostitute such as we encounter in the temples of the Near East, at Ephesus in particular, but also in the city of Magdala, the great center of worship of the divine woman. The collective unconscious has recognized in her this image of the prostitute virgin and, within a strictly Christian framework, she has become "Saint" Madeleine. How otherwise to justify that magnificent Romanesque basilica of Vézelay (Yonne), which will remain one of the masterpieces of sacred architecture? How to explain the determination of the abbot Saunière, at Rennes-le-Château (Aude), who restored his church in such a way so as to replace the Virgin Mary with Mary Magdalene throughout, and who also had a "Bethany" villa and a "Magdala" tower built in order to put together a library there? And that is to say nothing of that horrible Parisian church from the eighteenth century that is commonly called "La Madeleine."

It certainly had to be that the Magdalene exercised a real power over the popular Christian imagination for a woman to be so honored whom the official tradition considers to have gone astray, certainly returned to the right path, but no less stained by all her vices—in this case, what the Bible calls prostitution, but what was in fact the worship of a female divinity.[7]

By all evidence, it is because the Magdalene corresponded to a certain image of the Goddess of the Beginnings that she was thus exalted. To the absolute purity of Mary, the mother of Jesus, is added, to a certain extent, the ambiguity of Mary Magdalene, about whom it hasn't been forgotten that she was, first of all, a woman, with all the weaknesses and all the sensuality, however constrained, that that entails. But in opposition to this image, we cannot pass over in silence another face of this Goddess of the Beginnings, that of the mysterious Anne, the mother of Mary. Thus appeared the worship of the Grandmother, the "Old Woman," that is, the one who has always existed, even before creation. And never more than at Sainte-Anne-d'Auray has this worship of the "good grandmother" been emphasized.

Up until the seventeenth century, the site of Sainte-Anne-d'Auray, today the town and parish of Morbihan, was only a modest hamlet of the Pluneret parish going by the name of Keranna. To understand the renown of the current sanctuary, it is necessary to go back to the period when King Louis XII reigned over France—and, as an indirect consequence, Brittany, a country united to France under the same crown. Since the religious wars and the troubles of the League, particularly violent in the south of Brittany, the Catholic Counterreformation had not found any means to establish itself and win over the populations to its cause. Missionary zeal and "shock cures" pervaded the countryside as attempts were made to win back in the name of the true God—the one defined once and for all by Rome—those territories that were not so much contaminated by the Reformation, but more, by a return to a certain paganism. It is within this framework that the events of 1624 take place.

One evening, while he is working late in his field in Bocenno, Yves Nicolazic, a modest peasant of Keranna, sees a beautiful white lady appear holding a lit candle. He wonders if it was a dream[8] and speaks of this vision to no one at all. But the apparition manifests itself on many evenings just after nightfall. Nicolazic, who is very pious, and has listened carefully to the missionaries' sermons, is afraid he is witnessing tricks of the devil. Now, on the evening of July 25, 1624, the "white lady" speaks to him: "Fear nothing. I am Anne, mother of Mary. Tell your priest that on the piece of land called Bocenno, before any village was built, there was a chapel dedicated to me, the first in the whole country. It was destroyed 924 years and six months ago. I want it to be rebuilt and you to take care of it, because God wishes for me to be honored in this place." We cannot help but notice, in passing, the apparition's claim to honor and also her precision regarding the time of the destruction of the supposed chapel.

But Nicolazic does not seem to have much confidence in his priest. Perhaps, after all, the latter knew him too well. In any case, the "visionary" goes to find a Capuchin in Auray and tell him the whole story. The Capuchin takes him for a madman. Returning home, Nicolazic decides to clear the matter up in his own mind. He brings his brother-in-law to the places he saw the apparition in order to have a witness. But nothing happens, not that evening, nor for several months. Then, on Friday, March 7, 1625, while sleeping, Nicolazic is awakened by a strange noise and a bright light. He follows this light to the field of Bocenno and, there, the light disappears into the ground. With the help of his brother-in-law and a few neighbors rounded up for the occasion, he digs a hole in this spot and discovers a wooden statue, crudely made, and so eaten away that it is hard to recognize female features on it. Nonetheless, he declares this to be the statue of Saint Anne.

Of course, everyone proclaims it a miracle. The Capuchins of Auray come to examine it and are seized with doubt. Subsequently, after endless symposiums, these same Capuchins will date the statue to the year 701, using who knows what criteria. The precision must be admired. And the news of this discovery spreads to the surrounding area. People hurry to see the statue and, in a somewhat rudimentary way, to worship it. That is hardly to the clergy's liking, whether it be secular or religious. A complaint is lodged with the bishop of Vannes, Monsignor de Rosmadeuc. The latter has a closed inquiry carried out, the details of which are never made public. And, finally, not being able to stop the rising wave of popular fervor, the bishop officially sides with Yves Nicolazic, thus recognizing the reality of the apparitions and the identification of the statue as Saint Anne.

Nevertheless, nothing could be more uncertain. The statue, judged rough and ill-formed by the Capuchins of Auray, who, in this case, seem to have been in charge of the operation, was recut in such a way so as to give the impression of a Christian representation. Thus, we can ask ourselves if this wasn't simply a matter of a Venus or a Gallo-Roman statue of some kind, like so many others that have been found in Breton territory and throughout France. But this fact is certain: the Capuchins of Auray recut the statue before it was officially declared to represent Saint Anne, mother of the Virgin Mary. Of course, it is impossible to verify anything at all on this subject, since the statue was burned during the Revolution and only a tiny fragment of it remains, which was embedded into the current statue.

There is something else to consider: the name of the village, Keranna. That, of course, leads one to think that a statue found at this site could only be a representation of Saint Anne. According to the words pronounced by the white lady, according to Nicolazic, a chapel dedicated to Saint Anne would have existed in this place in the eighth century. Why not? Several years before Nicolazic's discovery, there was another discovery of this kind at Commana (Finistère). Not only was a statue, equally ill-formed, extracted from the ground, but with it, a stone trough. And the name of Commana ("trough" or "hollow" of Anne) obviously makes one predisposed to see a statue of Saint Anne. Why shouldn't the same be true at Keranna?

What is surprising in all this is that the worship of Saint Anne, of whom the canonical Gospels say nothing and do not even cite the name, did not develop in the West until the fourteenth century. This casts doubt on the existence of a sanctuary dedicated to Saint Anne and a statue representing her dating back to the year 701. It was not until 1382 that, under this name of "Saint Anne," the mother of Mary made her appearance on the official Roman calendar, and her liturgical holiday of July 26 was not established until 1584. These are the facts and not conjecture. So, who is this mysterious white lady then, who appeared to Yves Nicolazic and who claimed to be Saint Anne?

Whether or not the vision of Nicolazic was authentic, it must be acknowledged that the theme of the "white lady" refers back to the earliest mythologies and that it can be spotted almost throughout the popular local traditions of western Europe. But, in Brittany, as in all Celtic countries, it takes on very particular aspects, owing to the fact that a figure of divine motherhood exists in the Celtic tradition who bears the name of Anna, or Ana, or Dana, or even Don in Wales. Under these conditions, we can logically assume that at the Keranna site (and consequently, at Commana), a Gallo-Roman sanctuary existed, dedicated to this Goddess of the Beginnings. This is far from impossible, since the field of Bocenno was located right in the proximity of the Roman way from Angers-Nantes to Quimper. And we know that, in this period, sanctuaries were always built near major routes.

It is not only a vague homophonic connection that prompts this identification of the entirely hypothetical "Saint" Anne of Christianity with the ancient Anna of the Celts. Indeed, in genealogies of the Welsh—who belong to the same tradition originally as the Armorican Bretons do—we find very curious information on this point. As is true everywhere, historical figures wanted to trace their families back to mythological or divine beings, even to saints within the Christian framework. One of these genealogies, which appears in a manuscript from the tenth century, gives as an ancestor a certain Owen, chief of a part of Wales, *Aballac map Amalech qui fuit Beli magni filius, and Anna mater eius, quam dicunt esse consobrinam Mariae Virginis, matris domini Jessu Christi*, which means, "Aballac, son of Amalech, who was the grandson of Beli, and Anna, who was said to be cousin [or grandmother; the medieval Latin term *consobrina* carries both meanings] of the Virgin Mary, mother of Our Lord Jesus Christ." And this is not an isolated example, because again we find in the genealogy of a certain Morcant an entire lineage that goes back to *Aballach map Beli et Anna*, otherwise known as "Aballach [the Welsh name for the island of Avalon] son of Beli and of Anna." And when we know that Beli, the mythical ancestor of the Bretons, is none other than the god of light of the ancient Celts, who is often called Belenos, the "brilliant," we cannot help but be astonished. This conclusion must be drawn: in the Brythonic tradition (that is, Armorican Breton and Welsh), the one who later became "Saint" Anne was not only the grandmother of Jesus, but the ancestor of the Bretons. And she could have only been the Irish Dana, mother of all gods, or the Welsh Don, whose children play a large role in the mythological tradition, or again, if we go further back, Anna Parenna of the Romans or Annapurna of the Indians, the crystallization of all the concepts regarding the Mother-Provider, the Goddess of the Beginnings who gives life and nourishes those who issue from her womb.

What remains of this archaic notion at Sainte-Anne-d'Auray today? Many things, certainly, but subconsciously. Popular piety makes subtle analysis look foolish. This piety is lived in an everyday way that no one would consider denying. At the end of the twentieth century, most Breton families have a statue of the good Saint Anne in their houses, even if some members of these families allow themselves attitudes bordering on skepticism. Just as the Irish consider Saint Brigit, the mysterious Brigit of Kildare, to be mother of the Irish gods under all her various names, so the Bretons know that their protectress and their mother can only be Saint Anne. Beyond time and space, beyond the vicissitudes of religions, belief in the divine Mother is maintained. Here, it takes on the face of this "good" grandmother, the one whom everyone keeps safe and close in their secret gardens. But we cannot forget that she is the mother of the Anaons, that is, the deceased, as well. Goddess of the dead as well as the living, Anne could not represent any better the hidden anguish that twists the entrails of humanity in search of its identity.

This funerary aspect obviously calls to mind the representa tions of the tutelary goddess on the supports of the megalithic cairns, the one that is sometimes called the idol in the form of a shield, or the one that is stylized as an owl's head, forever keeping watch in the darkness of the burial mounds. But this idea does not only belong to the long-ago past, it is perfectly contemporary. On the western slopes of the forest of Réno, at La Chapelle-Montligeon (Orne), stands an immense church built at the beginning of this century in the form of a Gothic cathedral. This church, a basilica really, is the seat of "expiatory work," the members engaging in prayer for the most neglected souls in Purgatory, those anonymous souls sleepwalking in that vague place the mythological epics describe so picturesquely. This work began with a Percheron priest who led a pious and exemplary life, the abbot Guguet. And the latter has left a curious account of the circumstances that led him to devote himself to this unselfish love for others. Here is what he relates:

> For a long time, I loved to celebrate the Monday mass for the most neglected soul in Purgatory. . . . In May 1884 a person I did not know came to ask me to celebrate a mass for her benefit. Her face showed her to be about fifty years old; she was modestly dressed, wearing the clothes of a common woman; her manner inspired respect and confidence. Eight days later, at this mass that I celebrated according to her request and for her benefit at eight o'clock and on the day indicated, I was surprised to see her at the back of the church, dressed in a sky blue robe, her head covered by a long white veil, descending to her waist. Who was this? I have never known and no one has been able to inform me on this subject. For a long time she prayed before the altar of the Virgin Mary. At noon, how and at what spot did she disappear? I don't know, and although her presence had, by this point, attracted the attention of village people who came to the church during the morning to see her, no one was able to say where she had directed her steps.[9]

A strange story that raises many questions.

For this event had many witnesses, and all these witnesses are in agreement about never knowing where or how the mysterious woman left. Since we are familiar with the curiosity of village folk with regard to anything strange, we have every reason to doubt the actual, physical existence of this woman in the white veil. So, a collective hallucination, or a manifestation of a being who wished to appear long enough to draw the attention of humans in some forgotten town to the fate of sleeping souls, those souls waiting desperately for a sign of love to resume their way along the paths of the otherworld? Anything is possible, and on the hillside, this basilica now stands, dedicated to Notre-Dame-de-Montligeon, the Virgin who intercedes with her divine Son to lessen the suffering of souls in pain.

It is undoubtedly true that many sanctuaries have been built after a miraculous event occurred, not only the discovery of a statue buried in the ground or under a bush, but also the appa-rition of a "white lady" claiming to be the Virgin Mary. This is what happened in Paris, in the chapel of the Sisters of Charity on the Rue du Bac, in 1830. A nun, Catherine Labouré, who had already had two visions, one of the heart of Saint Vincent de Paul flying over a coffer containing precious mortal remains, and one of the Sacred Heart of Jesus, was awakened one night by a young child of astounding beauty. This is according to her account, at least. The child then invited her to go to the chapel where the Virgin would appear to her, dressed in a white robe, her head covered by a blue veil. The Virgin then predicted for her the misfortunes that were going to befall France, in particular the collapse of the monarchy and a great wave of anticlericalism, and then she encouraged her to come pray before the altar. During the course of another vision, in December of that same year, the Virgin appeared dressed in a robe entirely of white silk, with a white veil on her head, her feet resting on half a globe and trampling a greenish serpent. The Virgin extended her arms and hands, on which she wore rings covered with precious gems that cast rays of light toward the ground. The Virgin then explained that these rays were the blessings that she would grant to those who came to this place to ask for them. Finally, as an inscription with these words, "O Mary, conceived without sin, pray for us who appeal to you," appeared behind the altar, the Virgin asked her to have a medal coined, depicting what she saw, a medal that would be beneficial to all who wore it.

These Rue du Bac apparitions and the words pronounced have never been officially recognized by the Church, but in 1836, the archbishop of Paris, Monsignor de Quelen, ordered an inquiry regarding the medal, at the end of which he authorized its coining. Since then, this supposedly miraculous medal has spread throughout the entire world and the devotion to the Virgin Mary in this chapel has never ceased, making this sanctuary one of the most frequented in Paris. Here, it is the compassionate Virgin, the one who dispenses blessings, who is invoked, as mediator. The patriotic aspect of the discourse attributed to the white lady, and the monarchist connotations are more or less forgotten in order to retain nothing but her maternal indulgence toward all of humanity. We must note that this affirmation of the Immaculate Conception of Mary was made some years before the dogma was officially adopted. It is true that this notion had been under discussion for sometime in the councils and that it was certainly in the air.

We find these monarchist leanings again in the apparitions of La Salette (Isère), where another image of the Virgin Mary manifested itself, one that sheds tears over human iniquity and lack of fervor, even reproaching people for working on Sunday, and vigorously denouncing the attitude of certain ecclesiastics too ready to fall in with social-issues Christianity and aid and abet the diabolical democrats. All this seems a fabrication. The apparitions supposedly took place in the fall of 1846, and the two visionaries were shepherds, Mélanie Calvat and Maximin Giraud. The first ended her life a victim of mystical dementia, the other became an alcoholic. Moreover, Giraud vowed to the parish priest of Ars that he had never seen the Virgin. In fact, we now know that it was only a setup propagated by an elderly nun nostalgic for the ancien régime. That did not stand at all in the way of La Salette becoming an important sanctuary and a place of frequent pilgrimages. Yet, when asked to interpret the supposed secrets revealed by the Virgin to the two children, Pope Pius IX shrugged his shoulders and said that it was just a lot of foolishness. As for the writings attributed to the two "visionaries," they were only variations on a "letter of Jesus'" that had been circulating throughout Europe since the Middle Ages. At La Salette, it is not the image of the Virgin of Mercy that dominates, but one of a haughty avenger. This is, after all, one of the aspects of the Goddess of the Beginnings, since she represents a complete whole.

The Roman Church nevertheless mistrusts "apparitions" and all that is "marvelous" in general. It is popular tradition that seizes upon certain resolutely inexplicable events, interpreting them in their own way, and incorporating into them miscellaneous elements sometimes drawn from the most remote mythological and epic past. We know that Notre Dame Cathedral in Paris is an important Mary location, but we also know that it was built on the site of a Gallo-Roman temple. Claims have even been made for a temple to Isis having stood there, stemming from an aberrant etymology of Paris, *bar-Isis*, that is, "bark of Isis." We forget that the name of Paris belonged to the people who inhabited this region, while the place itself was called Lutèce, a name behind which lies, half-concealed, the god Lugh of Celtic mythology. But this appeal to legend with regard to Notre Dame of Paris is full of surprises.

Indeed,

> there exists a pious legend about the founding of the first church at the site upon which Notre Dame was built. In the year 464, Artus [Arthur], king of Great Britain, came to Gaul, where he caused great devastation. Gaul was then governed by the tribune, Flollo, who represented the emperor, Leon. Having withdrawn to Paris, the tribune fortified himself there. Artus challenged him to single combat. . . . An encounter took place on the eastern point of the city, with spear and ax. Artus, wounded first in the head and blinded by blood, implored the Holy Virgin Mary, who suddenly appeared before all, and covered him with the lining of her mantle, which seemed to be made of ermine,

Flollo was stupefied by this miracle. His sight failed him, and Artus killed him. In memory of the miraculous vision, Artus took the ermine for his coat of arms, where it remained for the kings and princes of Britain. He also wanted to perpetuate the memory of his triumph, and before the very place of the combat, he had built a chapel to the Virgin.[10]

We must point out that the ermine, before being Breton, was the arms of the Capetian prince, Pierre Mauclerc, husband of the duchess Alix de Bretagne, of the thirteenth century, and it is after this period that they were adopted by the Bretons. As to the supposed King Arthur, he never came to Gaul, much less to Paris. All of this stems from a misunderstanding in a passage from the *Historia regum Britanniae*, written in 1135 by Geoffrey of Monmouth: during the course of the battle of Mount Badon against the Saxons, Arthur wears the image of the Virgin Mary on his shoulders and obtains the victory. But it is never a question of an apparition. It is a simple tradition, probably of clerical origin, from the period when the Arthurian legends enjoyed lively success throughout Europe. Thus, the point was to give Notre Dame of Paris noble credentials, which, of course, it did not need, being sufficiently endowed already.

The legends are nearly as numerous as the places of worship. At Josselin (Morbihan), the story goes that a statue was found in the briars, next to a fountain, and that it returned there every night after having been moved to a safe place. That is why it is worshiped there under the name of Notre-Dame-du-Roncier (Our Lady of the Brambles) in the magnificent flamboyant basilica which stands near the no less superb castle of Rohan in a place very often visited on the day of the pilgrimage, September 8. At Boulogne-sur-Mer, the statue is said to have arrived on a bark, and the Virgin supposedly appeared to the inhabitants to ask them to take care of it. But, at the beginning of the Second World War, the statue was put in a safe place, and a curious pilgrimage resulted whereby it was the statue that made the journey and not the faithful. Becoming Notre-Dame-du-Retour (Our Lady of the Return), the Virgin of

Boulogne made long voyages before reclaiming her initial sanctuary at Pas-de-Calais. As for Notre-Dame-de-Liesse (Our Lady
of Jubilation), not far from Laon (Aisne), she is attributed with
the liberation of three crusaders from the Muslims in the Holy
Land and the conversion of a "Saracen" princess. The legend of
Notre-Dame-de-Liesse was so well known in the Middle Ages
that copies of her statue were erected nearly throughout France,
notably at Villeneuve-sur-Lot (Lot-et-Garonne) where it was
placed in a chapel situated almost right over the river.

The best known sanctuary dedicated to Mary in all of France,
one of the most visited in all of Christendom, is undoubtedly
Lourdes. There, the legend becomes blurred in the face of phenomena that not even a skeptic could deny. It is impossible to
doubt, even for an instant, the reality of the apparitions of
Bernadette Soubirous. She saw *something* and, on the advice of
what she saw, she made a spring burst forth at the entrance of a
cave. What is more debatable is the clerical interpretation that
was then given to the vision of Bernadette, and especially the
reference to the Immaculate Conception, the dogma of which
had been officially approved some years before. Of course, we
can refer back to the Pyrenean tradition regarding the "white
ladies" that appeared regularly in caves, and along the banks of
waterfalls and rivers. But it is nevertheless true that the worship
of Notre-Dame-de-Lourdes has far surpassed all other devotions
to the Virgin Mary and that "miracles," that is, "marvelous" and
thus, inexplicable, things have happened in this sanctuary, which,
if it is not divine, is nonetheless charged with such an aura that
anything is possible there.

But, outside all religious conviction and especially all aesthetic judgment that, in view of the bad taste deployed, would
be, frankly, unfavorable, Lourdes is one of those lofty places
where the Spirit breathes. And the image of Notre-Dame-de-
Lourdes is known worldwide, permeating the consciousness,
marking forever the imagination of the people. It is an undeniable fact: Notre-Dame-de-Lourdes is the representation that the
twentieth century has made for itself of the Goddess of the
Beginnings, and it would be very difficult, at the present time, to

substitute another shape, another face, another attitude, for hers.

Lourdes: it is the grandiosity, the masses of people, the hope of a miraculous recovery; it is an enormous liturgy echoing between the mountain slopes on the banks of the Gave. But to speak only of Lourdes is to ignore the rest, those sanctuaries that remain more modest but that reveal no less clearly that deep faith in Our Lady of all time. Lourdes has obscured Garaison and Bétharram, which are close by, in the same diocese, and even predate it. Lourdes has outshone Notre-Dame-d'Ay (Ardèche) in the very heart of Vivarais, on a strange fault in the earth's crust, a special place that, in the Middle Ages, was the meeting point for all pilgrims seeking cures for what ailed them. And how many fervent zealots of the Good Mother have come to Sion-Vaudémont (Meurthe-et-Mosell), this "inspired hill" so dear to Maurice Barrès? It is true that Barrès, in the heat of his vindictive patriotism, had forgotten that there, where the statue of Notre-Dame-de-Sion now stands, was once a sanctuary dedicated to the Gallic goddess, Rosmethera, the "Purveyor," in whom we can recognize the Goddess of the Beginnings, another face of Anna-Dana, the originator of all things. And how many pilgrims have gone to Aviot (Meuse) to pray to the Virgin whose statue was found in a hawthorn bush, a statue that, according to tradition, was sculpted by angels? Perhaps they don't know that, tradition-ally, hawthorn bushes are the dwelling places of fairies, and that fairies are nothing other than folkloric images of this divine mother from whom they seek tenderness. As to Notre-Dame-de-Pontmain, lost in the Le Mans countryside, on the Brittany border, she is the messenger of peace, having appeared, we are told, in 1871, to let some children know that the disastrous war against the Prussians was going to come to an end.

And there are many other sanctuaries, scattered throughout France, some known, others unknown or forgotten. In Folgoët (Finistère), Our Lady watched over the sleep of the "madman of the woods" (*fol-goët*), that is, Saluän, a poor vagabond who could only pronounce a few words to the Virgin and who lived there, insanely in love. One of the most beautiful flamboyant edifices in all of Brittany was built there. At the other end of France, at Tursac (Dordogne), the current statue of Notre Dame has succeeded a representation of a Gallic mother goddess, situated near a spring and a dolmen. At Douvres (Calvados), Notre-Dame-de-la-Délivrance (Our Lady of Deliverance), located on the border separating the territories of two ancient Gallic peoples, protects sailors and captives, and restores life to stillborn infants so that they can be baptized. At Noves (Bouches-du-Rhône), where the terrifying Gallic statue representing a man-eating monster is found, there is a statue of the Black Virgin that comes from a hill where formerly stood a temple dedicated to Hecate, the sinister goddess of the crossroads, who directs or leads astray according to fate, which is determined by what is above the gods, this mysterious energy that animates the universe.

We can feel this energy in certain places that are not very well known at all. This is the case in Querrien (Côtes-d'Armor), a small village situated in the remote regions of the mountains of Méné. Here, an Irish foundation appears in the heart of the Armorican peninsula. In 610, the monk Saint Gal, Saint Columba's companion, after whom the famous abbey in German-speaking Switzerland is named, built a small chapel in this desolate spot. Local legend reports that he caused a spring to burst forth that can still be seen there today. The chapel, it seems, was dedicated to the Virgin, whom Saint Gal greatly venerated. But time passed, and the chapel fell to ruins. Nevertheless, the worship of the Virgin Mary remained fervent in the country and, on August 15, 1652, the Virgin appeared to a twelve-year-old peasant, Jeanne Courtel, who was deaf and mute. Immediately, she began to hear and speak. The Mother of God supposedly told her to have a sanctuary constructed at this site, and four years later, this was done. The very simple building contains two beautiful retables in the side chapels, where a magnificent group composed of Saint Anne and the Virgin dating back to the end of the seventeenth century can still be seen today. This representation is completely original and stands in sharp contrast to the clichés that ordinarily accompany the images of Saint Anne. There is a Virgin with the child as well, which goes by the name of Notre-Dame-de-Toute-Aide (Our Lady of All Aid).

The name calls for some commentary. The same name designates a revered statue of the Virgin in Rumengol (Finistère) to which one prays for the healing of all diseases, in the image of the divine Mother who watches over her children and protects them from harm. We must note that this name is also found at Rumengol (Morbihan) and that it can be translated from Breton into French as "remedy for all." Now, this is one of the names given to mistletoe in Breton, which, if we are to believe the account of Pliny the Elder, was used by the druids to make a potion considered a panacea. There are curious coincidences here, but it is clear that Querrien is one of those very inconspicuous sacred places where the Theotokos, by whatever name, is honored in an enduring way by a population that has forgotten nothing of the great traditions of the Goddess of the Beginnings. This is only one example among many. How many modest chapels are the altars of repose like this for the mysterious Miriam-Mary, the Virgin of Virgins, the divine Mother in whom resides all grace, all beauty, all love, all compassion? Scattered throughout the countryside, the most humble religious structures from times past not only harbor very often obscure architectural treasures, but also the extraordinary splendor of the one whom the litanies call the "Star of the Sea," the "Queen of the Angels," or the "Consoler of the Afflicted." The worship of Mary, mother of Jesus, image incarnate of the Goddess of the Beginnings, has not died out at all, and the light that she radiates floods the most remote corners of the dark zones of the unconscious.

So who is this Goddess of the Beginnings, who is the Goddess of Dusk as well? Only the mystics and poets have been able, if not to comprehend her, at least to apprehend her in all her immensity. Human beings have never forgotten the trauma of their birth, nor the pain of being weaned. They search for their mother under names and aspects that are sometimes very diverse. But it is always the same, the eternal feminine that is the destiny of man. That is why, in the midst of his delirium, Nerval wrote, "I reported my thoughts to the eternal Isis, the mother and sacred spouse; all my hopes, all my prayers were united in this magic name, I felt myself brought back to life in her, and sometimes she appeared to me in the form of Venus of antiquity, sometimes with the traits of the Virgin of the Christians" (*Aurélia*, 2.6). There is no better way to express the universality of the Virgin of Virgins. And each of us can take this vision of Gérard de Nerval to heart: "It seemed to me that the goddess appeared to me, saying to me, 'I am the same as Mary, the same as your mother, the same as all the forms you have always loved. At each of your trials, I have abandoned one of the masks with which I conceal my traits, and soon, you will see me as I am' (*Aurélia*, 2.5).

Despite mask or veil, there is identity. Isis is said to be dressed in seven veils and that is why Salomé danced the dance of the seven veils for Herod before stripping herself bare into a vision of infinity. Of female infinity. Who dares to remove, one by one, all the veils enfolding the mysterious forms of the Goddess of the Beginnings?

PART 2
Our Lady
in All Things

INTRODUCTION

"From eternity I was established, from the first principle, before the beginning of the earth. When there were no depths, I was brought forth, when there were no springs abounding with water. Before the mountains were established, before the hills, I was brought forth" (Proverbs 8:23–25). This Hebraic definition of the Virgin, who is a pure emanation from the Creator as Wisdom personified, clearly shows the effects of Egyptian influence, even if it is formulated according to a masculine religion in which Yahweh is the absolute creative principle. But, just as Hegel insisted upon the fact that before the Creation, God was equivalent to nothingness, because he only became conscious of his existence when he faced the creature, Egyptian theology established a distinction between what came before and after that fateful moment that scientists have called the "big bang." Indeed, "in Egyptian thought, the divine spirit does not exist throughout eternity. It appeared when it became conscious of the fact that it was different from the primordial magma. It is only when it comprehends this difference, that the demiurge will initiate, of its own free will, its dissociation from the milieu in which it was inert."[1]

Thus it is that the absolute principle Atum "holds forth in the silence of the abyss. Then it begins a dialogue with the Nun and emphasizes its distinction from the unformed magma by naming it." It is by the Verb that creation is carried out, according to a process that, once set in motion, can never be interrupted. And divine Wisdom, the feminine face of an undifferentiated and asexual Creator, appeared; for this Wisdom is not only knowledge, it is also beauty, harmony, fecundity, and without it, nothing would exist, since existence depends upon a birth beyond the created and uncreated, a sort of parturition at the cosmic level. So then the primordial couple Tefnut (or Maat) and her son Shu will appear, which are the forms taken by the uncreated at the moment of creation. The Bible accounts for this creation by presenting this Wise Virgin as previous to all organization of the cosmos.

But it is a theme that will be thoroughly exploited by the Gnostics as well. In this Wisdom of whom Solomon sings, we can recognize the Pistis Sophia who will appear in all speculative thought from the beginning of the Christian era and who will be openly adopted under the name of "Saint Sophia" when it comes to building Christianity's greatest basilica in Constantinople, the capital of the Eastern empire. This "Saint" Sophia is none other than the Virgin of virgins, the "Virgin Throughout," the one who precedes all life and all knowledge because she is the immediate cause of it.

There is no doubt that, throughout the world, people have felt the need to represent this Goddess of the Beginnings with a maternal image, as simply as possible, an image that evokes this function only, like that small legendary object of ivory from the early Paleolithic (Gravettian, to be exact) found in Moravia, at Dolni Vestonice. There are two very recognizable breasts on an axis that terminates at a point evoking the neck. The head is missing, the belly and genitals as well, but the emphasis upon those two breasts makes this representation the very image of the mother who nourishes her children. Earth Mother or Virgin Mother, spiritual in nature? It hardly matters. The concept needs no further explanation because it involves all humanity, and we will find its equivalent in the Indian "churning the sea of milk" myth.

It is remarkable that, as soon as art objects appear—which are, at the same time, objects of religious worship and objects of meditation—a tendency to move from symbol to pure abstraction appears. Moreover, even if the representation remains realistic, just the fact of insisting on one detail over another, or on exaggerating this or that trait, clearly indicates this desire to impose a symbolic meaning onto the concrete, probably in order to encourage further thought. That is true with the famous Venus of Willendorf, discovered in Austria, which dates back to the early Paleolithic age, and is the same in nature and technique as the no less famous Venus of Lespugue, discovered in France. Here, it is a matter of a veritable "discourse" on the mystery of the woman. Because her breasts, belly, and thighs are so disproportionately large, we are obliged to consider the problem of procreation and to recognize that the woman is the one who possesses this power, as divine as it is magical, and therefore disquieting, but worthy of veneration, if not adoration.

Paleolithic sculptors and painters seem to delight in a certain exaltation of the "monstrous"—and not of the "monster," as in the Middle Ages—as a way of drawing attention to the exceptional nature of a being or a function attributed to this being. Archaeological examples prove that they were perfectly capable of representing human or animal forms in perfectly realistic ways. If they exaggerated their representations, it is because they had something more to say, a message to convey. In this respect, the group of Venuses, from Lespugue, Willendorf, and Grimaldi in Italy, constitute the most precise and oldest testimony to humanity's interest in the problem of creation. From all evidence, they have not supposed for a moment that the world and the beings that populate it could have been generated by a male god. If the Hebraic Yahweh appears as a completely solitary, all-powerful Father, it is, it seems, after a long ideological struggle resulting in the primacy of the male. But deeper analysis of Genesis bring to light more or less obscured speculation that coincides with other traditions. Even if an original female divinity is lacking, all theogonies and all cosmogonies allude to an ambiguous primordial being. The text of Genesis concerning the creation of Adam and Eve, at least the first version, clearly states that the human being was created in the image of God, at the same time male and female. It is much later that sexual distinctions intervene, that is, etymologically speaking, the break between the masculine and the feminine, each of these two elements being limited to a function determined within a universe that rests upon the opposition of two contraries, nevertheless united by a third term that can only be called divine energy.

Thus, as the divinities are represented, and this is since the appearance of art, there is a kind of fierce struggle between the partisans of a male god and the partisans of a female goddess. But, this is only a metaphysical quarrel that, if misunderstanding and intolerance have given it much importance over the ages, all traditions had resolved already in advance, including the Hebrew tradition. This Wise Virgin of Solomon is only the female part of God. But without her, nothing would exist. In the Egyptian tradition, the primordial god Atum masturbates, perhaps to spew out the two divine and, henceforth, sexual elements that are going to create the concrete. The separation takes place outside of the primordial chaos, outside of the hustle and bustle of beginnings, outside of all that the theologians call the *uncreated*, or again, the *undifferentiated*. Why is being made sexual? No one can explain it, nor even justify it metaphysically. But since this is the case, we must accept it and draw from it the necessary conclusions: no life is possible without the woman. Moreover, it is probable that, in primitive times, males were totally unconscious of their part in impregnation. From this arose the exaltation of the divine female, and then, as a reaction, the dismissal of femininity in favor of an aggressive and triumphant masculinity that had become conscious of its procreative role.

This chronology, however, has nothing to do with a debatable evolution in art. Realism and abstraction are always succeeding each other at more or less frequent intervals, and sometimes within the same ideological framework. In this domain, effectiveness is the only rule. The art work, which always has undeniable religious aspects, translates a metaphysical reflection into plastic forms. Its expression is a function of a method corresponding to the criteria of a society that has arrived at a certain state in certain circumstances owing as much to geographical as to historical contexts. The territories that constitute modern-day France have, since the early Paleolithic age, undergone continual change due to intrinsic conditions and outside influences. But other countries have experienced parallel changes, though not necessarily identical ones. Thus, countless specific formulations appear, which are only the multiple aspects of a single reality. The Goddess of the Beginnings has as many faces as she has names throughout the world.

7

THE INDIAN SUBCONTINENT, THE FAR EAST, AND THE AMERICAS

THE INDIAN SUBCONTINENT

Ever since the shared sociocultural origins of those peoples called the Indo-Europeans have come to light, there is, obviously, a strong temptation to look to India for representations of the mother goddess that might come nearest to the ones we know in France. There is no lack of them, but either they are not terribly ancient, or they are not necessarily Indo-European, so complete and successful was the assimilation between the early Aryans, coming from central Asia, and the aboriginal populations of the Indian subcontinent. Actually, the synthesis that took place between the Dravidian traditions of the south and the imported Aryan traditions was also a result of the mysterious Indus Civilization, which acted as an intermediary. This latter characterizes the Indo-Gangetic plain, and has been a kind of crucible in which originated the civilization we call Indian, marked as much by Buddhism, a relatively recent component, as by the various religions called Hindu, which incorporate numerous local adaptations, without taking into account a sha-manism always very much present in the thinking and the practices. But in spite of this incredible melting pot, the figure of the mother goddess springs forth from earliest antiquity, blithely crossing the ages, essentially considered the "Purveyor," the one who gives her name to the mountain of Annapurna, since this means "Anna the Purveyor," exactly like Anna Parenna of the earliest Roman times. Indeed, it is she who gives life to India by providing water to the Ganges and the Indus, without which the country would be only a vast desert.

But this is a mother goddess of the ancient kind, that is to say, perfectly ambivalent, dispenser of both life and death, nurturer and destroyer, giving birth to numerous children, but trying desperately to devour them. The Goddess is clearly the reflection of this region so full of contrasts and paradoxes, where life depends entirely upon the constantly threatened equilibrium between two antagonistic forces, fire and water, drought and flood, about which it is impossible to say that one is good and the other bad. One of the founding myths of Hinduism presents us with the divine male being, sacrificed, cut into pieces, and buried in the earth to make it fertile. For it is the earth that is the Mother: she gives birth, of course, but she takes back into herself what she has given in an unending cyclical process.

This ambivalence is not reserved for the Goddess. Shiva, the great god of the Indians, is also creator and destroyer, ascetic and master of eroticism. But he is a revealed god, incarnated in a relative, and thus sexual, world. Just by himself, he cannot govern the world in all its complexity. That is why a female form is associated with him, Devi, who is also perfectly ambiguous with her many different names: she is Sati, the Peaceful, or Parvati, best known as lover and companion to Shiva, when considered in her positive forms, but she is also Durga or Kali the Black when the poles are reversed. And if the terra-cotta statues from the second century B.C., that is, the pre-Aryan epoch, all represent attractive women, richly dressed, evoking wealth, plenty, and goodness, the representations that follow the arrival of the Aryans are much more complex and much less peaceful.

Because even Parvati possesses something disquieting when she evokes passionate violence. One of the places consecrated to this Parvati is a valley that goes by her name, near Kulu, in Himachal Pradesh, not far from the hot springs of Manikaran. Local legend holds that Shiva made love there for ten thousand years with Parvati. Then, after meditating for the next ten thousand years, he was well satisfied, and heated the nearby rocks for the well-being of all those who would come there in pilgrimage. But the name of Manikaran comes from another legend according to which Parvati had lost a jewel (*mani*) that was found by Shiva and thrown by him into a waterfall of hot water.

Nevertheless, the carnal union of Shiva and Parvati has become the very symbol of Tantric initiation. The Goddess is not only the Great Mother who gives life and nurtures her children. She is also Shakti, energy, that essentially female divine energy which is indispensable to any male god who wants to influence the world. Moreover, that is why, in numerous myths, the undifferentiated Devi becomes the wife of all the gods of the Indian pantheon; for this Devi is Bhu as well, the ancient earth goddess of pre-Aryan times, and again, Sati, who perished in a sacrificial fire, but whose corpse Shiva saved until it fell away to dust. From this dust, the Goddess was able to be reborn in new forms, because the metamorphoses of the divinities are so many symbols for a creative process that is never completed and that is an extension of the situation of the society in which it is found.

If the image of Parvati is linked to love and mystical sexuality, those of the two other forms of the Goddess, Durga and Kali, are terrifying and bloodthirsty. Nevertheless, these are the most widespread goddess images on the Indian subcontinent. It is interesting to note the transition from the purely positive aspect of Devi, known by the name of Sarasvati, the one who, according to the Rig Veda, "awakens the great wave in the consciousness and illuminates all thoughts," to that of the terrible Durga or the bloodthirsty Kali, who gave her name to India's largest city, Calcutta.

Regarding this transition, mythology relates that Durga was created by the gods to fight against the buffalo-demon

Mahishashura, who usurped their powers. Thus, the primitive function of Durga was to reestablish an equilibrium in a world threatened by a monster. And she was seen in her positive aspect as a good mother who protects her children. But in bringing down the monster, she committed an act of violence, and she very quickly became a sort of warrior goddess analogous to Maeve or Morrigan of Ireland, more infernal sorceress than guardian of celestial dwelling places.

In the popular iconography, this Durga, the incarnation of an ambivalent divinity, is usually represented as having a very pale complexion and many arms, sometimes ten, symbolizing her tireless activity. Also, we see her straddling a lion when she is fighting the buffalo-demon. Thus, she is the goddess of wild animals, as was the primitive Artemis of the Greeks, before becoming a pale lunar reflection. But, as Durga, the goddess never presents a terrifying face. It is in her aspect as Kali that she takes the most terrifying, fantastic, and bloodthirsty forms.

She is commonly called "Kali the Black," even though she is very often represented with a blue body and multiple arms. Her essential feature is her tongue, which is long and red, as if coated with the blood of the victims that she has just devoured. And if her face often reflects a certain serenity, her bloodshot eyes testify to the cruelty attributed to her. Moreover, she is carefully adorned with a necklace or a belt from which hang human heads, monstrous trophies that she delights in showing to her devotees. It is very likely that, originally, Kali was a Dravidian divinity, coming from the south of India, and once assimilated into the Indo-Aryan theology, was given all the aspects of a mother goddess, no doubt cruel, but also profoundly just toward all her children. Furthermore, she is considered to be beyond caste, thus untouchable. She is made to lurk about mass graves and is shown feasting on human blood, like a vampire. In fact, it really and truly is a matter of a vampire goddess. When she unites with Shiva, it is essentially to drain from him his vital energy in order to discharge his creatures out into the world. But when the union ends, Kali sits triumphantly astride Shiva who is stretched out on the ground, thus affirming the superiority of the female over the male principle. And, despite this ferocity, this bloodthirsty savageness, Kali is certainly the most popular and the most honored divinity on the Indian subcontinent, even to the point of becoming the "holy mother" under the pen of certain poets.

There is nothing surprising about that. India has always maintained an intimate familiarity with life and death, the positive and negative, and it certainly seems that Westerners have not understood this process by which life is born out of death. Indeed Kali represents what in alchemy is called the stage of the "crow's head." It is a matter of the "black stone," that is, of dissolution, an important step in the restructuring of the first matter in order to eventually arrive at the Philosophers' Stone. In India, everything happens as if human beings were conscious of this eternal transformation of beings and things that, through the cycle of reincarnations, leads the living to fullness, and not, as Buddhism teaches, to nothingness within a nirvana that is, moreover, very poorly conceptualized. Hindu religion, or to be more exact, the multiple religions that derive from Vedic tradition, are essentially a glorification of life going through its metamorphoses. Under these circumstances, Kali the Black can only be the best way of representing, visually as well as metaphysically, eternal creation carried out by superior powers that we call divine. And that remains true, no matter what abuses are prompted by such a conception. Kali the Black is not a murderer thirsting for blood, but an image of *natura naturans* that endlessly remodels living beings in order to lead them to their perfection. We could certainly call Kali "Our Lady of the Night." But, even as it did among the Celts, life surges from the night, as Being surges from non-Being. This notion is at the very heart of primitive Indo-European culture, and more than ever Kali the Black is one of the images of the Goddess of the Beginnings, the one who comes before and follows after, eternal creator of beings and things.

THE FAR EAST

The countries of Far Eastern Asia are so marked by Buddhism and various philosophical currents that it is difficult to discern what the image of the Great Goddess could have been in primitive times. In Japan, the goddess Amateratsu seems well obscured by the countless deities that are not divinities but projections of the human unconscious. However, by studying what remains of Far Eastern ancient religions, the claim can be made that almost throughout, in China, in Korea, and in Japan, indeed even in eastern Siberia, there was a sun-goddess cult dedicated to this Amateratsu who, with her Asiatic overtones, strongly resembles the solar divinities of the West, all originally feminine. We can then ask ourselves if, as certain anthropologists claim, the Ainus of northern Japan were not part of this Indo-European culture that disseminated so widely over the course of the first millennium B.C., throughout the great Euro-Asiatic plain, beginning from what is today a desert (the Tartars and the Gobi), but which was, we now know for certain, a fertile country, the probable base of this civilization.

But whatever name is given to the Goddess of the Beginnings, she is undeniably linked to the concept of fecundity and was represented very early in the plastic arts of Japan. A clay statuette from the middle Jomon period (toward the end of the second millennium B.C.), now at the Museum of Oriental Art in Rome, is clear and detailed evidence of this. The representation is closely related to those European Venuses of the Paleolithic period, except that the head is well defined, in a very realistic fashion. It belongs to an intermediary period between the Paleolithic—which lasted for a very long time in Japan—and the Neolithic, because the objects discovered in archaeological digs involving Jomon culture testify to obvious, if still rudimentary, agricultural and animal-breeding practices. The Goddess of the Beginnings is thus not only the mother of the world, but also the nurturer of living beings, animal as well as vegetable and human. She is the protectress of all life, the unfailing one.

We must also take into account those Chinese and Korean

influences that, to a large extent, conditioned both the metaphysical and the artistic approaches of the ancient Japanese. Chinese civilization is one of the longest continuous cultures that we can demarcate and analyze. Its complexity hardly makes it any easier to understand, and moreover, it is sometimes difficult to distinguish what is rightfully Chinese from what is Korean, Mongol, or even Vietnamese and Thai. In China, as early as the Paleolithic period, the Goddess of the Beginnings was represented with exaggerated sexual characteristics, as in Europe; hence, the abundance of statuettes, first stone and then ceramic, that could be classified as steatopygic. The emphasis is undeniably placed on fecundity, but we can find hardly any traces of an actual cult to the divine woman. It is true that the various cultures succeeding each other in the Far East have always manifested androcratic tendencies. The woman, as such, was considered, first and foremost, as reproducer, and her importance in more recent times has often been limited to that of a "beautiful object of art." So this is certainly not the place to search for the principle sanctuaries of Great Goddess worship, and Buddhism has hardly contributed to the exaltation of the woman. It is only in Indonesia and the Philippines that we can observe, within the local traditions, certain reminders of a time not matriarchal, perhaps, but at least more gynecocratic.

THE AMERICAS

We might be tempted to say the same thing about American Indian civilizations, but their diversity is such that we must abstain from all generalities. Certainly, it doesn't seem as though the woman had an elevated social standing or that she was considered a divine being among the Aztecs and Incas. These civilizations were undeniably patriarchal, but relatively recent, and they only involved a tiny part of this immense land mass. There again, the complexity is such that it doesn't allow for any exact assessment of the spiritual state of populations that were subsequently assimilated, in a manner of speaking, into the

Incan or Aztec framework, not to mention the Toltec or Mayan.

For a long time it was believed that America was not populated until recently, but no actual proof supports that claim.
Without prolonging this discussion, we can now assert that the
American continent was populated thanks to territory that is
now submerged under the Bering Strait, and that this population
movement, dating from 60,000 B.C. to 30,000 B.C., was Asiatic in
origin. Given these circumstances, it could well be said that from
the early Paleolithic to the Neolithic age, the beliefs and customs
of the American Indians were, if not identical, at least closely
parallel to those of the Asians. But everything depends upon the
region, and American archaeology, which has only just begun,
has very little to teach us about the various cultural strata that
succeeded each other over the course of time.

To look at an example, ten thousand archaeological sites have
been counted in Mexico, but only one thousand have been
investigated, and only one hundred carefully excavated. That is
not very many. However, it is enough to allow us to assert the
existence of a very ancient cult honoring a mother goddess.
Female statuettes have been discovered at Tlapacoya that date
from the middle of the second millennium B.C., and which are
undeniably fertility divinities. In a quarry near Mexico called
Tlatilco, an Aztec name meaning "hidden," countless female
figurines have been discovered, mostly naked or in short skirts,
which archaeologists have named "beautiful ladies." They appear in strange getup, with dyed hair, finely painted limbs and
faces, and lavish necklaces. And the most plausible hypothesis
concerning these "beautiful ladies" is that they were to accompany the deceased buried in the tombs where they were found.
Thus, this is a case of representations of the funerary goddess,
just as we see in the cairns of western Europe.

If representations are rare or limited, there is no doubt about
the female cults that preceded the great civilizations. Traces of
them are found in the pre-Columbian traditions themselves.
Thus, according to the Aztec legend of the sun, the first inhabitants of Mexico were born out of a deep cave and were nursed

by the spirit of the earth. Here we find the well-known theme of the uterus-cave (which is the theme of the Near Eastern Mithras), and also that of the megalithic cairn for which the funerary chamber is a womb intended for the regeneration of the dead in another world. All caves, whether they are natural or manmade, all crevices in a rocky mass, are indeed considered veritable female sexual organs. Among the Hopis of Arizona and New Mexico, an identical founding myth is passed down. The living beings emerged from the entrails of the earth by an opening called the *sipapu*. This primordial birth is still celebrated every four years through a ceremony known by the name of *wuwuchin*. A secret ritual is carried out in a vaulted hut, the *kiva*, which symbolized the maternal womb of the earth. At the center of the hut, a small opening represents the *sipapu*, and a ladder leads to another opening in the ceiling, symbolizing the umbilical cord linking the world of humans to the world of the gods. As for the Thompsons of British Columbia, they claim that the world results from a very ancient metamorphosis of the Earth-Woman. Her hair became the trees and vegetation, her skin the ground, her bones the rocks and mountains, and her blood the water dispersing life and fertility.

These traditions, still quite widespread among American Indian peoples and mestizos as well, testify to a very archaic conception that hardly differs from those found throughout Europe and much of Asia. Under these conditions, we can hardly be astonished that now, in the predominantly Catholic countries of Central and South America, there are so many customs and festivals surrounding the Virgin Mary. Certainly, the Spanish influence goes very deep here, but upon analysis, we can easily see that the image of the mother of Jesus rehabilitates—favorably and with impunity—the ancient face of the original mother goddess, so important is the tendency toward syncretism among all these peoples. But isn't this also an implicit recognition of the existence of a unique and universal primordial tradition with regard to the Goddess of the Beginnings, the one who existed before the world was created?

8

ANCIENT EGYPT
AND THE NEAR EAST

ANCIENT EGYPT

Egypt's contribution was essential to the theologies of classical antiquity, and then to Christianity itself. Gérard de Nerval understood this very well, even in his syncretic delirium of *Aurélia*, in which he deliberately and consciously confuses the Virgin Mary, Venus, Demeter, Cybele, and Isis, because, as he proclaims in one of his poems, "the thirteenth comes back, it is still the first." Nothing could be more true when it comes to trying to classify the female divinities of ancient Egypt, because if everything depends on time and place, the principle remains the same. Creation was only able to come about through separating the male and female elements of the divine at the time when the primordial couple, Maat and Shu, appeared. But from then on, multiple images overrun what is called the Egyptian pantheon, as if the divinities can only be apprehended in concrete forms.

As in India, in the beginning was the cosmic egg, from which would spring the spiral of existence, an egg laid by a mythic bird and thus symbolic (the famous swan, Hansa, of Vedic tradition).

Now, for the Egyptians, the egg was feminine. What's more, the sky was also a female entity. Thus, contrary to what would happen subsequently in Greece, the preexistence of the feminine over the masculine was affirmed, at least in the creation of a coherent and organized world, springing from an indeterminate chaos for which divine will alone was able to determine a polarity, otherwise called a current of energy, bringing forth—and in opposition to each other—two fundamentally contradictory forces. And it is this female sky which will become the goddess Hathor, sometimes represented by the characteristics of a woman to indicate her erotic nature, sometimes of a cow to show her as maternal and nurturing, sometimes as a lioness to emphasize her ferocity, even cruelty, and her untamable nature.

In this Egyptian theology, slowly elaborated over the course of the centuries and including various local contributions, notably those of Lower and Upper Egypt, we understand the celestial element to be feminine in nature, while the earthly element, its complement, is masculine. That might seem surprising, since, in general, the earth is considered to be a mother. But it is only a matter of symbols trying to explain a certain type of duality without which no existence would be possible. The sun is not said to be feminine (as is the case in ancient Germanic and Celtic languages), but it is represented by the eye of Ra, and this eye is essentially feminine, being very closely related, moreover, both formally and metaphorically, with the egg—and with the female genitals' outward appearance.

> Symbolizing the first luminous expression of the demiurge, the female entity was born of it. She incarnates the radiance of god, but also the principle that leads god to be manifest and to create the world. A projection of the vital energy of her parent, she herself is necessary to ensure the permanence of the universe that he has engendered. . . . Aid to the original female principle, her union with her "father" guarantees that the great cosmic cycle endlessly begins again. . . . Thus it happens that one entity appears by turn as the daughter, the wife, and the mother of the solar divinity.[1]

The first exegetes of Christianity would remember that when they tried to justify the birth of Jesus-God from the womb of Mary, daughter of God the Father, but wife of the Holy Spirit, which itself was God. Because the Virgin Mary is, at the same time, daughter, wife, and mother of the solar divinity.

But this "daughter" of the sun has many functions. To her erotic, maternal, and cruel aspects, she adds one more, still more cosmic, which is represented by the form of the cobra. Because she is the serpent-woman, *la vouivre,* feminine, Melusina, the goddess of the serpents of the Near East and of Crete, who uncoils herself in slow reptilian movements and who is finally nothing other than the spiral of involution and of evolution, the perfect symbol of the eternal respiration of the divine. From this serpent-shaped spiral bursts light, the light of the sun that spreads in curving waves over the earth, everywhere embracing it and giving it life. From time immemorial, the Egyptians have associated gold with the radiant heat of the sun, and that is why the serpent-woman-cow-lioness Hathor is often called "the Golden One." Hathor the Golden is the most astonishing expression of the female divinity. Born from the sun at the moment of conflagration of the universe (the big bang), her essential manifestation is the dazzling curve that surrounds the star without which no life would be possible. *Let there be light!* These words, or more, this Verb, is the magic act by which everything begins. The serpent uncoils, the tawny mane of the lioness is the emanation of the solar heat, the cow nourishes all creatures with her milk, and the woman sits enthroned somewhere, in a kind of convulsive beauty without which nothing would exist.

And so it is that at the end of many centuries, not to say millennia, over the course of which there is unrelenting speculation on this theme, the image of Isis, the best known of the Egyptian goddesses, finally appears. We hardly know her at all except through the Greek interpretation, especially the writings of Plutarch, but she is, no less, the ideal representation of this divine female entity that dominates the world. Sister and spouse to Osiris, the "black god," she is no other than Maat. But she is also Sekhmet, represented in the form of a languid cat, but ambiguous because she is always ready, her claws extended, to pounce. She is also Urt-Hekau, the "great magician," and, of course, Hathor the Golden One. The myth of Osiris dismembered, slowly reassembled by Isis, says much about the primordial role of this female divinity. Henceforth, the reign of Isis extends over the Mediterranean world, and there are few peoples who do not know this Goddess of the Beginnings by her many names and functions, even to the point of prompting the most extravagant fantasies, like the one that makes the name of the city of Paris into an aberration of a very problematic *bar-Isis*, that is, a "bark of Isis." We can see that, in the collective imagination, this image of the universal goddess mother forms an integral part of the human unconscious.

THE NEAR EAST

There is no denying that the most sacred, and perhaps the most secret, places of the Goddess of the Beginnings are in the Near East. Because it is not enough to note the preeminence of certain major sites, like Ephesus, to locate in this area of the world the origin of all Goddess worship. If this region is marked by the physical presence of sanctuaries dedicated to her, it is no doubt because this is where, in about the eighth millennium B.C., the essential change in human social structures took place, resulting in the transition from the Paleolithic to the Neolithic.

The beginning of agriculture was marked by a veritable revolution in lifestyle, and if the settling process very soon led to urbanization, it also led to a new vision of the woman, who became the pivotal figure in familial, indeed even tribal, life. Formerly, simply the man's procreative companion on his expeditions, the woman henceforth found herself the guardian of the home and distributor of community goods, from which emerged a new formulation of the role of the Goddess, by whatever name the different peoples of the Near East gave to her. This explains the importance of female worship in this region.

It is also a function of this fundamental change in the image of the divine woman that justifies the migration of Abraham and the birth of the Hebrew people. Actually, if we are to believe the Bible—and there is no reason not to—Abraham left Ur, in Chaldea, to honor his agreements with a father god whose worship was threatened by other liturgies favoring a mother goddess. Thus Abraham represents a conservative current that doesn't accept the new circumstances. He persists in being nomadic and refuses agriculture and all it brings with it in the way of changes. And in his wandering through the desert, he maintains the worship of the father god, sole protector of the tribe. In fact, he only repeats the drama of Cain and Abel, the first symbolizing the agricultural and artisan state, the second, the pastoral, but instead of letting himself be murdered, he prefers to take the initiative and flee. We know that over the course of their troubled history, the Hebrew people, in constant contact and often in conflict with neighboring tribes, will often be torn between fidelity to the father god and the temptation to worship the mother goddess.

However, parallel to this conservative attitude, we can observe a desire for reform among another people, not Semites like the Hebrews, but Indo-Europeans: the Iranians. It seems as though, in the earliest times, the Iranians actually had religious practices analogous to those of India and central Asia under Scythian, and thus Indo-European, domination. In establishing a dualistic theology (the universe is in perpetual conflict between Ahura Mazda, the Light, and Ahriman, the Darkness), the Zoroastrian reform made all the images of the Goddess of the Beginnings, the one who was named Anahit or Anahita, disappear. But despite that, she will not vanish, since we find her again much later in Greece, under the name of Anaitis, in central Europe under a Celtic name that was also given to the Danube, in the British Isles under the names of Anna, Dana, and Don, and even among the Semitic Phoenicians under the name of Tanit, the Great Goddess of Carthage. As for Arvi, the other name of the Indo-Iranian goddess, she will reappear among the Greeks in the form of the mysterious Artemis, probably through the mediation of the no less mysterious "Scythian Diana," by all evidence, a female solar divinity.

But it is especially among the countless newly settled Near Eastern Semitic tribes that the image of the Goddess of the Beginnings would be enriched in ways corresponding to the many functions attributed to her. She goes by many different names. In Babylon, a certain Anath was honored, probably the same as the Iranian Anahita, who is a sort of counterpart to the god Anu, at once Hittite, thus Indo-European, and Assyro-Babylonian, thus Semite. But she is also found in the form of Nanaï, or of Nanna before she is definitively established in the essential figure of the goddess Ishtar of Babylon, otherwise called Astarte by the Phoenicians. The distinguishing characteristic of this goddess is her sexuality, emphasized in such a way that could only shock puritans of all kinds and partisans of a unique procreating father god. The temple of Ishtar in Babylon was a sanctuary reserved for sacred prostitution. Not only could men engage in the sexual ritual there with the priestesses of the temple, but all women, at least once in their lives, were supposed to play the role of the priestess by going to the sacred enclosure to offer themselves to men. It was a matter, then, of a direct union between the human and the divine, this divine being incarnated by the priestess or the woman taking her place, either being the personification of Ishtar.

For Ishtar is not a "virgin" in the modern sense of the word: her virginity is not physical, it occurs on a higher plane. Etymologically, the word, "virgin," evokes strength and availability. And, in the mythological accounts that involve her, Ishtar represents life in all its intensity, especially considering her strange liaison with the god Tammuz—who may be her lover or her son, we do not really know, in all likelihood, both. Descending into Hell, the story goes, she was stripped of all her powers and treated as a simple mortal, which led to a rupture in the harmony of the world, and thus, to great disorder on earth. To remedy this, the celestial gods had to send her vizier, Namtar, after her, who succeeded in bringing her back to the surface after he had sprinkled her with the water of life. But Tammuz did not share her fate. He had to spend half the year in Hell. This basic myth is the same as that of Astarte, Cybele, and Demeter.

The representation of Ishtar and her various natures is most certainly erotic, and a woman going to prostitute herself in the temple performs a ritual that makes her sacred, or as Herodotus said, "the woman is sanctified in the eyes of the goddess." And forever after Herodotus, this Ishtar is the "goddess of desire, goddess of life, courtesan of love, and sacred whore of the temple." Moreover, she herself said, through the voices of her oracles, "I am a compassionate prostitute." But, as such, she is necessarily ambiguous and capable of taking on monstrous or terrifying aspects. Furthermore, the literary myth of Ishtar and Tammuz (also called Dumuzi), as it has come down to us, is far from clear. It can be taken to mean that Ishtar herself killed her lover, even if she later regretted it. If she gives life, she gives death as well. But in this case, it is a ritual death, since Tammuz, thanks to her, is reborn for half of the year. Thus, Ishtar is comparable to the Great Goddess represented symbolically in certain megalithic cairn engravings, this funerary divinity who is supposed to procure a new life in another world for the deceased by first swallowing them into her belly, then letting them mature there, before delivering them into a higher state. This is the dominant theme in all those strange Sheela-na-gigs, so numerous in Ireland and in one part of Great Britain, the wide open vulva being an invitation to be swallowed up inside.

But, in the Assyro-Babylonian representation, Ishtar, as completely "erotic" as she is, is defined as a divinity with many functions. Certainly the first role is handed down from Marduk, the tutelary god of Babylon, as well as Assur, an Assyrian god, strictly speaking, though we should not forget that in the primitive tradition, entirely defined by correspondences between the canopy of heaven and earth (we know that the Assyro-Babylonians were the creators of astrology), there exists an essential triad of Sin, the Moon, Shamash, the Sun, and Ishtar, the planet Venus. And in the complex theology of the Near Eastern Semites, these divine entities are only the results of the dismemberment of the goddess Tiamat, who corresponds to the original chaos. From these origins, the so-called classic divinities will retain some significant emblems. To Sin will be attributed the dragon and the lunar disc. The Hebrew Yahweh, ancient god of Mount Sinai, will long retain those same symbols, reappearing over the course of time, notably through the glowing cloud, which is nothing other than the flaming breath of the dragon. As for Shamash, his ambiguity makes him a universal divinity. As emblems, he has the lion and the solar disc, which is, in fact, energy personified, heat, life, but without any particular sexual identity. If Sin is incontestably a male god, and Ishtar a female goddess, Shamash is undifferentiated, androgynous.

It is, however, Ishtar who reigns over this divine world of Babylon and Nineveh. She is truly the goddess of a thousand aspects, often represented with winged arms, a conical robe, and a conical hat evoking a ziggurat, a kind of tower that decreases in size toward the top, which seems to have been the model for the famous Tower of Babel. And Ishtar possesses emblems that testify to her functions. She is the Lady of the Serpents (whom we will find again in the Aegean Sea), because she knows all the secrets of the subterranean world and thus presides over the germination of seeds. She is also the Lady of the Lion who bestows power and victory. And finally, she is the Lady of the Dove who gives rise to and protects love, and therefore, sexuality. Curiously enough, we will find these characteristics of Ishtar again in Indo-European territory itself, with the Irish goddess, Morrigan (the "great queen"), mistress of love, war, and fertility, who will become the fairy, Morgan, of the tales of the Round Table.

Along the shores of the Mediterranean, Ishtar is no longer known except by her distorted name of Astarte. And it is this Astarte who, once Hellenized, will become Aphrodite, or, again, Venus. Then, her son-lover will be Adonis, but the affair will be the same. A little further north, in present-day Turkey, this same entity will be the Phrygian Cybele, the mother, in fact, of all the gods. Just as her lover, Attis, castrates himself for her, her devoted priests, the galli, will make themselves eunuchs and will wear women's clothes to further identify with the goddess. Attis will be reborn each year, consequently becoming virile again, and will inseminate Cybele anew, that is, Mother Earth, in a sacred incest that shows the importance of the bond between mother and son, a bond subject to an absolute prohibition for the mortal community and that only the gods have the right and the duty to transgress to insure the equilibrium of the universe. During the Hellenistic period, Cybele will merge somewhat with the Greek Artemis—the Scythian Diana—and there will be a real attempt to erase the goddess's excessively sexual aspects by making her a chaste guardian of wild animals and by emphasizing her intransigent virginity. Thus, too bad for the one who sees the goddess completely naked! He will be condemned to death or castration. But this puritan evolution of the myth does not completely destroy its original meaning.

But if the Goddess of the Beginnings was particularly honored throughout the Near East, Christianity and especially Islam shamelessly drove her away. The terra-cotta figurines from Anatolia, representing the universal Mother with enormous hips, are scattered among the museums. The representations of Ishtar were stolen from the ruins of Babylon, to end up at the Louvre or the British Museum. If someone wants to make a pilgrimage to the sanctuaries of the Goddess today, they would have to go meditate at the excavation sites from which, for better or for worse, the remains of her former splendor have been extracted. Whether she is represented very simply and symbolically in the Neolithic age, more realistically in the Assyro-Babylonian era, or more chastely in Hellenistic times, she seems to have disappeared from the familiar landscapes of Asia Minor. Nevertheless, through the statues that show Cybele crowned with a crenellated tower symbolizing her power, or in the proximity of a pine tree, she awakens images forever fixed in the human unconscious.

The pine, moreover, will become her symbol, and this symbol will be explained perfectly by the authors of antiquity who described in great detail the kind of worship rendered to her. The great festivals in honor of Cybele began at the ides of March. There was a week of mourning in commemoration of the death of Attis, a week characterized by absolute sexual abstention. Then, on the day of the equinox, the priests of Cybele would go cut down a pine tree that they wrapped in bandages, like a mummy, and that they decorated with a statuette representing Attis, before carrying it in procession to the temple of the goddess. Thus, the pine represented the son-lover of Cybele. Then, on March 24, the Festival of Blood was celebrated. The most fanatic of the faithful slashed their shoulders and arms to water the pine with their blood, and thus to participate, themselves, in the passion of Attis. The pine was then lowered into a cellar in the temple where an evening of purification took place.

The next day, at the break of dawn, when the rays of the sun began to penetrate the sanctuary, the young god, revived, could be viewed, laid out on a ceremonial bed at the feet of the statue of Cybele, and incarnated as a young devotee. Thus began the triumphant day on which the rebirth of Attis was celebrated. On a chariot drawn by four horses were placed the images of Cybele and Attis, in a Phrygian cap and holding the pastoral staff. Then followed a procession made up of people playing flutes, tambourines and cymbals, singers, torch-bearers, priests and priestesses dressed in white and wearing gold crowns, who surrounded the high priest who wore a crimson pallium. The parade proceeded through the city, stopping in the temples of all the other gods, since Cybele was the Mater Deum, the "Mother of the Gods." The whole celebration concluded in endless drinking and feasting.

This, however, was only the visible part of the ritual. Other ceremonies took place, in the greatest secrecy, about which the historians only offer suggestions. We can surmise that the young initiates underwent a baptism of blood and participated in a meal of mystic communion, with the sharing of bread and wine, as in the Eleusinian Mysteries—and in the Christian Communion. Then they must have entered the nuptial chamber of Cybele, probably an obscure cave, image of the maternal womb, only accessible through a long corridor[2] symbolizing the vaginal passage. There, all the newly elected must have then identified themselves with Attis and wed the mother goddess in some mystical way, thus acquiring the confidence to share in the resurrection of the son-lover of Cybele.

We know the rituals for worshiping Cybele so well—at least their external aspects—because they very soon spread throughout the Roman Empire, merging with the worship of Mithras and becoming what has been called the Metroaic religion. We also know that, during the first and second centuries A.D., this Metroaic religion found itself in direct competition and vicious rivalry with emerging Christianity. But if the towns of the Roman Empire, which then included most of the Near East, gave a warm welcome to the worship of the mother goddess, Cybele, the greatest Metroaic center was incontestably Ephesus, where the Goddess had been honored under the names of Anahita, Tanit, Astarte, and of course, Cybele, successively, but also as Aphrodite and Artemis.

Given these circumstances, we can hardly be astonished that the authors of the Acts of the Apostles were anxious to make Ephesus the place where, after the ascension of Jesus, the Virgin Mary was supposed to have withdrawn in the company of the apostle John. The Cybele-Attis couple gave their place to the Mary-John "couple." Nor can we be any more astonished by the solemn acceptance of the Theotokos dogma during the famous council of Ephesus, in 435. As for the emperor and empress Justinian and Theodora, they knew exactly what they were doing in ordering the construction of the greatest church in Christendom at Constantinople, and dedicating it to Saint Sophia, otherwise known as the Virgin Mary, the Virgin of the Beginnings who existed even before the world was created by the Word—and the breath—of Yahweh Adonai. The Near East is not only the place of the Jesus Christ's birth. It is also the place of the Virgin.

9

GREECE AND THE AEGEAN SEA

The Greek world is not limited to Hellas, that jagged, mountainous peninsula that seems a southeastern extension of Europe. It includes all of the eastern Mediterranean, as well as the
Asiatic coasts and the islands of the Aegean Sea. And it is precisely in these islands that the first outlines appear of what was
called Hellenism, which was, in fact, a succession of very diverse
civilizations that were built one upon the other before attaining
some kind of unity, thanks to the harmonious synthesis of very
disparate tendencies. Here, like the Near East, is the domain of
the Goddess of the Beginnings.

It is very difficult to recognize her face, since her reflections
have multiplied over the centuries. We are only familiar with
Greek mythology through very recent literary adaptations that
give us an imperfect account of earlier theological realities. The
great divinities of the Olympian pantheon are fixed figures,
bearing no relation to their original counterparts, and it is more
interesting, sometimes, to focus on the minor figures of the
Greek period than on the too well-known "stars" that the Romans assimilated because they had nothing else to fill their
places. That is the case with Penelope, who, before being considered the model of wifely fidelity, was, first, the personification of

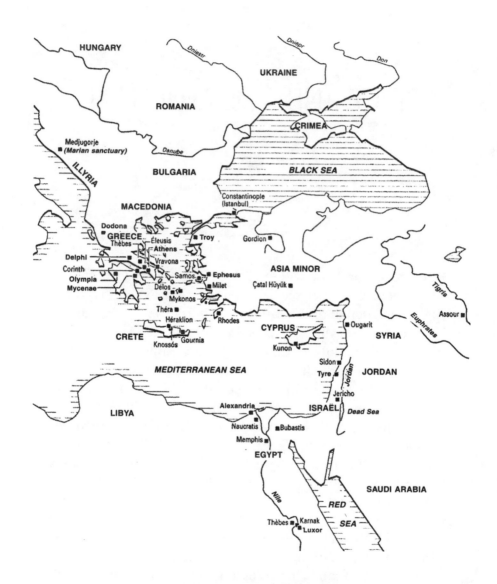

GODDESS SITES IN GREECE AND
THE EASTERN MEDITERRANEAN
(Locations of Discoveries, Monuments, and Museums)

the mother goddess of Ithaca, mother goddess and possessor of absolute sovereignty at the same time. The persistence of the suitors proves this, without requiring more in-depth analysis, and Odysseus's vengeance against them is thus easily explained. The same is true for Circe, reduced to the role of evil sorceress in the *Odyssey*, who nevertheless represents the great transformer, the mother of metamorphoses, the very one whom the builders of megaliths honored, confident of her regenerative powers. But Circe, like her "colleague," Calypso, is relegated to an island, as the fairy Morgan will later be. This is indicative of her precedence over all the other female representations of the divinity.

The link with Asia Minor is undeniable. In Anatolia, in the ancient city of Çatal Hüyük, many Neolithic sanctuaries were found, their walls showing the breasts of women sculpted in relief. These forms were modeled around skulls of vultures, foxes, weasels, and necrophagous animals whose beaks and pointed teeth represent the nipples. Strange comparison: femininity and death seem to rise from the same entity. And nevertheless, the representation of breasts also signifies life in all its fullness. The countless terra-cotta idols discovered in the Cyclades are mother goddesses, but also protectresses of the deceased, and more than ever, life and death are only two aspects of the same reality.[1]

The Neolithic civilization of the Cyclades remains very mysterious, and that of Crete even more so. The Cretans were not Indo-Europeans, but neither were they Semites. Perhaps they had the same origin as the ancient Egyptians, who, we know, were Hamites, whose modern-day descendants are the Bedouins, the Tuaregs, and the Kabyles (or Berbers). We cannot deny that Crete was an important cultural melting pot between Egypt and Greece proper, even in those periods when Hellenic civilization was only in its infancy. And Crete, especially, can be called the holy island of the Goddess.

It was between 3000 and 1400 B.C. when the Cretan civilization developed, in a period that included the end of the Neolithic and a part of the Bronze Age. Then it abruptly disappeared, no one knows how, and the Greeks would only retain very vague memories of it through legends that present more problems than they resolve. All hypotheses could be true, in particular, a natural catastrophe, or a foreign invasion, putting an end to the Cretan culture.

Thus, we can speak of these mysterious "peoples of the sea" who also appeared in Egypt, without knowing where they came from exactly, but in whom we can recognize, not without reservations, of course, the survivors of Atlantis, if we take seriously the two essential accounts Plato gives us in the *Timaeus* and the *Critias*. First, the Atlanteans were supposed to be peerless navigators, thus "peoples of the sea," and secondly, their power was derived from the sacred union of Poseidon, god of earthquakes (and not of the sea!) and the daughter of a native Atlantean named Clito, that is, "magnificent," an obvious symbol for the Goddess of the Beginnings.

As to the gynecocratic nature of the Cretan civilization, proven by the worship of a female divinity, mistress of serpents and wild animals, we find the same thing again in a very clear, but no less mysterious, Breton-Armorican legend of the city of Is. This city, perhaps more historic than mythic, was indeed ruled by a princess Dahud, derived from the Gallic, Dagosoitis, meaning "good sorceress," a princess cursed and demonized in the Christian version of the legend, swallowed up with her city by the wrath of God—displaced and obscured by androcratic forces crystallized in the father-god religion.

Though documents written by the Cretans themselves have been found, their language still remains incomprehensible. But archaeological digs done at the beginning of the twentieth century by the British archaeologist Evans have brought to light certain essentials about this culture. The Cretans were a peaceful people, navigators, a very gynecocratic community ruled by a king-priest, the *minos*, a term that has been taken to be a proper name, but that was, in reality, only a title. And it seems very much as though the Cretans had only a single divinity, the mother goddess, for whom the *minos* was interpreter and principal head priest.

This Cretan goddess seems to have been the absolute mistress of all living beings. She was represented as a very beautiful woman, dressed in a long robe richly decorated, but leaving her breasts uncovered, with her arms raised, holding in each hand a serpent and the head of an animal that might be bird or a cat. That is how she appears in the magnificent statue from Knossos, now at the Herakleion archaeological museum. We also know that this goddess had no temple, strictly speaking, and that she was worshiped in the open air, on hills or mounds, and that often the officiating priest-king or priestess sat on a throne flanked by two horns. This feature, for which there is archaeological proof, and the certain fact that the ceremonies included bullfights, though the bulls were not killed, calls for a close look at the myth of the Minotaur.

We have only poor knowledge of the Minotaur through the imagination of the Greeks, but certain elements convey indisputable evidence of an earlier reality. According to the legend, Minos was a king of Crete, a king-priest of course, and was married to a certain Pasiphae. Poseidon had presented him with a magnificent bull that Pasiphae fell in love with. She was then changed into a heifer and mated with the bull, subsequently giving birth to a cruel half-human, half-bovine monster, the Minotaur. To hide his shame, Minos then had a labyrinth constructed at Knossos, his capital, in which the monster was imprisoned. To this legend the Greeks grafted the legend of Daedalus and Icarus, and then, a bit later, that of the Athenian Theseus.

All evidence suggests the labyrinth to be a sacred enclosure. Its name probably comes from the Greek name for the ax, *labrys*, but what was its Cretan name? Rather than getting lost in the symbolic significance of the ax, it is better to examine the form of the labyrinth, which is necessarily derived from that of the octopus, a marine animal well known to the Cretans and of which there are numerous representations on the Aegean pottery of the Neolithic period.[2] From a purely geometric point of view, it is like a spiral. Now, the spiral conveys exactly the fetus's position in the maternal womb, and, if we take this further, it constitutes the most perfect representation of the expanding universe.[3] Here is something to think about: the labyrinth is the image of the maternal womb, and the fact that the Minotaur was placed at its center signifies that the primitive being—the fetus or the primordial seed—is still undifferentiated, half-human, half-animal, the result of a conjunction between the animal and the human world, reminder of the Golden Age when, in an earthly paradise, humans and animals understood and mixed with each other.

Taking these considerations into account, the adventures of Icarus and of Theseus can only be linked to the concept of the divine maternal womb. Supposedly imprisoned in his own creation, Daedalus, the builder of the labyrinth, is, in reality, confined within the womb and cannot be born into earthly existence. And when he sends his son, Icarus, furnished with wings held together with wax, into the air, he is trying to ignore the stages: wishing to be born, here through an intermediary (Icarus is only his double), he naively believes that it is enough to leave the womb to acquire an autonomous existence. Now, Icarus is immature, and the heat of the sun that makes the wax melt and causes his fall corresponds to the fierce burning in the lungs of the newborn in contact with the air's oxygen. The lungs of Icarus have not reached the stage that would allow him to exist with impunity in the free air. This is the first lesson to draw from the myth.

But if Icarus wanted to leave the maternal womb, Theseus, on the other hand, wants to return to it. Certainly, on a political and historical level, Theseus's adventure conveys the Athenians' desire to lay claim to the Cretan heritage and integrate into their own traditions the worship of the mother goddess. Now, all myths have various meanings according to the level we consider, and, in this case, the metaphysical (or religious, or mythological) level seems much more important. Theseus the hero, destroyer of monsters, hero of light, and thus civilizing hero, decides to obliterate this monster who lies in the darkness and whose fury seems formidable because it is an unknown, buried deep in the human unconscious. Theseus wants to do away with the ancient world, the uterine world, and create from it a new one (on the Greek model, of course, according to the legend) that will emerge *from the murky depths of the unconscious*. That is the goal of his expedition. But the fact that Ariadne gives him a thread that allows him to find his way—to return with impunity from this *regressus ad uterum*—is significant: Theseus is afraid of being swallowed up in the original womb and of being destroyed there. So, he turns for recourse to Ariadne, herself a personification of the Cretan goddess. In short, he secures Ariadne's complicity, with whom he has sexual relations, in order to explore the womb, otherwise known as the female mystery, par excellence.

He is victorious over the monster. Psychoanalytically speaking, he has vanquished his ancestral fears, he has penetrated to the very heart of the mystery, but he has returned from it, thanks to Ariadne's thread. But what has he gained from his experience? Very little, certainly, since he abandons Ariadne for her sister Phaedra. That could mean that, unsatisfied with his exploration, he looks for another image of the woman whom he believes he has discovered in Phaedra. Here, the Greeks have extended the story and demonstrated the complete failure of the hero who will see himself supplanted—symbolically—by his son, Hippolytus, himself a priest of the Goddess, but going by her new name of Artemis. Still, it remains no less true that the palace of Knossos continues to be a sanctuary of the Goddess, not the center of the world, but the absolute center around which are arranged the spirals that lead to existence.

The Cretans, under the name of Minoans, left traces in the Greek domain proper. On Crete itself, the town of Gournia, which is very recent and whose ancient name we don't know, was a sanctuary for the Goddess of the Beginnings. But it was especially to the ancient island of Thera that the Minoans brought their religion, in particular, to the city of Akrotiri, whose ruins contain countless representations in the form of frescoes. The goddess of the serpents is always present and watching over her distant descendants, because the Greeks, entirely Indo-European as they were, and subject to a particularly restrictive patriarchal system, had, without being aware of it, assimilated the worship and beliefs regarding the ancient Neolithic goddess of the Aegean Sea. Thus, she will reappear under different names, according to the period, and especially according to the various influences the Hellenic world undergoes.

Provided that we go back far enough in time, and if we are to believe Hesiod's accounts, we can acknowledge that Greek theology was built upon a sacred union between Oranos, the Sky (the Vedic Varuna) and Gaia or Ge, Mother Earth, the same one as was honored in the Cyclades. From this union issued many separate lineages of divine entities, as would be expected from a society that, in a few generations, was supposed to be rational. That is how we arrive at the Titanic couple, Cronus-Rhea, from whom are born all the gods and all the humans. But Cronus, who can be viewed as the incarnation of time, the youngest of the Titans, dethrones his father and replaces him, a symbolic act that marks the evolution of metaphysical speculation. That is why, to avoid being dethroned in his turn, Cronus devours his children as soon as they are born. But he is fooled by the woman, the mother goddess Rhea, who makes him swallow stones, a substitution he doesn't notice because of his gluttony. Then appear the divine entities that are going effectively to succeed the Goddess of the Beginnings, with different names and different functions, becoming, according to the circumstances, the new faces of the same divine reality.

In his turn, the son of Cronus, Zeus, is going to dethrone his father, and even castrate him, before sending him into exile, according to Plutarch, to an island west of the world. And he will organize the Olympian pantheon with his brothers, Poseidon (Neptune), to whom he will entrust the unstable elements (water and earth, which is subject to earthquakes) and Hades (Pluto) to whom he will entrust the underground and invisible world. But it is his sisters who will inherit the greater part of divinity. Demeter will be Mother Earth, the provider and nurturer of beings and things, Hestia (Vesta), not the goddess of the home, as some have wanted to make her, but actually the possessor of the sacred and divine fire that allows for all life, and finally, Hera (Juno), who embodies the maternal and domestic functions, and whom Zeus will make his wife. Another goddess should, nevertheless, be added to this first list, Aphrodite (Venus) who is born from the waves at the moment when the testicles of Cronus fall into the sea. Mistress of feelings, passions, and sexual desires, queen of unsettling beauty, at once alluring and formidable, Aphrodite is none other than the Greek representation of Ishtar-Astarte, and her name, no doubt coming from the Indo-European term meaning "wild boar," makes her the mistress of the wild animals, and so, of the impulses stemming from what is now called the "reptilian brain."

The divinities take on more specific names when they are considered according to more and more precise criteria based on their functions. Thus, myth makes them into products of such and such a union, this union always taking on symbolic value. But that does not mean that the other great Olympian divinities are the legitimate children of Zeus and Hera. Far from it, because adultery and incest are the rule in the divine lineages and constitute transgressions, forbidden to humans, but necessary to the evolution of the world and without which it would soon sink into a static state of nonexistence. Thus will appear figures like Athena (Minerva), Artemis (Diana) and Hecate, emblematic female figures, all three of which are going to represent one of the aspects of the primitive Goddess.

Athena is presented as the protectress of Athens, the city that bears her name (a plural name, moreover, as if there were many Athenas, which recalls the Elohim of the Bible). She is said to have been born, completely armed, from the brain of Zeus, and she has been made into a warrior goddess. Yet that is not her essential role, because this miraculous birth means simply that she embodies Zeus's thought, divine intelligence at its highest level. It is not by chance that her Latin equivalent, Minerva, has been considered the expression of wisdom, above all—in a Christian or even Gnostic language, we would say "Saint" Sophia—and that Caesar, in his *De bello gallico*, easily likened her to the Celtic goddess of poetry, arts, and crafts, the Irish Brigit, who became "Saint" Brigit of Kildare with the coming of Christianity. But Athena was not only honored in Athens; it even seems as though she was a Panhellenic goddess, for whom the temples of the Sunion cape, near Athens, at Lindos on the island of Rhodes, and especially at Mycenae, provide sites for numerous pilgrimages. In fact, Athena is Artemis's double, the primitive Artemis, another face of Ishtar-Astarte, and merged here with the ancient solar goddess of the Scythians. The best hypothesis on this subject is to consider Athena as borrowed from the Scythian peoples, especially the Sarmatians, because the descendants of these last, the Ossets, have retained in their mythological traditions the name and the adventures of a certain Sathana, sorceress goddess but wise, warrior but nurturer, with multiple functions and formidable powers.

Now, as Jean-Claude Lozarc'hmeur has proven by taking as his starting point Georges Dumézil's studies on the ancient period of the Nartes, this legendary Ossets clan who are the present-day descendants of the Scythians, the name, Sathana, derives from a Christianization, or more accurately, a demonization of the traditional proper name that had already become Athena in Greek.

The most celebrated sanctuary of Artemis was, we know, at Ephesus, in Asia Minor, the true center where the many diverse religions surrounding the Goddess of the Beginnings crystallized, and where Greek influence dominated in the so-called Hellenistic period. Moreover, it should not be forgotten that the whole Asiatic coast of the Aegean Sea was Greek for many centuries. What we call Greek civilization took shape in these places. The account of the Trojan War made this cultural community apparent, since it was actually a case of political and economic rivalry between two branches of Hellenic peoples. The cause of this war is, in itself, perfectly eloquent, since the legend of Paris, forced to choose among three goddesses, shows us that the latter were only three faces of a single entity. Hera, Athena, and Aphrodite are actually three functional aspects of the Goddess, and when Paris gives the apple (called the apple of discord!) to Aphrodite, he only privileges the erotic side of the divinity. But we should note that if Artemis is absent from this "competition," she soon reappears in the course of the tragedy in relation to Iphigenia, the Greek Europa, daughter of Agamemnon, who must sacrifice her to obtain victory for his clan.

For Artemis—who is, in fact, this triple goddess of the judgment of Paris, or, if we prefer, the goddess of the three names and three faces found in Irish mythology (the triple Brigit)—is an all-powerful, and consequently, cruel divinity. She is the famous "Scythian Diana" whom we will later see in the Greek legend of Iphigenia in Tauris, obliging her priestess to spill the blood of every young man arriving in her holy city. It is Artemis who kills the audacious one who sees her naked and thus learns the secrets that she reserves for initiates. But the image of Artemis was very watered down by the Romans who made her into their huntress, Diana, when originally, she seems to have been the protectress of savage beasts. Moreover, it is probable that her name comes from an Indo-European term that is the source of the Gallic *artio*, "bear" [*ours* in French] (from which comes the name of the famous King Arthur). In this case, the famous statuette in the Berne museum, the "Goddess of the Bear," of Gallo-Roman make, is only the Celtic vision of this Artemis of the Near East and Greece, such as she was before her transformation by the Romans.

The very probable link between Artemis and the bear makes her into a great queen, analogous to the Irish Morrigan, because the bear is a royal emblem (as the wild boar a priestly emblem). But she was dethroned. The mythological account of her birth harbors elements that make this clear. According to the Greek legend, Artemis and her brother Apollo are the children of Zeus and Leto (Latona), a very mysterious goddess who is surely not originally Greek and may well have been passed down from the earliest Indo-European times, if not, more precisely, pre-Indo-European times. Actually, according to Diodorus of Sicily, the country of Leto's birth is the British Isle, in the vicinity of the Stonehenge solar monument. Leto is undeniably linked to a solar worship inherited, at least, from the Bronze Age. The fact that her son Apollo was considered a sun god is obvious proof of this. But all of this needs to be qualified.

Zeus does not have a reputation for fidelity to his wife, Hera, and his liaisons, no matter how fleeting, arouse her violent jealousy. Thus, when Leto is pregnant, Hera hounds her vindictively, delaying her delivery considerably. It is only on the island of Delos—we may wonder why—that Leto finds shelter from the fury of Hera and that she can bring into the world her twins,

Apollo and Artemis. This legend allows the god Apollo to be assimilated into the Greek tradition, who, all evidence suggests, was a stranger to the Hellenic tradition. All the commentators of antiquity, including Cicero himself, are in agreement that Apollo is a "hyperborean" god, that is, that he came from the north. And he is considered, first of all, a poet, a scholar, and a doctor. The primitive Apollo, whose name, furthermore, refers to "apple," is not, in any case, a solar god, and if there is a relationship with the sun, it is his sister, Artemis who maintains it, pure and simple, following her mother, herself a solar divinity, making Artemis her rejuvenated double (as in Egypt, Horus is to Osiris). Now, the legend of Leto appears at the time when the polarity is reversed, as recorded in all Mediterranean traditions. The sun, which was originally feminine, became masculine, and of course, the moon, which was masculine, saw itself linked to feminine sexuality and consigned to the night as a secondary figure, a simple reflection of the star of the day. In the same way, Artemis lost her primary position to her brother Apollo. The one who was the solar Great Goddess of the ancient Scythians is reduced to the role of mirror, and decked with a crescent moon. It is a sign of the times, the triumph of patriarchy not over the matriarchal, but over the gynecocratic conceptions of earlier societies living under the gaze of the all-powerful Goddess of the Beginnings.

And thus, Artemis-Diana will be the moon. Still, we are left to interpret that crescent moon, which figures emblematically over her head or on her forehead when she travels through the darkness of the forest at night accompanied by wild animals. The bear was quickly replaced by the doe, which is more comforting and more feminine. The inversion of symbols, however, parallels the inversion of metaphysical polarities. It is likely that the crescent moon was always one of the emblems for Artemis, the all-powerful, the one who possesses the secrets of life and death, the one without whom the man, the male, would be plunged into the darkness, since she, herself, represents the sun. In fact, the crescent moon over the head of Artemis represents the man, the son-lover Adonis, Attis, or Tammuz-Dumuzi, over whom the goddess is mistress and who cannot live more that twenty-eight days without her, as in the Celtic legend of Tristan, who would die if he did not have physical relations each month with Isolde the Blonde, the incarnation of solar forces.

It seems that the most ancient temple dedicated to the primitive Artemis is in Vravona, on the eastern coast of Attica, about forty kilometers from Athens. Part of the sanctuary dates from nearly 1300 B.C., and, near a sacred spring, one structure, now in ruins, is supposed to be the tomb of Iphigenia. The archaic nature of the Artemis cult here is explained by a tradition that returns the goddess to her position as mistress of the wild animals. Indeed, the story goes that Artemis, furious because a mortal killed one of her bears, demands as compensation that the Athenians send their young girls to her sanctuary. These girls, aged five to ten, were called *artoi,* that is, "bears." In fact, they were supposed to imitate the sacred animals during a ceremony that included a "dance of the bears." The etymology of Artemis's name, which we have already discussed, can leave no doubt about this: she is the bear-goddess.

There are countless temples in honor of Artemis, in continental Greece, in Sicily and southern Italy, which constitute what is called "greater" Greece, and in the islands of the Aegean Sea. But at Delos, she stands side by side with the other goddesses: Hera, who protects the family and maternity, Demeter, the other face of Gaia, and Aphrodite, the wild-boar goddess, whose high priestess maintains the link between the visible and the invisible, which is symbolized by love, beauty, and sexual desire. The Greeks have given great importance to their representations of Aphrodite, the most well known being the celebrated Venus de Milo, because this divinity corresponds perfectly to their desire to make exterior beauty coincide with inner goodness, which is expressed remarkably well by the formula *kalos k'agathos,* "beautiful and good." This desire for perfection never clashes in the least with the idea of guilt. Aphrodite is "amoral" in the sense that sexuality is neither good nor bad, but an integral part of being human. And Delos can convince us that the various names given to the goddesses are only so many expressions on the face of a single Goddess.

This Goddess remains the prehistoric Gaia whose shadow forever haunts Delphi, a sanctuary nevertheless marked by Apollo's victory over the serpent, Python. This legend of the celestial god vanquishing a telluric, and somewhat demonized, being explains the transition from a feminine cult to a masculine cult, and marks the reversal in polarity that occurs among Mediterranean peoples at some point in history, probably in the Bronze Age. But, even as the Goddess of the Beginnings emerges from the very center of Christianity as the Virgin Mary, the Gaia of the dim past is the eternal mistress of Delphi, *omphalos* of the world, where divine will is revealed by a priestess who has retained the name of the serpent, since she is called the Pythia. The Greek world consecrated the triumph of man over woman, that is clear, but the woman remains very powerful in the unconscious, and especially omnipresent in the kinds of worship rendered to the divinity.

The example of Eleusis is certainly the most significant in this regard. It is not the only sanctuary dedicated to Demeter, but it is the one that best conveys the Greek attitude toward the divine female. In the Olympian pantheon, Demeter occupies a place apart. She is a daughter of Cronus and Rhea, but in all aspects she most resembles her grandmother, Gaia, and her name means exactly *goddess mother*. According to the myth, she had one daughter, we don't know by whom—because she can be considered a virgin—named Kore, or, again, Persephone, the Latin Proserpina. This Kore is essentially only a double of Demeter, her younger self. The idea of renewal expresses itself here with the aid of a daughter, whereas, in the case of Cybele, it was a matter of a son-lover. The myth of Demeter is apparently more ancient, since it refers to a sort of matriarchy, while the myth of Cybele shows androcratic tendencies, the emphasis being on the role of Attis. But as the myth unfolds, Kore, who is carried away by Hades and eats of the fruit of Hell, is no longer completely of the surface world and Zeus's will is powerless to make her return to that world for good. She must remain in Hell for half the year. It has been said that this theme reflected the changing seasons. Perhaps, there is also something else. It also reflects the certainty that above is as below, that there is a kind of equivalence between the obscure, underground world, and the luminous world of the surface, between the visible and invisible. And it is this basic idea that leads to the celebration of what have been called the Eleusinian Mysteries.

The ceremonies in honor of Demeter began in Athens on September 22, the beginning of autumn. They started with a general purification of the *mystes*, or initiates, notably by a bath in the sea. Then the procession toward Eleusis took place. But after that, despite all the research that we have been able to do on this subject, it is a *mystery*. The most we know is that, for nine days, which correspond to Demeter's wandering in search of her daughter, there were liturgies with songs and incantations, all of it ending in a *communion*, the *mystes* sharing bread and wine. What was affirmed was not only a special relationship between humans and their divine Mother, but also the community of all living beings. The asceticism demanded of the adepts was probably both individual and collective in nature, and surely had points in common with the asceticism required of the first Christians. But the mystes of Eleusis knew how to guard the secret, because all breaches of the rule of silence could be punished by death.

It seems that Demeter represented the nurturing, beneficent, maternal aspect of the female divinity, being much more of a divine "generalist" than Hera, for whom numerous sanctuaries existed nevertheless. In fact, Hera was public, exoteric, whereas Demeter was private, esoteric, reserved for those few who had delved into their own inner beings to find their inner source. The descent into the labyrinth must have been the same sort of thing, and perhaps Demeter had the same face as the Cretan goddess of the origins. But Demeter, as completely mysterious as she was, has a still more secret, more unmentionable nocturnal double in the form of Hecate, a sort of terrifying "demon" who presides at the crossroads, or more precisely, at the *triforia*— where three paths meet—the true crossroads *(quadriforia)* being the domain of Hermes of the four faces. Hecate is often compared to the dark moon and expresses all the terrors that a traveler can experience in the darkness. Also, it is necessary to ward off the goddess through offerings and incantations. Hecate probably recalls a devouring mother, analogous to the Indian Kali, and in the medieval imagination, she more or less merged with Diana and became a true sorceress. She was sometimes even made masculine and appeared with the traits of the devil, whom one meets at crossroads where he proposes his famous pact.

All these divine female representations from the Greek world are the result of reducing an invisible entity to her functions. Moreover, the same process can be observed with regard to the masculine divinities, but it seems that the human unconscious was made very uneasy by the mystery of the woman herself, sweet lover and admirable mother, model of beauty, but, at the same time, shrewish wife, devouring and castrating mother, and especially, repulsive old woman. Thus appear what are called the secondary goddesses, the Erinyes, the Furies, and the Eumenides, then the Marcae, the Moirai, and the Sirens, but also the Muses, the Nymphs, and so many other immortal beings who populate dreams and nightmares. And in borrowing the whole of Greek mythology from the Greeks and adapting it to their own mentality, the Romans were only going to facilitate the disintegration of the Great Goddess's primitive image into multiple fantastical constructs.

10

CONTINENTAL EUROPE

Central and southern Europe were populated very early and the early Paleolithic people left abundant traces there. Among these, the female representations seem to be some of the most ancient in the entire world, and the statuettes known as the Venus of Willendorf, in Austria, and the Venus of Grimaldi, in Italy, very similar to the French Venus of Lespugue, number among the most beautiful and noble religious objects relating to the universal Great Mother. This tradition continued over time. The Neolithic age left an impressive number of female statuettes representing this goddess, in ceramic as well as in stone. The same is true for the Iron Age, as the strange Strettweg cart, at the Graz (Austria) archaeological museum, makes clear, consisting, as it does, of a series of warriors surrounding a female form whose divine nature is beyond doubt. What goddess is this? Probably the goddess of war, of magic, and of love, who so often reappears under various names in Celtic mythology. Finally, beginning with Christianization, those places formerly consecrated to the Great Goddess became sanctuaries dedicated to the Virgin Mary, and thus survived, essentially in the predominantly Catholic countries, because the Protestant Reformation often did away with all traces of whatever the reformers considered to be vile superstitions. There where, in the past, partisans of the Goddess officiated, visionaries perceive the Virgin who delivers messages to them and invites them to turn their gaze toward heaven. But, this being the case, what has changed since the distant prehistoric past?

To tell the truth, very little, except the outer aspects and inner values attributed to the Goddess. If the vestiges of the Celtic religion of the two Iron Ages remain buried underground, in Austria, at Frauenberg (the "Mountain of the Ladies") south of Graz, the ruins of the temple of Isis-Noreia still stand. But this is an Isis already very different from the one who was honored on the banks of the Nile. She has been Romanized to a great extent, and bears more resemblance to the one invoked by Lucius, the hero of *The Golden Ass,* by the Late Empire Latin writer Apuleuis, or the one who took over of the fevered mind of Gérard de Nerval, that synthesis of all the mother goddesses of antiquity and of the Theotokos herself. Thus, it is not astonishing to discover her once more, again in Austria, under the name of Our Lady of Mariazell, not far from Vienna, at a very popular pilgrimage site. But here, we should note, the statue of the Theotokos is a Black Virgin, and well before the pilgrimage began here in 1366, this place was already called Mariazell, the "cell of Mary." It is likely that this site has been consecrated to the Goddess for thousands of years. Austria is a land that was populated in the past, a land of loess where diverse populations established themselves and paid homage to the richness of the soil through regular worship to a fertility divinity. This is what the Paleolithic statuettes at the Natural History Museum of Vienna attest to, a group to which the famous Venus of Willendorf belongs, discovered near Krems. But the latter should not make us overlook her neighbor, called the "Lady of Pazardzik." From approximately the same period (25,000 B.C.), this is a seated female form, with enormous hips and buttocks, evoking a violin, and a very clearly marked pubic triangle. This statuette is not Austrian. It was discovered in Bulgarian Thrace and belongs to the representations of the Cyclades. Another neighbor, this one Austrian and recently discovered at Krems, the dancing Venus of Galgenberg, seems much more ancient, going back to 30,000 B.C.

France is the European country with the most Black Virgins, or figures called by that name, but they exist in other countries, in Belgium for example, in Brussels, Halle, and Scherpenheuvel. The Brussels statue, found in the Saint Catherine church, seems to be an ancient Diana or Gallo-Roman Aphrodite that must have been retouched many times over the course of the centuries. The one in Halle sits enthroned over the main altar of the Saint Martin basilica, which is very often called the "Our Lady of Halle" basilica. The one in Scherpenheuvel (Montaigu) is also over a main altar in the Onze Lieve Vrouw basilica, at the very center of the city, and there is proof of its worship since the eleventh century. It is, indeed, a healing Virgin, invoked to spare the inhabitants of the region from the plagues. Each year, the first Sunday after All Saints Day, a procession takes place by candlelight. The date and the ritual recall ancient Celtic worship of a female divinity who heals and protects people from illness during the winter months.

At Beauraing, also in Belgium, a cult to Mary was very recently established. In 1932, in fact, on December 8—the day on which the Immaculate Conception is celebrated—five children from the little village of Beauraing, not far from Dinant, testified to having witnessed the apparition of a woman dressed in a long white robe, whom they recognized as the Virgin Mary. And for many weeks, at regular intervals, the same vision seized the children, which set off a movement of extraordinary fervor in all of Catholic Europe. A sanctuary was built where the apparition took place, and, close by, a museum to Mary that receives many visitors. Today, Beauraing is a veritable Belgian Lourdes, thus testifying to the endurance of mother-goddess worship on territory often ravaged by invasions and seemingly permeated with Celtic spirituality.

The link with the past is at Walcourt, south of Charleroi, in a country that can no longer be very clearly identified as either French or Walloon. The surroundings are particularly rich in Gallo-Roman remains, but in the center of the town of

Wallencourt stands the basilica of Saint Materne. Tradition claims that this Materne, bishop of Tongres, discovered a statue of the Virgin Mary in this spot and had the first sanctuary built here, which would be rebuilt many times before becoming the present basilica. This statue, if it is indeed authentic, having escaped the wars and the Reformation, is the object of great veneration. But if we reflect a little on the tradition, we would be right in affirming that this "Saint" Materne is none other than the masculinized and canonized (only by the voice of the people!) figure of a Gallo-Roman Matrone discovered in the ground by chance, and identified, like so many others, by popular piety, as a miraculous statue of the Virgin. This only makes the permanence of Goddess worship more evident.

In this exploration of the Goddess's domain, Germany occupies a very particular place. The ancient Germanic cults left hardly any visible traces, destroyed and obliterated as they were by the forced Christianization of Charlemagne and his successors. As to the Virgin Mary, she doesn't seem to have been very important. Certainly, after the Lutheran Reformation, the northern countries did not look upon her very favorably, and the countries of the south that remained Catholic, Bavaria in particular, contain hardly any important sanctuaries devoted to the Mother of God. Germany is not Mary country—that is a fact—but that does not imply that the Goddess of the Beginnings was never honored there at all.

At the time of the Roman Empire, which modern-day western Germany was part of, many sanctuaries were built in new towns, which were really "colonies," like Cologne, and all along the imperial frontier, called the *limes*, for the troops stationed there to use. That is the case in Aalen, east of Stuttgart. The discoveries there have been particularly numerous and interesting, and an outdoor museum has been established, which gives a striking picture of what the *limes* might have been like. Here, the Great Goddess is present, but in an astonishing syncretism. Indeed, she bears the traits of the Celtic Epona, the divine horseback rider, the traits of Diana-Artemis, the inheritor of a Germanic divinity for the wild kingdom, and the traits of the Roman Vesta, who protects the eternal flame. The Limesmuseum is one of the most revealing sites for what has been called Germano-Roman culture.

However, it is in the Rhine region that Germano-Roman vestiges are most numerous, in particular, around Cologne. Pesh has certainly been one of the great centers for pilgrimages in honor of the famous Matronae, these triads of anonymous mother goddesses who testify to a tradition Celtic in origin, and the sanctuary, partially restored, presents a great quantity of these representations, which are also very numerous in eastern France. But as time passed, these primitive Matronae seem to be have merged with a new representation from the East (because many legionaires were originally Easterners), thus making Cybele of Phrygia the universal symbol of the Mother. Local worship of the Matronae resisted foreign influence, however, as another sanctuary shows, the one in Nettersheim, where the triads of women are particularly numerous and moving. Of course, many of these statues, taken from the original site, are found in the Römische-Germanische Museum of Cologne, where their neighbors are the goddesses imported from Rome—Minerva, Venus, Diana, Cybele, of course, but also Isis, herself an eloquent symbol of intransigent maternity—and whose representations are very often prototypical of what will become the Christian Madonna.

Neither are the Scandinavian countries affected to any degree by Mary worship, on account of Lutheranism, and the old divinities of the Germano-Scandinavian pantheon are buried away in the museums. The Uppsala site in Sweden, which was once a great pagan sanctuary, is nothing more than an archaeological curiosity and tourist attraction now. As to the famous Gundestrup Cauldron, at the Aarhus museum in Denmark, that is an entirely Celtic creation, a perfect illustration of the mythology at the time of the druids, with the strange representation of the one whom the Welsh call Rhiannon, the "goddess of the birds." Women hardly play a part in Germanic mythology, with three exceptions: the figure of Freya, in whom we can recognize one of the aspects of Aphrodite; Erda, the Earth personified, who is the equivalent of Gaia; and He, the goddess of the infernal world, who has some of the characteristics of Hecate and others of cruel Persephone, recalling Kali the Black.

But we find Virgin Mary worship again in the Netherlands, a territory very split between Catholics and Calvinists. It is in the extreme south that we find the principal pilgrimage centers, notably at Maastricht, where the Sterre der Zee, also called the Stella Maris, can only be concealing an image of Isis in her bark, in the midst of her passionate quest to find the dismembered body of Osiris. And, north of Maastricht, in Roermond, Our Lady of the Sands is honored in a chapel that has been destroyed and rebuilt many times. Maastricht and Roermond are some distance from the sea, but it seems as though the Virgin there retained some aspect of the ancient goddess of nurturing and healing waters. Not far away flows the Rhine. And isn't it true that this river has its source in those mysterious Alpine regions where delicate transformations give birth to water, this substance that flows throughout the earth and all living organisms, the guardian of the soul of the world?

Divided between three languages and two religions, Switzerland presents a picture similar to that of the Netherlands, and it is clearly in predominantly Catholic, German-speaking Switzerland that Goddess worship held its own. Moreover, this worship goes back to earliest antiquity, as the town of Berne attests to. We know that the name of Berne comes from the Germanic term for "bear." Now, it is in Berne where a small grouping known as "the Goddess of the Bear" was discovered. It is a representation of Gallo-Roman design featuring a woman seated before a bear. This is indisputably the goddess Artio of the Gauls, the result of the evolution of a divine figure symbolized by the bear. It is clearly the Celtic aspect of the eastern Artemis, the mistress of wild animals. In modern-day Berne, no one would think of connecting the name of the town to the worship of this savage goddess anymore, but the unconscious acts by itself. The most visited place in Berne, and the one that Berne residents are most proud of, is the famous Bear Den. This observation needs no commentary.

That doesn't keep the Catholic Swiss from having their Black

Virgin. She is found in Einsiedeln, about forty kilometers south of Zurich, in the middle of the mountains. There again, a vague memory of the savage goddess seems to linger, but she has been entirely Christianized, and the place has become an important pilgrimage site for the Virgin Mother, who protects and nurtures. Tradition has it that a penniless hermit, a certain Meinrad, settled there among the wild animals, and that he was killed by bandits. Where the hermitage was, a monastery now stands, and in the chapel is the interred head of Saint Meinrad, under the feet of one particularly venerated Black Virgin.

There are few sanctuaries in central Europe as celebrated as those of the east. In Hungary, a country both Catholic and Calvinist, there is the especially important ancient sanctuary of Szombathely, near the Austrian border. But this is an entirely pagan site, dedicated to the Isis who came from the shores of the Nile and metamorphosed during her passage to Rome. And, in the Czech Republic, again along the Austrian border, not far from Brno, is another pre-Christian site, dedicated this time to a mother goddess from the early Paleolithic age, of whom there is a statue and who has been called the Venus of Vestonice, from the name of the neighboring village, Dolni Vestonice. This baked-clay Venus is related to the one of Willendorf, but she expresses even more clearly the nurturing aspect of the divinity. She is standing, proudly planted on her legs. Her hips are very large, her face well carved, with clearly marked eyes. Her two breasts are especially prominent, drooping over her belly as if they were heavy with milk. The name Venus does not seem adequate here, because it is indisputably only the maternal aspect that is being emphasized. But given that this region was the primitive melting pot from which the Hallstatt, the first Celtic civilization, came, who can say what form the Goddess took in the imagination of those peoples who would become the Celts?

In Poland, the Catholic country par excellence, squeezed between Lutheranism and Orthodoxy, the image of the Goddess rises from the darkness as the Black Virgin of Czestochowa, in the south, between Wroclaw and Cracow, the great religious metropolis of this region that was also once heavily influenced by the Celts before succumbing to "Slavic charm." Czestochowa is the spiritual center for all of Poland, and Czestochowa's Black Virgin, popularized by an icon that is known worldwide, is a kind of "mother of the afflicted," the latter being the Polish who, after a period of independence—and of conquest, it must be added—found themselves torn apart by the desires of all their neighbors. Supposedly brought back from Palestine in 1384, this Virgin of Czestochowa is, in some way, the very soul of a Poland that, through the vicissitudes of history, searches endlessly for its identity.

Would the border zones between different cultural systems be auspicious places for Great Goddess worship? The case of Medjugorje, in Bosnia-Herzogovina, would seem positive proof. It involves a spot, located south of Mostar, in an indisputably Catholic region that was originally Croatian, but which is in direct contact not only with Orthodox Serbs, but with Islamic Slavs firmly established there since the Ottoman Empire. Here we find no pre-Christian sanctuary, no miraculously discovered statue, but an "apparition" that, though never officially recognized by the Roman Church, nonetheless poses certain questions that are difficult to resolve. The difficulties are compounded because the apparition of the Virgin Mary is, in some way, permanent, and at some moments, very detailed. It all began in 1981. Some children perceived a female form on the mountain that they recognized to be the Virgin and that delivered messages to them. The content of these messages, as is always true in such cases, was very prosaic. However, the phenomenon, reverberating through the media—and the economy!—remains unexplained and can lend itself to multiple interpretations, all equally unsatisfactory as far as reason goes, but all equally plausible. Perhaps these "apparitions" of Medjugorje can be understood as a desperate cry for world peace from the Mother of all humanity. That is, for now, the only observation to make on the subject.

On the other side of the Adriatic, Italy has the densest concentration of ancient religions, and since Roman society was one of the most tolerant with regard to religion, a rich mosaic of Goddess worship developed there. Furthermore, the southern end of the peninsula and Sicily bear heavy marks of Hellenism, since they constituted what has customarily been called "greater" Greece. Thus, we should not be astonished to discover Mediterranean female divinities here in their Greek forms. That is what we find in Agrigente, the primitive Akragas, in Sicily, where three sanctuaries dedicated to Demeter still stand in ruins, which may seem a bit surprising, but which can be explained by the fertility of a volcanic soil constantly turned by the labor pains of an ancient earth goddess. Sicily is covered with feminine sanctuaries. At Gela, there are temples to Demeter, again, and to Athena, in her aspect as divine wisdom. Again in Sicily, at Selinonte, there is a sanctuary to Demeter Malaphoros, "bearer of fruit," an expression that could describe the fertile nature of the goddess, and also allude to her daughter, Kore, eating the pomegranate of Hell, a symbolic episode that is parallel to the one in Genesis concerning the apple of the Tree of Knowledge. But danger threatens, and in this same temple of Demeter, we find a representation of Hecate, the queen of the night, mistress of nightmares and magic spells. As for Syracuse, a curious superimposition transpires there. The Catholic cathedral standing there today is built on the foundations of an ancient temple dedicated to Athena. Here again, no commentary is needed.

This Italian "greater" Greece resurfaces in the north, and we know, moreover, that the Greeks first settled in the center of the peninsula before moving south and leaving such indelible marks on the Pouilles and Sicilian countryside. The area around Naples is simultaneously Greek and Latin. It is, in fact, much more Greek than Latin. The Baia site is particularly rich, since the discoveries there include the remains of a temple to Diana (who is very like the Artemis of Ephesus), a grotto of the Sibyl, that divine prophetess-priestess who can introduce humans to the other world and who thus reveals her regenerative role, and an enclosure dedicated to Hecate, the pale goddess of the *triforia*, where it is possible to enter into pacts with the infernal powers. But we must not forget the temples of Athena and Hera at Paestum, these two complementary aspects of the initiator goddess who reigns in semidarkness near the slopes of Vesuvius, from which the fire of the earth surges, the source of both fertility and destruction. As for Pompeii, the city engulfed by Vesuvius's ashes, for religious centers, it boasts a temple dedicated to a faithful and maternal Isis, as well as a temple to a slightly wild Venus whose sanctuary turned into an authentic bordello, richly decorated with very suggestive frescoes.

Romanization is still more apparent in the north, in Rome and around what has appropriately been called the Eternal City. Like the churches and basilicas dedicated to the Virgin Mary, the sanctuaries dedicated to a female divinity cannot be counted. In seizing on Rome and making it the center of the new religion stemming from the apostles' preachings, Christianity entirely subsumed—and most of the time, entirely unconsciously—not only all the rituals of an earlier paganism, adapting them to its own uses, but also and especially this idea of Bona Mater, which would soon give birth to the concept of Madone, extremely rich in interpretations of all kinds, and charged with all the inner anguish of the human soul with regard to the birth and death of the human being. More than ever, the Virgin Mary would take the place of all the goddesses of antiquity, watering down their traits, giving up their sexuality, but remaining always the one who gives life and nurtures. And when, at San Damiano, the Virgin Mary appeared and made a pear tree blossom in the very heart of winter, she was no more and no less than the "baptized" image of the Roman Ceres, goddess of fruit and the harvest—Demeter, of course, but even more: the mother goddess of all times and all countries.

Italy is a propitious country for the worship of the Madone, and its Catholic roots can only favor the construction of sanctuaries dedicated to the Virgin Mary, the development of artwork taking for its themes the birth of the Virgin, the Annunciation, the Nativity, the Assumption, without forgetting the grieving pietà, or Our Lady of the Seven Sorrows. Also, we must take into account the numerous miracles that are attributed to the Virgin Mother, and the many apparitions of Mary, as witnessed by her devotees—though rarely ratified by the official Church, which is very cautious in this regard and very conscious of Italian devotees' propensity for fantastic imaginings, so well have they been nourished on traditions handed down since the beginning of time.

The Iberian Peninsula, and especially Spain, possesses a comparable tradition. But there, the problem is clearly more complex, because on top of the primitive Iberian foundations— Celtic foundations in the northwest—are superimposed very different, even contradictory, cultural layers: the Carthaginian, and thus Phoenician influence, with its Semitic origins; the very strong Roman influence; the Islamic influence, without which Spain cannot be explained; the limited but no less real Basque influence; and, in addition, the Jewish influence, particularly important in the Middle Ages, even if the Jews had as their base an exemplary community that knew no equivalent, before the stakes of the Inquisition were set on fire. In this melting pot out of which emerges the contemporary Spanish nation, a strange, heterogeneous assemblage, taking cover under an intransigent and ostentatious Catholicism, it is very difficult to locate the worship of the Virgin as a function of the various pre-Christian cults. It is especially in Catalonia, a country that escaped Islamic domination, that this worship seems most ancient. Indeed, throughout Catalonia, the number of Black Virgins is impressive. Where did they come from? Probably from very ancient Great Goddess religions. But none of these Black Virgins has acquired as much fame or aroused as much fervor as the Virgin of Montserrat, near Barcelona, this center of Iberian spirituality.

Montserrat is a very popular pilgrimage site, and the Catalan museum of Barcelona is known for containing the most extraordinary collection of Black Virgins in all of Europe. Of course, once they have been displaced, lifted from their original sites where they served supporting and complementary functions, these statues do not have the same mysterious value as those that remain in sanctuaries, but they constitute eloquent testimony to the enduring worship of the Virgin of the Beginnings in a country that has so often been wracked by invasions and reversals in circumstance. It is impossible to believe that the memory of this ancient female goddess could be erased from the popular imagination. Indeed, throughout Spain, during certain festivals, especially in February, there are ceremonies accompanied by processions that seem to fall within the domain of women. That is the case in Escatron, not far from Saragossa, in Zamarramata and Sotosalbos, near Segovia, and in Miranda del Castamar, near Salamanca. Thus, ancient Spain reawakens at the time of the festival of Saint Agatha, and this Agatha is none other than a very archaic epithet (meaning "good") for the Bona Dea of the past, whatever name is given to her. Within the collective unconscious, Spain has retained the memory of a cult rendered to the universal Great Mother.

The inhabitants of Portugal did not spring from exactly the same mold as the Spaniards. The Phoenician, Roman, and Islamic influences were not as strong there. In contrast, the native elements, probably Celtic as in Galicia, were maintained over the centuries. Classical antiquity has left traces there, in particular at Evora, in the south, where the ruins of a temple to Diana survive, upon which later stood a mosque, at the time of the so-called Arab occupation. Diana probably conceals an indigenous divinity, a mistress of wild animals, a sort of queen of the night analogous to the primitive Artemis, the one who demanded the blood of the young travelers in Tauris who dared to come to her sanctuary.

It is not clear what the Virgin Mary requires of the many pilgrims who gather at Fatima, in central Portugal, in a poor and disadvantaged region. She is content—or rather, the clergy who watch over her sanctuary are content—with a generous offering dropped into a sacred enclosure that has become, along with Lourdes, one of the most important centers of pilgrimage in all of Christendom. Here, everything is recent. It was in 1917 that the apparitions of the Virgin took place, to three children standing near an oak tree. From there, a whole mythology was constructed, sometimes appearing very questionable because of its clearly fascist political repercussions and its financial takings that bordered on the scandalous. The cult of Our Lady of Fatima has developed over the years, nourished by strange phenomena that have remained inexplicable, but the apparitions of the

Virgin to the three shepherds has never received official recognition by the papal authorities. More than ever, Fatima is a symbol, the symbol of a popular fervor deeply rooted in the collective unconscious. Even if it never openly admits to it, humanity is engaged in a perpetual quest for the Mother who nourishes her children, consoles them in their misfortune, and guides them along the shores leading to the other world.

11
FAR WESTERN EUROPE

What touches upon the northwest of Europe, that is, all of the British Isles, we need to set apart, because the relative distance of these islands from the Continent has always contributed to the continuation of a state of mind that goes back to pre-Christian epochs, even beyond the Celtic period, a state of mind that manifests itself as much in the customs as in a written and oral tradition which is particularly rich in thought. Here, the spiritual life, entirely permeated with Christianity as it is, seems very different from that of the continent, and this is true as much among the various Protestant groups as among the Catholics, even if these latter display—at least at the present—an unfailing submissiveness to the Roman authority.

What is surprising about Great Britain is the complete absence of a place of pilgrimage dedicated to the Virgin Mary. Now, Anglicanism, the official religion of the United Kingdom, over which the queen reigns, has never rejected the worship of Jesus' mother. It is true that the influence of Scottish Calvinists, who are called Presbyterians, as well as that of the Welsh Methodists, has contributed to decline of Mary worship, especially over the course of the religious troubles in the sixteenth and seventeenth centuries, and the country's Catholic minority, despite its fair

GODDESS SANCTUARIES IN GREAT BRITAIN

amount of power, has never succeeded in reversing this trend. Worship of the Virgin took refuge in popular ancestral customs and in the evocation of a pre-Christian past.

We know that the Celts, the incontestable occupants of the British Isles since at least 500 B.C., built no temples at all, and that their druids officiated in natural surroundings, in what were called the *nemetons*. We also know that they did not want to represent divinity using anthropomorphic figures, and that they contented themselves with symbolic or geometric forms, thus following their predecessors, who built the megaliths and represented the funerary Great Goddess with lines, curved, concentric or spiraling, on the walls of numerous Neolithic burial mounds. We must wait for the Roman conquest to witness the appearance of stone temples and statues representing the divinities, which are the result of a synthesis between local beliefs and forms borrowed from Mediterranean art. Because if the Romans did not really conquer the British Isles in any profound way, they nevertheless left very important vestiges, in a style we could call Anglo-Roman.

The best known Anglo-Roman ruins are those in Bath, a much visited spa, the ancient Aquae Sulis, which bore the name of the goddess Sulis, comparable to the Gallo-Roman Minerva. This Sulis, whose statues are found in Bath, is, in fact, the Sun personified, female, as would be expected in the ancient Celtic languages. Thus, her patronage of the healing springs of Bath was essential, even if the wisdom and the knowledge attributed to Minerva were added to her principal functions. Everything seems to have happened as if to incorporate the primitive Great Goddess under this name, the one who dispenses warmth, fertility, and as a result, life, and also, knowledge.

In southern Wales, at Caerleon-on-Wysg (made famous by the tales of the Round Table), the ancient Isca Silurum, a strategic Roman position in the midst of the Silurian people, we find Anglo-Roman vestiges as well, scattered throughout a very large area. And there a temple once stood, dedicated to the goddess Nemesis, the result of a curious Greco-Roman-Celtic syncretism. In Greece, Nemesis was one of the functional aspects of the

Great Goddess, by whatever name she was called, in this case representing vengeance or immanent justice. In the British Isles, she no doubt embodied the very abstract concept of destiny, which the Greeks called *ananke,* and the Romans *fatum.* It seems that the occupying Romans were very keen on this notion of destiny, no doubt as a result of their contact, as amicable as it was antagonistic, with the British populations and their metaphysical speculations. For sanctuaries dedicated to Nemesis are not uncommon in Great Britain. We find one in Chester, another important Roman settlement between Wales and the north, and this sanctuary is neighbor to a temple to Minerva, who here again, it seems, embodies all those functions attributed to the female divinity.

To protect themselves from incursions by the Picts and the British from the north, the Romans constructed an immense stone wall, known as Hadrian's Wall, between the Irish Sea and the North Sea, going from Carlisle to Newcastle-on-Tyne, and flanked by imposing fortresses in which the garrisons lived. One of these fortresses, situated in modern-day Carrawburgh, about forty kilometers west of Newcastle, was built near a sacred fountain, under the wall itself, upon which there appears an inscription and an engraving revealing that it was dedicated to the goddess Coventina. This goddess is shown stretched out on a sort of island, her breasts prominent, a palm leaf in her right hand. This is the only mention of this Coventina. No doubt she masks a divinity that protects sweet water, a goddess whose principle functions were to bring life and fertility to those who came beseeching her.

The worship of springs and sacred wells is always very important across the entire expanse of Great Britain. These fountains were often Christianized by associating them with the name of a saint, and especially a female saint, which clearly indicates the earlier patronage of a female divinity. Moreover, fresh water is an object of true devotion in a more general way. If we are to believe popular legend, many small rivers are linked in one way or another to a magical or divine being. That is the case with the Severn, which is the Roman Sabrina and the Welsh Hafren;

223

with the Mersey, consecrated to the goddess Belisama, the "very brilliant"; with the Clyde, which conceals the name of the goddess Cluta; and again, with the variations Braint and Brent, in which it is not hard to recognize the name of Brigantia, otherwise known as the Irish triple Brigit, but, in fact, pan-Celtic, similar to the Gallo-Roman Minerva.

The legends recounted throughout the British territory involving a water fairy, or a white lady, or a sorceress who lives in a palace under the surface of a lake are reminders of very archaic rituals dedicated to the Goddess of the Beginnings. Certain places have held on to this tradition more firmly than others, notably in Scotland or Wales, mountainous regions a bit cut off from socioreligious change. One of the most famous of these places is the Bala lake, in Gwynedd (northwest Wales), also called Llyn Tegid in Welsh, not far from the town of Bala. According to the legend of the bard Taliesin, it is there, in the middle of the water, where Keridwen had her home, who was one of the somewhat frightening faces of the divine Mother, possessor of all the secrets of the world, unwitting mother to the hero of this story. But many other lakes harbor marvelous palaces, like the one in Llyn Barfod, also in Wales, where a fairy people reside whose women can marry mortals, provided the latter agree to respect certain prohibitions, Melusinian in nature. And what can be said about that mysterious Black Annis, that "Anna the Black," who wanders in the night above Yorkshire, indiscriminately bringing joy and misfortune, according to whether the humans are well or badly disposed toward her? She is none other than the western aspect of Anaitis of the Near East, the one we find in Armorican Brittany under the name of "Saint" Anne, and in Ireland, under the name of Dana.

The Goddess's ambiguity, which the legend of Keridwen and Taliesin point up, is illustrated in an exemplary fashion by those strange representations found on the walls of certain churches, only in Ireland and in the west of Great Britain, representations that have been given the Gaelic name of Sheela-na-gig. It is difficult to date them. Some of them go back to the pre-Christian epochs, others to the Middle Ages, until about the twelfth century. They are distinguished by a remarkable consistency in expression and technique. It is always a matter of a female form viewed from the front, with a more or less frightening head, more or less developed breasts, and her two hands invariably spreading the lips of her vulva, thus exposing a deep and mysterious cavity. Clerical and moralizing commentaries consider these representations of lust in its most demonic aspect. Alternatively, archaeological commentaries consider them fertility goddesses. It seems that either interpretation leads to a third.

Actually, the exaggeration of the vulvar opening is an invitation to be swallowed up into the depths of the maternal womb of the woman. This then invites comparison with the architecture of certain megalithic cairns in which a long vagina-like corridor leads to a funerary chamber evoking the womb, where the bones and ashes of the deceased are deposited. And the fact that, at a certain time of the year, generally at winter solstice, the rising sun penetrates this chamber through the corridor and lights it up entirely makes us think in terms of a symbolic ritual of regeneration, of rebirth. Given these circumstances, the Sheela-na-gig would be the image of the mother goddess who takes creatures back into herself to let them grow again and to give them another life in another world. Thus, it is not astonishing to find these representations on the exterior walls of churches, very often beside a cemetery.

Some 115 examples of Sheela-na-gigs have been counted in all of Great Britain, but the most famous is certainly the one found on the south wall of the Saint Mary and Saint David church in Kilpeck (Herefordshire), twelve kilometers southwest of Hereford in the direction of Abergavenny, on the border between Wales and England. But others are just as characteristic, notably on the church of the Holy Trinity at Holdgate (Shropshire), on the church of Saint Lawrence in Church-Stretton (Shropshire), and on the church of Saint Catherine (there are even two of them there) in Tugford (Shropshire), also on the Welsh border, as well as on the church of Saint Michael at Oxford. But it is sometimes difficult to discover them because in these puritanical countries, modesty requires that they never be indicated with any kind of a sign.

The Sheela-na-gig is just as common in Ireland, but, as on the neighboring island, she is often been kept an absolute secret. It was not until recently that two Sheelas made a discrete appearance in the National Archaeological Museum of Dublin, in the room where the most beautiful treasures of Irish art are shown. But visitors have to know what they are looking for. And, at the Cashel site, visited constantly by tourists from all over the world because of its magnificent location, the exceptional Cormac chapel, and the grandiose ruins of the cathedral, who would imagine that on the wall of the restored choir school building, now serving as a museum, could be found a superb representation of this goddess opening wide her vaginal lips? In Ireland, the burden of Catholicism has obscured a good number of so-called pagan divinities. But the latter do themselves no disservice by springing up behind the stereotypical image of the Virgin Mary.

The Virgin Mary is particularly honored in the Irish Republic, which is ninety-five percent Catholic, but outside of a recent sanctuary in county Mayo, which is more a commercial operation than a spiritual one, there exist practically no places of pilgrimage in honor of the Theotokos in Ireland. Nevertheless, at every curve in the road, in the smallest village, we can discover a "grotto of Lourdes." The artistic taste displayed here is more than a little doubtful, but they testify to the faith of the Irish in Our Lady. The fact is that Lourdes has cast such a spell over the Irish that they have not felt the need for a Mary sanctuary on their own soil. On the other hand, they have annexed Lourdes, so to speak, where great numbers of them go in pilgrimage and where they have had a traditional, authentic Celtic cross erected. In fact, "Notre Dame" takes on very diverse aspects in which the tradition inherited from the druidic past mixes harmoniously with the most rigorous Catholicism.

A meaningful example of this is the town of Armagh, in the part of Ulster that belongs to the United Kingdom, the seat of the archbishop primate of Ireland (Anglican just as well as Catholic), thus a holy city for certain, which honors the memory of its founder, Saint Patrick. The name Armagh means "powerful

Macha," and this town was once a primitive Ulate settlement, their principal fortress being a few kilometers away, at the site now called Emania, and which was formerly called Emain Macha. Now, Macha is one of the aspects of the ancient Gaelic mother goddess. The myth concerning her tells how Macha was going to find a certain Crunniuc, a poor widowed peasant who had many young children. She proposed marriage to him, promising him wealth and happiness on the condition that he never speak of her to anyone. Here we can recognize a familiar prohibition, Melusinian in nature. Everything went well until one day when, during an assembly of the Ulates, the king of Ulster claimed that no one was capable of beating his horses in a race. Crunniuc, no doubt a little too drunk on mead, rose to the challenge, saying that his wife could run faster than the king's horses. Of course, the king made him go find Macha and prove his words. Now, Macha was pregnant and asked for a delay, which the king refused. So she ran, beat the king's horses with her speed, but died on the spot, giving birth to twins, Emain Macha, from which the name of the royal fortress comes. But before dying, she uttered a curse against the Ulates and their descendants, according to which they would suffer the pains of childbirth for nine days every year.

This Macha has been recognized as one aspect of the Great Goddess under one of her many names. She is called Badb, Morrigan, and, again, Brigit the "powerful" as well, and she has been compared to the Gallo-Roman Epona, protectress of horses, as well as the Welsh goddess of riders, Rhiannon. Under the name of Brigit, daughter of the god Dagda, goddess of the arts, skilled crafts, poetry, and wisdom, she reappeared in the Christian era as "Saint" Brigit of Kildare, considered to be the founder of an abbey for both men and women and whose responsibility it is to watch over the eternal flame. At Kildare, the vestiges of this monastery are many, and there we also find the fountain of Saint Brigit, which is supposed to be miraculous. Kildare is another holy city for Catholic Ireland, a pilgrimage site for many. What is more, we know that Brigit is the second patron saint of Ireland, after Saint Patrick. Now, neither of these two

ATLANTIC OCEAN

■ Grianan
Ailech

ULSTER

■ Sligo
Maeve's Mound
(Knocknarea)
Carrowmore

Emain ■ Armagh
Macha

Rathcroghan *(Cruachan)*

Lough Crew

CONNAUGHT

Knowth ■ Dowth
Newgrange
Boyne
Tara ■
Liffey

Galway

Shannon
Clonfert
Killinaboy
(Sheela-na-gig)
Kildare
(Brigit)
Dublin *(Museum)*

LEINSTER

IRISH SEA

Grania's Bed
MUNSTER
Kilkenny

Paps of Ana
Cashel
(Sheela-na-gig)

50 km

GODDESS SITES IN IRELAND
(Locations of Discoveries, Monuments, and Museums)

"saints" are officially recognized by the Roman Church, which shows how well Christianity and paganism get along together here. Indeed, the name of Kildare (*cill-dara* in Gaelic) means "hermitage of the oaks," which suggests the existence of a sacred enclosure from the time of the druids. As to the "fires" that Brigit is responsible for maintaining, they more closely resemble the fires of Beltaine, the Celtic festival at the beginning of May, than the Easter fire lit by Saint Patrick on the hill of Slane in 433, the date that marks the conversion of Ireland to the Christian faith. But that doesn't in anyway impede Brigit from having many sanctuaries, even very modest ones, as well as sacred springs, throughout the country. We must remember that Brigit, under her other name of Boann (from *bo-vinda*, the "white cow"), is a goddess who provides fertility and wealth. She has given her name to the Boyne River, sacred river par excellence, on the banks of which still stand the great megalithic sanctuaries of Newgrange (Sidh-na-Brugh or Brugh-na-Boinn), Dowth, and Knowth, where the Goddess of the Beginnings is represented by geometric forms, especially spirals and concentric circles that evoke the maternal uterus, the original womb of the world. Moreover, the festival of "Saint" Brigit, at the beginning of February, coincides not only with the Christian Candlemas, but also with the druidic holiday of Imbolc, the middle of the winter season. That says something about the importance of this "Saint" Brigitte of Kildare to the spiritual life of the Irish. She is a little "Notre Dame of Ireland."

But she is a somewhat unnerving Our Lady, because she is continually changing form and function. Mistress of the water and the fire, she is also the sun, with the traits of the young Grainne, prototype of the beautiful Isolde the Blonde, in fact a formidable enchantress who has the power to cast spells (the mysterious druidic *geisa*) over the man she has chosen in order to lure him to her. This Grainne, or Grania, has a name that derives from the Gaelic term meaning "sun," and many megalithic monuments are dedicated to her throughout all of Ireland. What is more, another fortress of the Ulates, situated on a summit overlooking the town of Derry and the north of Donegal, is named Grianan Ailech. Its circular construction and privileged location suggest that this residence of Ulster kings beginning from the seventh century was once a sort of solar temple. Now the sun, which gives warmth and life, which is also itself a healer, can cause death by its fierce rays, unless it contents itself by putting humans into a state between life and death. Then, the Lady is going to change her aspect and her name, becoming the mythic queen of Connaught, known as Maeve (Medb in Gaelic, whom Shakespeare made Queen Mab), which means "drunken ecstasy," but also "medium."

This queen Maeve occupies an important place in ancient Irish epics. Wife of King Aillil of Connaught, she is the one who actually holds sovereign power, the king being only a figurehead for the society she represents. And we are told that she "lavished the friendship of her thighs on every warrior she needed to assure the success of an expedition." Warrior queen, devourer and castrater, cunning and cruel, she is presented as the model of sovereignty, but this sovereignty is ambiguous, since it takes place as much on the sexual as on the political level. Thus, we may ask ourselves if the image of the Sheela-na-gig doesn't suit her perfectly, especially the one that can be seen on the ruins of the abbey of Killinaboy, near Corofin, in county Clare, and thus in Connaught. Doesn't the Sheela promise, in effect, "the friendship of her thighs" to her devotees? The name of Queen Maeve, however, remains attached to two sites important to the Gaelic tradition. The first is that of Cruachan, Rathcroghan today, in county Roscommon. This is the site where ancient accounts locate the residence of Aillil and Maeve, and certain texts even specify that under the Celtic fortress of Cruachan can be found a sidh, a megalithic mound, the supposed location of the otherworld haunted by the gods and heroes. Thus, Maeve is clearly linked with the Irish druidic divinities. The second site is Knocknarea, a small mountain above Sligo, overlooking the ocean to the west and the vast Carrowmore megaliths to the east, the greatest funerary enclosure of prehistoric Ireland. On the summit of Knocknarea stands a dry-stone cairn that is called the "tomb of Maeve." Now, for various reasons, no archaeologist has wanted to undertake the excavation of this megalithic mound that would, nonetheless, provide important information on the civilization of the dolmen builders. Everything goes on as if there were a magic prohibition on this mound, and we cannot help but note that this is clearly a matter of a sacred place. Moreover, popular custom calls for each individual who climbs the summit of Knocknarea to bring along a small stone and deposit it on the cairn. Isn't that evidence of the astonishing and unconscious permanence of the worship of the Goddess of the Beginnings?[1]

If we are to believe the long mythological tradition of Ireland, conveyed to us through written accounts of Christian monks from the early Middle Ages, the name of the Goddess of the Beginnings was Dana. The great Irish gods whose actions these accounts involve were the Tuatha de Danaan, the "peoples of the goddess, Dana," who came from the "islands north of the world," clearly a symbolic location, The name of Dana, often simplified to Anu or Anna (and to Don in the Welsh tradition), indisputably recalls the Carthaginian Tanit, the Tanaïtis and Semitic Nanna of the Near East, the Indian AnnaPurna, the Roman Anna Parenna, the Greek Danae and her daughters, the Danaides, as well as one of the names of the Greeks, the Danaeans, and of course, the names of the rivers Don and Danube, without mentioning Anne, the mother of the Virgin Mary, about which the canonical Gospels say nothing, but Breton traditions are particularly long-winded. And, not far from Killarney, in county Kerry, are twin summits, called the "Paps of Anu," where the Irish sometimes go in a strange pilgrimage. There are too many coincidences for this collection of similar names surrounding the Goddess of the Beginnings to be the result of chance, even if Semitic terms are not usually compared to Indo-European ones. Because they themselves are universal, the divinities laugh at racial differences.

Pre-Christian Celtic spirituality is characterized by an absolute and unconditional refusal of any concept giving rise to duality. For the druids, there was neither good nor bad, but complete freedom of choice for human beings in two directions, that of negative forces and that of positive forces. This *monism* is found again in the doctrine of Pelagius, in the fourth century, the British theologian who argued against Saint Augustine in favor of absolute free will. This tendency is manifest in the way in which the Irish live and practice Christianity (and the Celts, too, in a more general way). Blind faith in human will to secure one's salvation can only lead to a complete surpassing of the individual and the negation of any principle of absolute Evil. Under these conditions, the image of the Great Goddess can only be "black" or "white," her gaze turned upward or downward. That is why the image of the Theotokos that springs from the Irish collective unconscious, no matter how marked it is by endless conflict between deviationist Protestantism and steadfast adherence to Catholic orthodoxy, is very different from the one that is honored on the European continent. The Virgin of the Irish is not necessarily the Virgin of the Armorican Bretons, even though they often share the same characteristics. And popular Irish tradition makes no mistake in making use of a sort of female ghost, given the name of *banshee*, literally, "woman of *shee*," this *shee* being the Anglicization of the Gaelic term, *sidh*, which means "peace," but which designates the otherworld, the one found in the mysterious universe of the megalithic mounds. Thus, the *banshee*, is, in some way, the folkloric image of the ancient Goddess. Those who encounter her may fear her, because she often announces misfortune, but they may also invoke her, because she is the all-powerful of the female divinities of the past. She ceaselessly wanders the Irish countryside, especially at night. So perhaps, this is Our Lady of the Night, the one who was thrown into the darkness by a patriarchal society, but who continues to haunt the dreams of humans in their endless quest for their Mother?

Essential evidence for exactly this image of the Irish Virgin of virgins exists. It is found in the cathedral—Anglican—of Kilkenny, the seat of the ancient bishopric of Ossory (the name means "realm of the serfs," which is typically Celtic), but out of the way, hidden in a corner of the sanctuary, since it is a matter of an engraved plaque dating from the twelfth century, which belonged to the ancient building and that was moved during the nineteenth-century restoration. Here we find an entirely odd representation of the Trinity. Generally, the Trinity is composed of God the Father holding between his knees the Cross on which is nailed the Son, and over his head is the dove that symbolizes the Holy Spirit. Here, in this Saint Canice cathedral, a mother goddess replaces the father god, and on her right appears a bird resembling much more closely the one found on the famous Gundestrup Cauldron (one of those birds of the goddess Rhiannon who puts the living to sleep and awakens the dead) than the usual dove. If there is something to see in Ireland, it is this modest bas-relief relegated to a place among second-rate archaeological curiosities. Nevertheless, it lets us understand how the Venus of Lespugue and Our Lady of Lourdes are the two faces of the very same Goddess of the Beginnings.

NOTES

Introduction

1. See J. Markale, *Women of the Celts,* trans.A. Mygind, C. Hauch, and P. Henry (Rochester, Vt.: Inner Traditions, 1986).
2. André de Smet, *La Grande Déesse n'est pas morte* (Paris, 1983), p. 81. We should point out that the author is actually a Catholic priest.
3. Ibid.
4. Ibid., pp. 81–82.
5. On this subject of Lilith, see J. Markale, *Mélusine* (Paris; Albin Michel, 1993).
6. Walter Schubart, *Eros et religion* (Paris: Fayard, 1972), p. 36.
7. André de Smet, *La Grand Déesse,* p. 117.
8. Ibid., pp. 120–21.
9. This will be found again in the Middle Ages in the theme of the Holy Grail, of which the written form, on the manuscripts, is *sangréal*, with the double meaning "Holy Grail" [*saint Graal*] or "royal blood" [*sang royal*]. And the Grail is supposed to contain the blood of Jesus.
10. This is perhaps the real cause of Judas's betrayal. The ridiculous sum of thirty pieces of silver effectively rules out financial interest. Rather, it is because, according to Judas, Jesus was supporting a cursed religion that the Iscariot decided to deliver him to the representatives of the official religion.
11. See Jacques Lacarrière, *Les Gnostiques,* (Paris; Albin Michel, n.d.)

12. Christiane Marchello-Nizia, trans. *La Légende arthurienne* (Paris: Laffont, 1989), p. 132.
13. And not "In the beginning was the Word." It is not a question of time since God is eternal. Since everything is contained in the origin, why should only the Word exist at the beginning of time? This Word *logos* is only the creative breath inherent to the eternal God. This argument is clearly gnostic, but not to acknowledge it would be to call the edifice of Christian dogma into doubt.
14. Grillot de Givry, *Lourdes, ville initiatique* (Paris, 1979), p. 30.
15. Ibid., p. 29.
16. Ibid., p. 31.
17. *The Golden Ass*, Paul Valette trans. (Paris, 1947), 12.3–4.
18. Catherine Millot, *Horsexe, essai sur le transsexualisme* (Paris, 1983), p. 79.

Chapter 1

1. This is the title I gave to one of the chapters of my work, *Women of the Celts*. Also see my study, *Mélusine*, with regard to the relationship between Mélusina and Lilith.
2. See J. Markale, *The Grail*, (Rochester, Vt.: Inner Traditions, 1999), as well as *Le Cycle du Graal*, (Paris: Pygmalion, 1992), second period, 1993, a complete rewriting of all the texts relative to the Arthurian legend.
3. Paule Salomon, "L'émergence du couple androgyne," in *Question de* 92 (Paris: Albin Michel, 1993), p. 37.
4. Stella Cherry, *A Guide to Sheela-na-gigs* (Dublin: National Museum, 1992), p. 2. This little work includes a list of all the Sheelas, as well as an important bibliography on the subject.
5. Marija Gimbutas, "The 'Monstrous Venus' of Prehistory," *In All Her Names*, J. Campbell and C. Musès eds. (San Francisco: HarperSanFrancisco, 1992), p. 42.
6. Rosé Ercole, *Le Premier Langage de l'homme* (Paris, 1988), p. 89. Numerous illustrations of this theme can be found in this work devoted to prehistoric Corsica.
7. It is necessary to note that this Venus of Laussel was presented to the Academy of Medicine (its discoverer was a doctor) where, in this regard, a gynecologist brought up the "steatopygia" of certain African women, the Bochimans in particular, that is, the accumulation of fat in the region of the buttocks. At the Musée de l'Homne in Paris, there is a life-size casting of Sarah Bartmann, the famous Hottentot Venus from

the beginning of this century.

8. Joseph Campbell, "The Mystery Number of the Goddess," *In All Her Names*, p. 101.

9. Ibid., pp. 100–101.

Chapter 2

1. At present many monuments have been restored and rebuilt according to their original plan, largely because stones were found right at their bases or in the vicinity. Such is the case with the cairn at Dissignac in Saint-Nazaire (Loire-Atlantique), at Gavrinis in Larmor-Baden (Morbihan), and the famous Table des Marchands of Locmariaquer (Morbihan), and the whole megalithic structure of Bougon (Deux-Sèvres), and, at least in part, with the great cairn of Barnenez in Plouézoc'h (Finistère).

2. In my work on *Carnac et l'énigma de l'Atlantide*, (Paris: Pygmalion, 1988) I have developed an entire hypothesis on the origin of megalithic constructions, which could very well be the work of survivors of a catastrophe that would have engulfed Atlantis. It is only hypothesis, but it is based upon interesting findings.

3. The serpent represents the gynecocratic religion of the Goddess struggling against the phallocratic religion of Yahweh characterized by its absolute prohibitions. This is one of the plausible interpretations—and not the least plausible of them— of "original sin."

4. See Markale, *Mélusine*.

5. L'Helgouach, *Préhistoire de la Bretagne*, pp. 310–12.

6. Fernand Niel, *Dolmens et menhirs* (Paris, 1957), p. 105.

7. See Georges Dumézil, *Romans de Scythie et d'alentour* (Paris: Payot, 1978), as well as *Le Livre des héros* (Paris: Gallimard-Unesco, 1965–89). Also see J. C. Lozac'hmeur, *Fils de la veuve* (Villegenon, 1990).

8. Alfred Jarry, "La princesse Mandragore," in the *Tapisseries* collection.

Chapter 3

1. In a very strange—and truly encoded—work on a so-called search of the country of the "ants who find gold" in the western Himalayas (on the borders of Pakistan and India), entitled *L'Or des fourmis* (Paris: Laffont, 1984) Michel Peissel is not far from believing himself to have rediscovered the mysterious people of the Dardicae, cited by Herodotus in relation

to the Amazons. These people are, without a doubt, white and Indo-European, in the midst of Asiatic populations. Are they the last survivors of the primitive Aryans? These people of Minaros (their current name) have an Indo-European language, matriarchal customs, notably, polyandry, and a very archaic religion that is feminine in nature. "The two principle divinities of the Minaros . . . are Gyantse-Lhmamo and Shiringmen-Lhamo, the fairy-goddess of Fortune and the fairy-goddess of Fertility, respectively. Two women. . . . The principle divinity, called Gyantse-Lhamo in Tibetan, and Mun-Gyantse in Minaro, which means "fairy embracing all," resides . . . on the summit of a montain" (p. 118).

2. Except, let us remember, in the Celtic and Germanic languages.
3. André Varagnac, *L'Art gaulois* (La Pierre-qui-Vire [Yonne]: Zodiaque, 1956), pp. 220–21.
4. On the subject of Gallic coins and their significance, see Lancelot Lengyel, *L'Art gaulois dans les médailles* (Paris, 1954), a fundamental work constructed around numerous enlargements of Gallic coins found in the Cabinet des Médailles of the National Library of Paris; also, by the same author, *Le Secret des Celtes*, (Forcalquier, 1969), a very ambitious thesis in which certain interpretations rely entirely upon the author's imagination. This book's interest rests in the meticulous description of raised details on Gallic coins and their comparison with elements of Irish mythology.
5. It is not only a matter of the Breton peninsula, but also of the neighboring English Channel and the Atlantic, from the Seine to the Garonne (in Gaulish, *Aremorica* means "turned toward the sea").
6. Cabinet des Médailles, Paris.
7. Ibid.
8. Ibid.
9. Ibid. See L. Lengyel, *L'Art gaulois dans les médailles*, plate 60, fig. 436.
10. Archaeological Museum of Bourges.
11. Orléans History Museum, Orléans.
12. The ancient Indo-European sound *qw*, which was maintained in Latin and in Gaelic Celtic, became *p* in Greek and in the Brythonic Celtic languages (Gaulish, Breton, and Welsh).
13. See J. Markale, *L'Epopéé celtique en Bretagne* (Paris: Payot, 1985), 3rd edition.
14. See J. Markale, *L'Epopéé celtique d'Irlande* (Paris: Payot, 1993), new edition. [The Ulates, or Ulaides, were the people of Ulster.]

15. See Markale, *Women of the Celts,* pp. 93–103.
16. This statuette is part of the collection of the Bretagne Museum, Rennes.
17. Kept in the Dijon Archaeological Museum.
18. See Markale, *L'Epopée celtique d'Irlande.*
19. The Latin inscription, as well as the visible workings of the spring, date from the seventeenth century.
20. I do not believe this statue is authentic. It resembles nothing else. It must be the work of a forger from the beginning of the eighteenth century, commissioned by the count of Lannion. But it must replace a more ancient statue that was the true "couarde," the object of this erotic cult denounced by the clergy of the period.
21. Paul-Marie Duval, *Les Dieux de la Gaule* (Paris: Payot, 1976), p. 106.
22. See Markale, *L'Epopée celtique en Bretagne*, pp. 27–42, and *Women of the Celts,* pp. 111–117. This "mistress of the birds" reappears in the tales of the Round Table in the features of the famous fairy, Morgan. See Markale, *Le Cycle du Graal*, vol. 4, *La Fée Morgane.*
23. Varagnac, *L'Art gaulois*, p. 321.

Chapter 4

1. Actually, in the sixth century B.C., Buddhism delivered an analogous message, but for an Oriental society completely different from classical European society, insisting more on *compassion*, that is, *sympathy* ("to suffer together"), than on the merging of beings that Christian *agape* supposes. The suffering of Christ on the Cross does not represent a single share, but is the subsumption of all human misery by one being who sacrifices himself for the pure love of others in order to free them from the weight of destiny.
2. Moreover, very often the persecutions against the Christians were provoked by zealots of Cybele, who saw them as dangerous rivals. That was the case in Vienne (Isère) notably, and Lyon, where Metroaic worship was solidly established.
3. This statue has nothing to do with the drawing executed in 1778 by Faujas de Saint-Fond, which is supposed to represent the ancient statue of Puy burned during the Revolution. But this drawing takes into account the Virgin's dress. The rustic replica of Notre-Dame-du-Puy belonged to a private individual in Craponne-sur-Arzon (Haute-Loire). I have seen it myself, but I don't know what has become of it. The only photo of it

is found in the work of E. Saillens, *Nos Vierges noires* (Paris: 1945), figs. 1 and 2, after p. 274, a front view, and in profile.

4. Statue discovered in 1976 in an attic. Photo published in Jacques Bonvin, *Vierges noires* (Paris, 1988), plate following page 160.

5. Grillot de Givry, *Lourdes, ville initiatique.*

Chapter 6

1. Saillens, *Nos Vierges noires*, p. 57.
2. Ibid., p. 58.
3. For more details on this subject, see J. Markale, *Chartres et l'énigme des druides* (Paris: Pygmalion, 1988).
4. Anonymous report published in the review, *Cosmos* (1980), p. 161.
5. Ibid., pp. 161–62.
6. This is the case at Bé-er-Sant ("tomb of the Saint") in the forest of Floranges (Morbihan), where the socks and slippers of children are left so that they will be able to walk correctly, or at the "tomb of the Girl" in the forest of Teillay (Ille-et-Vilaine and Loire-Atlantique) where women who want to marry or win back a man leave one of their undergarments.
7. On this subject, see J. Markale, *Rennes-le-Château et l'énigme de l'or maudit* (Paris: Pygmalion, 1989).
8. Certain psychomedical studies on the behavior of Nicolazic suggest that he was the victim of attacks of alcholic delirium.
9. *Petite histoire de Notre-Dame-de-Montligeon*, (n.p., 1938), p. 8.
10. François Bournand, *La Sainte Vierge dans les beaux-arts* (Paris, 1895), p. 266.

Introduction (Part 2)

1. Isabelle Franco, *Mythes et dieux, le souffle dud soleil* (Paris: Pygmalion, 1996), p. 127.

Chapter 8

1. Ibid., pp. 142–43.
2. Here we again find the arrangement of the megalithic cairn, in which the funerary chamber represents the womb, and the corridor the vaginal passage. See J. Markale, *Dolmens et menhirs* (Paris: Payot, 1995).

Chapter 9

1. More than one hundred of these female representations are now kept in the Archaeological Museum of Athens, and they

testify not only to the worship of the mother goddess in all the islands of the Aegean Sea, but also to extremely subtle philosophical reflection on the female function. Most of these figures are somewhat analogous to the Paleolithic Venuses found on the Continent, but they are much more detailed.

2. Similar representations are found in the engravings of the megalithic cairns in western Europe.

3. The spiral and the series of concentric circles are constant motifs in the decoration of the great megalithic cairns, especially in Ireland.

Chapter 12

1. On this subject, see Markale, *L'Epopée celtique d'Irlande,* as well as *Women of the Celts.*

INDEX OF SITES, MUSEUMS, SANCTUARIES, AND PILGRIMAGES

(the numbers refer to pages containing information on these places)

AALEN. Not far from Stuggart. The Limesmuseum is an outside museum containing many relics from Roman times on the borders (the *limes*) of the empire, notably statues of the female divinities. 210.

AARHUS. City in northern Denmark whose museum houses the famous Gundestrup Cauldron. 96, 211.

AGRIGENTE. Sicily. Three sanctuaries dedicated to Demeter.

AIX-EN-PROVENCE. Bouches-du-Rhône. In Saint-Sauveur Cathedral, the famous painting known as *The Burning Bush*. The Granet museum holds many Celto-Ligurian sculptures coming from the Entremont site. 122.

AKROTIRI. Island of Thera, Aegean Sea. Many Minoan frescoes representing the goddess of the serpents. 197.

AMIENS. Cathedral in honor of the Virgin Mary. 118.

ANGLES-SUR-L'ANGLIN. Vienne. Grotto containing cave paintings, among them a triad of female divinities. 58.

ANVERS. Belgium. The museum is particularly well endowed with representations of the Virgin Mary, especially by Flemish painters. 117.

ARMAGH. Northern Ireland. Episcopal seat founded by Saint Patrick where there was probably once a sanctuary to the goddess Macha (Armagh = Ard Macha, the "powerful Macha"). 226–27.

ARZON. Morbihan. Many megalithic cairns containing symbolic representations of the Great Goddess. 67.

ASCO. Upper Corsica. Megalithic stones representing female symbols. 55.

ATHENS. Greece. At the National Archaeological Museum, countless statues of goddess from all epochs, particularly the Mycenaean. A collection of many hundreds of representations from the Cyclades.

AUTUN. Saône-et-Loire. Lapidary museum very rich in Gallo-Roman statues, representing, notably, the goddess Epona. 86.

AUXERRE. Yonne. Archaeological museum.

AVENY. Near Dampmesnil (Eure), above the valley of Epte. Dolmen with symbolic engravings representing the Great Goddess. 86.

AVIOT. Meuse. Statue of the Virgin. Pilgrimage site. 159.

AY (Notre-Dame d'). Saint-Romain-d'Ay (Ardèche). Sanctuary dedicated to the Virgin Mary. Pilgrimage site. 159.

BAIA. Near Naples. Temple of Diana, sacred enclosure to Hecate, and grotto of the Sibyl. 128.

BALA LAKE. Also called Llynn Tegid. Lake south of the town of Bala (Wales) where the legend of Taliesen and the goddess Keridwen takes place. 184.

BARCELONA. Capital of Catalonia. The Catalan Museum holds the richest collection of Black Virgins in all of Europe. 180.

BARENTON (fountain of). In the area of Paimpont (Ille-et-Vilaine) in the forest of Brocéliande. This is where the legends about the fairy Vivien and the Lady of the Fountain take place. 77.

BARNENEZ. In the area of Plouézoc'h (Finistère), above the river of Morlaix. Double megalithic cairn, with many symbolic representations of the Great Goddess. 56, 60.

BATH. Great Britain. Ancient Anglo-Roman city, sanctuary of the goddess Sulis, patron of healing springs. 78, 170.

BAUD. Morbihan. In the area of Quinipily, mysterious statue called the Venus of Quinipily. 79.

BEAULIEU-SUR-DORDOGNE. Corrèze. Magnificent statue of the Virgin in the parish church. 99.

BEAUNE. Côte-d'Or. At the archaeological museum, a representation of the Gallo-Roman goddess, Epona. 72.

BEAURAING. Belgium, near Dinant. Very important Mary pilgrimage on December 8, since the apparition of the Virgin there in 1932. 173.

BELLÉE. In the area of Boury (Oise). The name Bellée comes from that of the Gallic solar divinity. The dolmen of Bellée contains symbolic representations of the Great Goddess.

BELLÊME. Orne. This name comes from that of the Gallic goddess, Belisama, the "very brilliant." In the forest of Bellême, near the Herse pond, a sacred spring dedicated to the *infernal* gods, belonging to the goddess Venus. 78.

BERNE. Switzerland. This is where the famous Gallo-Roman representation of the Goddess of the Bear was discovered. The name Berne comes from the Germanic name for bear, and the town is famous for its "Bear Den." 74, 166, 176.

BIBLIOTHÈQUE NATIONALE. Paris. The exhibit of medals contains numerous bronzes representing the female divinities. Countless Gallic coins, some of them illustrating the theme of the warrior goddesses. 73.

BOUISSET-EN-FERRIÈRES. In the community of Ferrières-les-Verriries (Hérault). Stela from the Bronze Age representing the goddess with the face of an owl. 65.

BOULOGNE-SUR-MER. Pas-de-Calais. Miraculous statue of the Virgin Mary. 157.

BOURY. See BELLÉE.

BOURGES. Cher. At the archaeological museum, famous Gallo-Roman representation of a weeping goddess. 72.

BRASSEMPOUY. Landes. The famous Venus of Brassempouy was discovered in the Cave of the Pope. 51.

BRENNILIS. Finistère. In the parish church, a strange statue of Notre-Dame-de-Bréac-Ilis. 109.

BRITISH MUSEUM. London. One of the best collections in the world, including representations of female divinities from all periods and all countries. 82, 156.

BRUSSELS. Belgium. Musée des Beaux-Arts is particularly well endowed with representations of Mary. 173.

CABRERETS. Lot. In the Pech-Merle cave, engraving of a female divinity. 43.

CAERLEON-ON-WYSG. Wales. Ancient Anglo-Roman fortress. Ruins of a temple dedicated to the goddess Nemesis. 183.

CALCUTTA. Bangladesh. The name of the city undoubtably comes from that of the goddess Kali the Black. 206.

CARNAC. Morbihan. The most extensive prehistory museum in the world. Numerous representations of female divinities, both realistic and symbolic.

CARRAWURGH. Great Britain, near Hadrian's Wall, not far from Newcastle. Sanctuary of the goddess Coventina. 183.

CASHEL. Ireland. On the wall of an annex of the Episcopal site, a representation of a Sheela-na-gig. 186.

ÇATAL HÜYÜK. In Anatolia (Turkey). Many Neolithic sanctuaries dedicated to female divinities. 159.

CATEL (Le). Isle of Guernsey. In the Catel cemetery, a strange female stela dating from the megalithic era. 91.

CHANGÉ-SAINT-PIAT. Eure-et-Loir. In the Eure valley, not far from Maintenon, a dolmen, with a support upon which the Neolithic goddess is represented. 60.

CHANTILLY. Oise. At the Condé museum, many representations of the Virgin Mary.

CHAPELLE-MONTLIGEON (La). Orne. Sanctuary of Notre-Dame-des-Ames-du-Purgatoire (Our Lady of the Souls in Purgatory). Pilgrimage. 153.

CHARRECEY. Saône-et-Loire. This is where a stela representing the goddess Epona was discovered, now kept in the Musée Lapidaire in Autun. 73.

CHARTRES. Eure-et-Loir. One of the most beautiful cathedrals dedicated to the Virgin Mary. Statue of Notre-Dame-de-Sous-Terre (Our Lady of the Underground). A much debated tradition concerning a Virgo Paritura honored by the Gaulois druids. 76, 101, 114–19.

CHESTER. Great Britain. Ancient Anglo-Roman fortress. Remains of sanctuaries dedicated to Minerva and to Nemesis. 183.

CHISSEY. Saône-et-Loire. In the church, magnificent statue of Notre-Dame-des-Avents. 108.

CHOREY-HAUT. Côte-d'Or. This is where a stela representing Epona as mother goddess was found. The stela is now at the museum in Beaune. 72.

CHURCH STRETTON. Great Britain. On the wall of the church, a represention of a Sheela-na-gig. 185.

CLERMONT-FERRAND. Puy-de-Dôme. In the cathedral, a Black Virgin called Notre-Dame-de-Clermont. In the Notre-Dame-du-Port church, a statue of Notre-Dame-de-Tendresse (Our Lady of Tenderness). 99.

megalithic cairn that contains symbolic representations of the Neolithic goddess. 55.

DIVONNE-LES-BAINS. Ain. Ancient sanctuary of a female healing divinity. The name Divonne means "divine." 77.

DOLNI VESTONICE. Czech Republic, on the Austrian border, not far from Brno. Paleolithic sanctuary in which was found a strange statue called Venus of Vestonice, now in the Prague museum. The Vestonice museum contains many female representations. 167, 176.

DOUVRES. Calvados. Miraculous statue of Notre-Dame-de-la-Délivrance (Our Lady of Deliverance). Important pilgrimage site. 160.

DOWTH. Ireland, in the valley of the Boyne. Important megalithic cairn containing symbolic engravings of the Neolithic Great Goddess. 187.

DUBLIN. Ireland. The National Museum contains magnificent religious objects from the Neolithic, the Bronze Age, and the Celtic epoch. Female representations called Sheela-na-gigs, and medieval statues of the Virgin. 185.

EDERN. Finistère. At the place called Koat-Kaer, a granite cross bearing a strange pietà from the eighteenth century. 109.

EINSIEDELN. Switzerland. Black Virgin. Very popular pilgrimage site. 176.

ELEUSIS. Greece. Famous sanctuary of Demeter where the Eleusinian Mysteries took place, famous initiation rites under the protection of the divine Mother. 37, 170.

EMAIN MACHA. Northern Ireland, west of Armagh, now Emania (Navan). Ancient royal residence of the Ulates, bearing the name of the goddess Macha. The site was restored and has become a Celtic museum. 73, 186.

EPHESUS. Turkey. Indisputably the greatest sanctuary of the mother goddess throughout antiquity, becoming one of the major sites of Christianity and Mary worship since the famous Council of Ephesus, which likened the mother of Jesus to the Great Goddess. Supposedly the location of the house in which Mary lived with the apostle John and where she experienced her "assumption." 11, 13, 14, 24, 27, 36, 48, 91, 95, 122, 158, 166, 178.

EPINAL. Vosges. Archaeological museum. 83.

ESCATRON. Spain. Sanctuary of the Virgin Mary. Pilgrimage site.

FATIMA. Portugal. Since 1917, the date of some apparitions of the Virgin, famous sanctuary and very common pilgrimage site for Mary worship. 181.

FOLGOËT (Le). Finistère. Magnificent church in the flamboyant style dedicated to the Virgin. Pilgrimage site. 159.

FONTBOINE. In the town of Saint-Jean-d'Aubrigoux (Haute-Loire), Gallic sanctuary dedicated to a mysterious goddess of springs. 77.

FONTVIEILLE. Bouches-du-Rhône. Covered megalithic passageway containing a representation of the Neolithic goddess. 54.

FRAUENBERG. Austria. Not far from Graz, Germano-Roman sanctuary dedicated to Isis-Noreia. 172.

GAGARINO. Italy. A Paleolithic Venus was found here, comparable to the one of Lespugue. 43.

GAVRINIS. Morbihan. Island in the gulf of Morbihan, in the town of Larmor-Baden. Very famous megalithic cairn containing engraved supports with symbolic representations of the Great Goddess. 58.

GELA. Sicily. Temples to Athena and Demeter. 178.

GLANUM. In the area of Saint-Rémy-de-Provence (Bouches-du-Rhône). Ruins of an ancient city, one part of which was Gallic, one part Greek, and one part Roman. Remains of a cult to healing female divinities near springs located in the Gallic section. 81.

GRAND. Vosges. The name comes from the Celtic name for the sun. This is an ancient sanctuary dedicated to a healing solar divinity linked to springs. Gallo-Roman bas-relief representing a sort of medicine goddess. 77, 83.

GRAZ. Austria. Schloss Eggenberg Museum is particularly rich in votive objects from the first civilizations of the Iron Age. 171, 172.

GRIMALDI. Italy. Paleolithic grotto in which a Venus of the Lespugue type was found. 34, 141, 171.

GUIDEL. Morbihan. Female stela representing the Neolithic goddess in a megalithic cairn. 61.

GUNDESTRUP (Cauldron of). Famous Celtic ritual object made entirely of gold and engraved with mythological scenes. Kept in the Aarhus museum in Denmark. Copy at the Musée des Antiquités Nationales in Saint-Germain-en-Laye. 82, 175.

HALLE. Belgium, south of Brussels. Honored statue of Notre-Dame-de-Halle, also called Siège de la Sagesse. 173.

HERAKLEION. Crete. National museum has large collection of relics from the Minoan epoch, notably bas-reliefs and paintings representing the goddess of the serpents.

HISSARLIK. Neolithic site in Turkey, on the Anatolian plateau. Many vases with representations of goddesses with owl faces. 64.

ILE-LONGUE. In the town of Larmor-Baden (Morbihan). Megalithic cairn containing many representations of the Neolithic goddess. 57, 60.

JOSSELIN. Morbihan. Beautiful flamboyant-style church containing a statue of Notre-Dame-du-Roncier (Our Lady of the Brambles). Famous pilgrimage, September 8, for the Breton "Gallo" country. 157.

KILDARE. Ireland. The name means "church of the oaks." Druidic sanctuary that became a monastery for both men and women in the fifth century. The mysterious figure of "Saint" Brigit was substituted for that of the ancient goddess Brigit, of the three faces. The remains of the sanctuary and fountain of Saint Brigit can still be seen there, a place venerated by the Irish. 187, 188.

KILKENNY. Ireland. In the Anglican cathedral of Saint Canice, a curious stone engraving representing the Trinity, in which God the Father is replaced with a perfectly recognizable female figure. 190.

KILLINABOY. Ireland. Sheela-na-gig. 188.

KILPECK. Great Britain. The most perfect representation known of a Sheela-na-gig. 45, 185.

KNOCKNAREA. Small mountain overlooking Sligo (Ireland). At its summit, a megalithic cairn called the Tomb of Queen Maeve, the name Maeve being one of the names of the Great Goddess in the Gaelic tradition. 189.

KNOSSOS. Crete. The most beautiful remains of the Cretan-Minoan civilization, with many representations of the Great Goddess. 161, 163.

KNOWTH. Ireland. In the valley of the Boyne, superb megalithic cairn with symbolic engravings representing the Neolithic goddess. 163.

LACAUNE. Tarn. Female menhir-statue of Granisse. 63.

LANISCAT. Côtes-d'Armor. Female menhir-statue of Trévoux. 61.

LANGON. Ille-et-Vilaine. In the Saint Agatha chapel, an ancient Gallo-Roman temple, there is a fresco representing Venus. 79.

LANRIVAIN. Côtes-d'Armor. Chapel of Gueodot (or Guiaudet), containing the curious representation of a recumbent Virgin with child. 111.

LAON. Aisne. Honored statue of Notre-Dame-de-Liesse (Our Lady of Jubilation). 133.

LAUSSEL. Dordogne. Paleolithic shelter near the Eyzies in which the famous Venus of Laussel holding a bison horn was discovered. 47–49.

LESPUGUE. Ariège. Paleolithic site where the famous steatopygic statue called Venus of Lespugue was discovered. 4, 43, 44, 47, 51, 140, 141, 171, 191.

LOCMARIAQUER. Morbihan. Many megalithic cairns in which certain supports are engraved with symbolic representations of the Neolithic goddess, notably at the Mané Lud, at the Table des

Marchands, at the Mané Rutual, at the Pierres Plates, as well as at the Mané-er-Hroëg. 56 57.

LOS MILLARES. Spain. Neolithic grouping with engraved slate plates and pottery decorated with symbolic representations of the Neolithic goddess. 64.

LOURDES. Hautes-Pyrénées. Since the apparitions of the Virgin to the young Bernadette Soubirous in a grotto, on the shores of the Gave, this is the most famous sanctuary to Mary in all of Christendom. Continuous pilgrimages. 77, 133, 159, 181, 191.

LOUVRE (museum of). Paris. Countless representations of ancient goddesses and portraits of the Virgin Mary from all epochs. 102, 104, 105, 156.

LYON. Rhône. Ancient capital of the Gauls. Archaeological museum and temple to Cybele. In the Saint-Jean cathedral, strange bas-relief representing a *Chasse à la Licorne* (Hunt of the Unicorn) which very much seems to be the symbol of a mystical union between the divine Mother and the creature, represented here by the hunter. 103.

MAASTRICHT. The Netherlands. In the basilica, a very beautiful statue of the Virgin, called Stella Maris here, an object of great veneration. 175.

MARGUT. Ardennes. Celtic site where a statuette of the goddess Arduinna was discovered, now in the Cabinet des Médailles in Paris. 74.

MARIAZELL. Austria. Particularly venerated Black Virgin. National pilgrimage site for Austrians, Hungarians, and Slovaks. 172.

MARSAT. Puy-de-Dôme. Black Virgin.

MARSEILLE. Bouches-du-Rhône. Sanctuary of Notre-Dame-de-la-Garde. Black Virgin in the ancient abbey of Saint-Victor.

MAS-CAPELLIER. In the town of Calmels-et-le-Viala (Averyon), female menhir-statue, now in the Musée des Antiquités Nationales. 63.

MAURON. Morbihan. The ancient doors of the parish church, now in the interior of the sanctuary, present a curious image of the serpent from Genesis, with the head of a woman at one end and the head of a serpent at the other. 109.

MEDJUGORJE. Bosnia. Very famous Mary sanctuary since recent apparitions of the Virgin. 177.

MEIN-GOAREC. In the area of Plaudren (Morbihan). Megalithic female stela with no face in the Mein-Goaric vicinity. 61.

MESNIL-SUR-ORGE. Essonne. Hypogeum with stylized representation of the funerary goddess. 54.

MEURSAULT. Côte-d'Or. A bas-relief representing the goddess Epona was discovered here. It is now in the Beaune museum. 73.

MIRANDA DEL CASTAMAR. Spain, near Salamanca. Curious ceremonies in honor the Saint Agatha held in February. 180.

MONPAZIER. Dordogne. A strange Paleolithic Venus of the Lespugue type was discovered here. 43–48.

MONTSERRAT. Spain. Near Barcelona, an important place for Mary worship. Festivals and pilgrimages to the Black Virgin. 180.

MURI. Switzerland. Bronze statuette of the Gallo-Roman goddess Artio. 109.

MUSÉE DES ANTIQUITÉS NATIONALES. Saint-Germain-en-Laye (Yvelines). The best French archaeological museum for the Celtic and Gallo-Roman periods; numerous objects from earlier epochs are found here. 51, 63.

MYCENAE. Greece. The most beautiful archaeological ensemble from the first Greek civilization, called the Mycenaean period. 165.

NEUVY-EN-SULLIAS. Loiret. Gallic sanctuary where astonishing bronze statuettes of female divinities were found. These objects are now in the historical musuem of Orléans, in Orléans. 72, 84.

NEWGRANGE. Ireland. In the Boyne valley, this is no doubt the most beautiful and most impressive of all the megalithic cairns.

Many symbolic and geometric representations of the Neolithic goddess on interior and exterior stones. 55, 187.

NOVES. Bouches-du-Rhône. Black Virgin discovered at the site of an ancient sanctuary of the goddess Hecate. 160.

OSTIA. Italy. Remains of temples to Ceres, Bellona, the Bona Dea and the Magna Mater.

PAESTUM. Italy. Remains of temples to Athena and Hera. 178.

PAPS OF ANU. Ireland. Kerry Mountains, not far from Killarney, with two hillocks that tradition says are the "breasts of Anna," the Great Goddess. 189.

PARIS. Notre Dame Cathedral. 100–101, 154–55.

PARIS. Chapel of the Miraculous Medal, rue du Bac. 112, 154.

PECH-MERLE. See CABRERETS.

PENMARC'H. Finistère. Prehistory museum.

PÉRIGEUX. Dordogne. Tower of Vésone, remains of a Gallo-Roman temple dedicated to the goddess Vesuna. 80.

PESH. Germany. Not far from Cologne, sanctuary dedicated to the mother goddesses, presented in triads. 174.

PIERRE-TURQUAISE. In the forest of Carnelle, in the area of Saint-Martin-du-Tertre (Val d'Oise). Famous dolmen, one of the supports shows a symbolic representations of the Great Goddess. 60.

PLOUÉZOC'H. See BARNENEZ.

POMPEII. Italy. Temples of Venus and Isis. 179.

PONTMAIN. Mayenne. At the Maine and Brittany borders, famous Mary sanctuary. Pilgrimage site. 192.

POULAN-POUZOLS. Tarn. Female menhir-statue from Coutarel. 75.

PUY-EN-VELAY (Le). Haute-Loire. One of the most famous sanctuaries of the Virgin. Superb cathedral at the site of an ancient temple dedicated to the Great Goddess Anna, whose ancient name was Anicium. Major pilgrimage on August 15. 98–99, 116–17.

QUERRIEN. Côtes-d'Armor. In an isolated spot in the Méné mountains, monastic establishment, Irish in origin, which became a sanctuary to Mary. Pilgrimage site. 160, 161.

QUINIPILY (Venus of). See BAUD.

RATHCROGHAN. Ireland. Formerly Cruachan. Legendary domain of Queen Maeve, one of the Gaelic images of the Great Goddess. 189.

REIMS. Marne. Superb Virgin in Majesty on the northern portal of the cathedral. 100.

RENNES. Ille-et-Vilaine. Musée de Bretagne.

RENNES-LE-CHATEAU. Aude. Strange church dedicated to Mary Magdalene. 124.

RIOM. Puy-de-Dôme. Black Virgin in the Notre-Dame-du-Marthuret church.

ROANNE. Loire. Dechélette Musuem devoted to prehistory.

ROCAMADOUR. Lot. Great sanctuary to Mary. Black Virgin which seems to have succeeded an ancient divinity. 119–20.

RODEZ. Aveyron. The Musée Fenaille rich in prehistoric monuments, especially menhir-statues. 63.

ROERMOND. The Netherlands. Sanctuary to Mary and pilgrimage of Our Lady of the Sands.

ROME. Italy. Countless relics. Musuems, in particular, the Oriental Museum and the Museo Nazionale Romana, also called Museo delle Terme. 147.

RUMENGOL. Finistère. Mary sanctuary. Site of ancient pilgrimage to Notre-Dame-de-Toute-Aide (Our Lady of All Aid). 161.

TOURNUS. Saône-et-Loire. Very beautiful statue of Notre-Dame-la Brune. 99.

TRÉBEURDEN. Côtes-d'Armor. Female stela in the Prajou-Menhir mound. 61.

TRESSÉ. Ille-et-Vilaine. Stela representing the Neolithic Great Goddess. 61.

TRÉVOUX (Le). See LANISCAT.

TUGFORD. Great Britain. Curious Sheela-na-gig. 185.

TURSAC. Dordogne. Where a Paleolithic statuette called the Venus of Tursac was discovered. Statue of the Virgin inspired by a Gallic goddess found near a spring and a dolmen. 43, 160.

UPPSALA. Sweden. Sanctuary dedicated to the Germano-Scandinavian divinities. 175.

VALLETTE (La). Malte. National Museum of Archaeology.

VANNES. Morbihan. Musuem of the Polymathic Society of Morbihan. 80.

VERRIÈRE (La). Aveyron. Female menhir-statue, now in the Musée Fenaille in Rodez. 66.

VÉZELAY. Yonne. Magnificent abbey-church dedicated to Mary Magdalene. 121, 124.

VIENNA. Austria. Ephesus Museum and Natural History Museum. 172.

VIENNE. Isère. One of the most ancient religious center of Gaul. Remains of the temple of Cybele.

VICHY. Allier. In the Saint Blaise church, statue of Notre-Dame-des-Malades.

VRAVONA. Greece. This is where the most ancient temple of Artemis is found. 168.

INDEX